A Global Racial Enemy

A Global Racial Enemy

Muslims and 21st-Century Racism

Saher Selod, Inaash Islam, and Steve Garner

polity

Copyright © Saher Selod, Inaash Islam, & Steve Garner 2024

The right of Saher Selod, Inaash Islam, and Steve Garner to be identified as Author of this Work has been asserted in accordance with the UK Copyright, Designs and Patents Act 1988.

First published in 2024 by Polity Press

Polity Press
65 Bridge Street
Cambridge CB2 1UR, UK

Polity Press
111 River Street
Hoboken, NJ 07030, USA

All rights reserved. Except for the quotation of short passages for the purpose of criticism and review, no part of this publication may be reproduced, stored in a retrieval system or transmitted, in any form or by any means, electronic, mechanical, photocopying, recording or otherwise, without the prior permission of the publisher.

ISBN-13: 978-1-5095-4019-8
ISBN-13: 978-1-5095-4020-4(pb)

A catalogue record for this book is available from the British Library.

Library of Congress Control Number: 2023937138

Typeset in 10.5 on 12.5pt Sabon
by Fakenham Prepress Solutions, Fakenham, Norfolk NR21 8NL
Printed and bound in Great Britain by TJ Books Ltd, Padstow, Cornwall

The publisher has used its best endeavours to ensure that the URLs for external websites referred to in this book are correct and active at the time of going to press. However, the publisher has no responsibility for the websites and can make no guarantee that a site will remain live or that the content is or will remain appropriate.

Every effort has been made to trace all copyright holders, but if any have been overlooked the publisher will be pleased to include any necessary credits in any subsequent reprint or edition.

For further information on Polity, visit our website:
politybooks.com

Contents

Acknowledgments	vi
Introduction: Muslim Global Racialization: 21st-Century Racism	1
1 Muslim Histories: Contextualizing the Global War on Terror	30
2 The Media and the Racialization of Muslims: Constructing a Global Threat	62
3 The Global Racialization of Muslims and the Rise in Nationalism and Populism	106
4 Global Counterterrorism Policies: Racializing Muslims via Surveillance, Policing, and Detention	137
Conclusion: Where Do We Go from Here? Possibilities for Resistance and Further Securitization	166
References	178
Index	211

Acknowledgments

We would like to thank Polity Press for the opportunity to publish this book. In particular, Jonathan Skerrett has been incredibly patient and encouraging, and we are incredibly grateful to have worked with him. We are indebted to him for his graciousness and understanding on the multiple occasions that we asked for deadline extensions. We would also like to thank Karina Jákupsdóttir for her guidance and support over the last few years. We are incredibly grateful to Deepa Kumar for her feedback and insights on the manuscript and for being a trailblazer through her own work on Muslims and racism.

Collaborating on this book has been an exceptionally rewarding experience. Not only have we pushed one another intellectually, we were able to support one another through the trials we have all faced dealing with a pandemic, family illnesses, and professional changes.

For Steve, the last section of this book project occurred during a particularly tough time, and he would like to thank people who went out of their way to help him through it: his great family of course; his fantastic wife and children, Anne, Dani, Gabriel and Morganne, and his parents, Chris and Chris. Thanks also to Lisa Jones, Christi Barrera, Marisa Winking, Emilce Santana, Kelly and Sara Davidson, Derald Young, Lori Vesperman, Heili Pals, and Warren Waren for their kindness. He would like to thank Saher Selod, David Embrick, Sin Yi Cheung, David Brunsma, and Nasim Vaseiezadeh (and her new daughter, Arta) for their faith in

Acknowledgments vii

him. He really appreciates Wendy Moore of New Orleans, who goes the extra distance to be an epic friend. Finally, as we received proofs for this book, he got the horrible news that his former colleague, Mark Fossett had passed. He would like to include Mark for his help and hospitality when he was working at A&M.

For Inaash, first and foremost, she is indebted to her co-authors for taking a chance on her when she was still a doctoral student at Virginia Tech. She would like to thank Saher and Steve, for bringing her on to this important project. She has learned so much from them and is grateful for their guidance, mentorship, and support. She would also like to express her gratitude to David L. Brunsma for being a brilliant friend and mentor over the last few years. To her family, Izza, Haneen, Ammi, and Abbu, their constant encouragement and belief in her has meant everything. She thanks them from the bottom of her heart.

Saher would like to thank first and foremost Steve and Inaash for their dedication and commitment to this project. Thank you to Jyoti Puri and the Hazel Dick Leonard Fellowship at Simmons University for their support. Aaron Rosenthal, Jessica Parr, Laura Prieto, Sarah Leonard, Felipe Agudelo, Lena Zuckerwise, and Sumayya Ahmed provided thoughtful and critical feedback during the early stages of the book. Saher is grateful to Marilyn Rodriguez for her work as a research assistant. Saher is indebted to Sahar Aziz and John Esposito for their invitation to publish on ethnonationalism and populism and the racialization of Muslims in their forthcoming edited manuscript, which greatly helped in formulating some of the ideas presented in this book. She would also like to thank Margaret Hicken for the invitation to present on this project at the Racism Lab at the University of Michigan. Saher would like to give a huge shout out to Fatema Ahmed and the Muslim Justice League for being the true superheroes in doing the hard work on surveillance and policing of Muslims on the ground through their advocacy. Finally, to her husband and daughter, Eben and Isra English, Saher owes everything. They continue to provide the encouragement desperately needed to continue pushing forward with this work. Saher hopes this book honors the memory of her parents, Farooq and Sayeeda Selod, whose histories of forced and voluntary migration from Myanmar (formerly referred to as Burma) to Calcutta, to the newly created Pakistan, to the United States, continues to inspire her work. Their resilience in the face of discrimination and racism and their dedication to social justice is what sustains her commitment to this work.

Introduction
Muslim Global Racialization: 21st-Century Racism

Introduction

Rushan Abbas, a Uyghur activist living in the United States, has been speaking out against the crimes against Uyghur Muslims in China. She is the founder of the organization Campaigns for Uyghurs, and has spent years advocating for the human rights of Uyghur Muslims. In a podcast with Al Jazeera, she discussed how millions of Uyghurs are being placed in camps simply because they are Muslim (Al Jazeera Podcast 2022). Her husband's family had been disappeared in China and after she started speaking out about forced sterilization, rapes, and camps for Uyghur Muslims, her own sister, Dr. Gulshan Abbas, was placed into a camp and sentenced to twenty years in prison for "terrorist activities" (Cadell 2021). In the podcast, Abbas noted the long and complicated history of Uyghur Muslims in East Turkestan (referred to by the Chinese government as Xinjiang) with the Chinese state, one that she characterized as colonialist. But she also discussed how the Global War on Terror shifted the way the state framed Uyghur Muslims as a threat to the nation by labeling them as terrorists. Once this label of terrorist is applied, individuals are dehumanized to the point where they are no longer thought to behave with any rationality, and instead reduced to bloodthirsty, evil, and irrational actors. This marker justifies the Chinese government's draconian and cruel policies put in place to prevent terrorism. As we show in this book, it is the Global War on Terror (GWOT) that has led to the imprisonment of a retired doctor and mother, Dr. Gulshan Abbas, for twenty years.

The racialization of Muslims in the 21st century is global in nature. Although the terrorist attacks that incited this war took place in the United States, this new war, one that is waged against terror as opposed to a nation-state, has allowed for counterterrorism laws and policies that rely on the construction of a Muslim as a threat to both national security and cultural values to be reproduced and cross borders. The deeper motivations for the oppression of Muslims are unique to their histories within each nation, chronicled in this book, but the current global call to weed out terrorism has triggered anti-terrorism laws resulting in unprecedented levels of state-led discrimination and human rights abuses of Muslims internationally. In this book we unpack how the Global War on Terror has led to a global enemy as a result of the global racialization of Muslims.

The way that racism via attitudes, representations, and policies crosses borders while at the same time retains its uniqueness within a particular sociopolitical context requires us to identify this process across various spaces and contexts. For example, Pakistanis in the UK have a history of racialization that is tied to the history of colonialism in India. The derogatory use of the term "Pakis" was used prior to the attacks of 9/11 reflecting the anti-South Asian sentiments that derive from a history of colonialism (Taylor and Gillan 2009). However, since 9/11, counterterrorist policies that target South Asian Muslims in new ways have been appearing in the UK. Kundnani and Hayes' (2018) report on the history of a surveillance policy in the United States, Countering Violent Extremism (CVE), exemplifies the global nature of counterterrorist policies. After 9/11, European countries began to develop theories of radicalization to understand the motivations of terrorism, which the United States later adopted. One program that Prime Minister Tony Blair put into place was called Preventing Violent Extremism (PVE), later named PREVENT. This policy aimed at surveilling a British Muslim population, by targeting mosques and

Introduction

individuals that the government thought was susceptible to "extremism" as a way to prevent the radicalization of Muslims and consequently violence. But PREVENT is deeply problematic because it relies on stereotypical associations of Muslim=radicalization=potential terrorist. The policy was based on these stereotypical associations.

> From 2005, the analysis of extremism among UK security officials shifted away from references to formal groups and movements and towards an emphasis on attitudes, mindsets, and dispositions – similar to the shift in the Netherlands and the US at this time. Attention turned, above all, to concern about a free-floating Islamist ideology that did not spread through organisational recruitment but through a radicalisation process in which it captured the minds of the young and made them into "violent extremists" – the term had been adopted from the US by UK policy-makers in 2006. Extremism was pictured as a virus, flowing from radicalizer to radicalized, infecting, spreading, infiltrating. (Kundnani and Hayes 2018: 7)

The way people are perceived to think is tied to their religious identity, which becomes criminal via this policy. PREVENT racializes Muslims because of the construction that Islam is a violent ideology, therefore anyone who practices this religion is susceptible to radicalized ways of thinking and behaving. Kundnani and Hayes (2018) trace the lineage of Countering Violent Extremism (CVE) in the United States under the Obama administration back to PREVENT. PREVENT was created in England, inspired by Dutch policies that were put into place after the murder of filmmaker Theo Van Gogh. Theo Van Gogh was known for making films that vilified Muslims as misogynists, barbaric, and violent. His killer, Mohammed Bouyeri, was twenty-six at the time and a Dutch citizen of Moroccan descent. Although the Netherlands experienced few terrorist attacks, compared to other European countries, the response to this one isolated violent act was to institute a community-based surveillance program, Preventing Violent Extremism (PVE), to stop radicalization in individuals. PREVENT in the UK drew on the Dutch version, which then influenced CVE in the United States. In the first iteration of CVE in the United States, federal grants were given to organizations that aimed to weed out radicalization in their communities. Not surprisingly, mosques and Islamic community centers were some of the first recipients of these grants. Communities who received the grant were expected to monitor their population for extremists. While we revisit CVE and PREVENT in more depth in later chapters, the point that we make here is that counterterrorist policies do not exist in a vacuum but have a global domino effect. These policies rely on the racialization of a Muslim identity that transcends borders. While Muslim experiences in the UK are different to those in the United States due to their unique histories, the counterterrorist policies that have arisen in each country are similar to one another and rely on a global bogeyman, or the global racialized Muslim.

The global racialization of Muslims entails certain tropes about Muslims that are shared across nation-states even though they thrive under very different contexts. Uyghur Muslims, Indian Muslims, American Muslims, and British Muslims are all framed as misogynists, violent, irrational, and a population that should be watched, monitored, deported, or even detained. It is important to note that it is not just Muslims in these countries who have been impacted by the racialization of Muslims that has been used to justify the Global War on Terror. Every country that is a member of the United Nations was tasked with participating in the GWOT after 9/11, which resulted in human rights breaches against Muslims in these other countries as well. These policies that appear to target Muslims have a much wider net and have impacted other racialized and marginalized groups, which we touch on later in this book. Furthermore, the global racialization of Muslims is not a one-size-fits-all, but rather is a deeply gendered construct. Throughout the book, we identify the ways that Muslim women encounter forms of gendered racialization that are unique from Muslim men. Finally,

Introduction 5

we show how racism against Muslims is not owned by the "West" but is a global phenomenon that exemplifies racism in the 21st century.

Rethinking Islamophobia

Since 9/11, Islamophobia has become the go-to term to encapsulate the encounters Muslims have with racism and discrimination (Sayyid and Vakil 2010; Love 2017; Beydoun 2018). Although the original application of the term centered on a fear of Islam, several scholars have articulated the ways that race and racism are central to the concept, allowing it to capture anti-Muslim racism (Tyrer 2013; Love 2017; Kumar 2021). Making race central to the concept of Islamophobia became more widespread, particularly in the years after 9/11. Prior to 9/11, Islamophobia was used by scholars to describe anti-Muslim discrimination, without much analysis of whether it is a form of racism (Gottschalk and Greenberg 2008; Shryock 2010). While some scholars argued that Islamophobia could be used to incorporate structural racism, others have noted the limits of this term when it does not adequately address histories of race and racism for Muslim populations (Halliday 1999; Garner and Selod 2015; Husain 2021b). One of the critiques of the term is that it focuses too much on the religion, Islam, rather than on Muslim experiences (Garner and Selod 2015). Another issue with the term is that within the US context it makes invisible anti-Black racism because the concept has been rooted in the experiences of Arabs and South Asians (Husain 2021b). Indeed, to date, the majority of research on Muslims and racism, particularly since 9/11, has been mostly conducted on Arabs or South Asians (Naber 2007; Cainkar 2009; Alsultany 2012; Bayoumi 2015; Selod 2018). This argument is best reflected in the idea that Muslims are being racialized as "brown" (Zopf 2018), revealing the focus on South Asians and Arabs in the current literature. Furthermore, some of the scholarship on Islamophobia situates it in relation to whiteness (Razack 2022), making the term difficult to use in countries like

Nigeria, where Muslims experience discrimination but are phenotypically similar to the dominant population (Ejiofor 2023). As a result, there has been a call to decolonize the scholarship on Islamophobia because it centers whiteness and is Eurocentric (Ejiofor 2023). We argue that racialization is a better theoretical analysis because it allows us to show how religion is racialized and interacts with other identities, such as religion, gender, race, ethnicity, sexual orientation, ability, class, etc., in unique ways. As we show later in this chapter, racialization of a religious identity via Muslim men as terrorists and Muslim women as cultural threats justifies security practices that are deeply racialized.

Another reason we steer away from the term Islamophobia is because of the problematic ways in which it reinforces the idea that racism is an illness. The suffix "phobia" in Islamophobia participates in the continued stigmatization and vilification of mental health issues whereby racism is continuously characterized with words and phrases that denote disabilities, highlighting the problems with these negative attitudes. A Google search of the term "phobia" provides a definition as an extreme or irrational fear of something. This definition perpetuates the idea that this is an individualistic practice and one that is not rational – ignoring how it is a systemic issue and an intentional act with material consequences. Anti-Muslim racism is structured into laws and policies with concrete political, social, and material effects, something that a phobia does not capture. And while Love (2017), Beydoun (2020), Kumar (2021), and Kazi (2021) do the work of identifying how Islamophobia can also refer to structural racism, we feel the term can detract from the concept of structural racism. Finally, we view racism against Muslims as part and parcel of racism at large. In other words, although Muslims have not been theorized about enough in race scholarship currently or historically, their encounters with racism have always been there. These experiences have not been uniform, but are complicated by race, ethnicity, sexual orientation, gender, and religion. African Muslims who came over to the US via slavery have very different experiences with racism because of their religion and race than do the South Asian migrants who came over as cheap labor in the 19th century (Bald 2013). Just as an indigenous population has been ignored in the construction of critical race theory (Byrd 2011), so have Muslims and other racialized religious groups. The ways that race theory has been and continues to be constructed often leaves out issues around immigration, colonialism, and settler colonialism. Settler colonialism predates slavery in the United States, and this should be built into theories about racism that often treat slavery as the starting point in critical race theories (Byrd 2011). Without dismissing the important work that current scholars and activists are doing around Islamophobia, we argue that Muslim racialization is a better way to understand and theorize a 21st-century racism that is global. Racialization allows us to build on existing theories of race and racism, bringing in intersectional and global perspectives that are rooted in the existing scholarship on race, racism, and colonialism.

Orientalism and Neo-Orientalism: Foundations for the Global Racialization of Muslims

The association of Muslim men with terrorism has a long history that predated the Global War on Terror. Arabs, and consequently Muslims, have always been portrayed as uncivilized, barbaric, and violent. Edward Said's (1978) concept of "orientalism" provides a starting point to situate the racialization of Muslims as a global project. One of the most renowned theorists of postcolonial thought, Said showed how ideas about the Orient, which he referred to as the Arab world, were constructed through a colonizing epistemology. In *Orientalism*, Said convincingly writes that the construction of the Arab/Muslim via literature, aesthetics, and scholarly texts produces the "us" vs. "them" mentality that is incorporated into laws and policies that make up the governing structure of colonialism and imperialism. The epistemological construction of "the Orient" is done in such a way that the creators of knowledge need not ever step foot into the cultures and countries they represent. In his text, Said refers to paintings by European artists that depict the Arab world as static, unchanging, and inherently unmodern. Some of the paintings include harems of white women in submissive positions to the darker skinned Arab men wearing what appears to be traditional attire, like a turban. What Said discovered is that many of these artists had never been to an Arab country, thus these images were from their imagination.

The title of Zareena Grewal's book, *Islam is a Foreign Country: American Muslims and the Global Crisis of Authority* (2014), further exemplifies the ways the Arab world and Islam are constructed. The first part of this title reveals how a religious identity is conflated with spatial geographies. "Americans have inherited this centuries-old discourse. When Americans refer to the 'Muslim World,' they reproduce, amend, and complicate Colonial Europe's moral geography of the Orient" (pg. 5). The creation of the "West" and the "Orient" is a construct that is not based in reality. There is no Muslim world with specific boundaries and a unified national and cultural identity. The Global War on Terror is not one that is engaged with one specific nation-state, like past wars, but one that extends its reach to wherever terror may be found, making war's scope limitless. Because the terrorist is not worthy of human rights, state-sanctioned violence against Muslims is seen as necessary. But to be clear, it is not just the United States or the mythical "West" that participates in this subjugation. It encompasses a multitude of countries that inherit and adapt the construct of the terrorist to expand their authority on their population. This imaginary geographic location, the "Orient" or the "Muslim world," is viewed as a place where terrorists are produced.

Orientalism in the 20th century laid the groundwork for its use in the GWOT in the 21st century. Samuel Huntington's work best exemplifies how orientalism was used to set the stage for the GWOT. Huntington, a Harvard political scientist, was influenced by Bernard Lewis (1990), a British American historian, who wrote about the "Roots of Muslim Rage," arguing that Muslim men naturally tended

Introduction 9

toward rage and violence. In 1993, Huntington made a prediction about what the next global war would be in his article "The Clash of Civilizations." Huntington states that clashes between distinct cultures would create the context for the next major world war. But rather than characterizing the war as between nations, he identified eight "civilizations" that make up the globe. Huntington defines civilizations as,

> the highest cultural grouping of people and the broadest level of cultural identity people have short of that which distinguishes humans from other species. It is defined both by common objective elements, such as language, history, religion, customs, institutions, and by the subjective self-identification of people. (pg. 24)

Huntington's thesis is what Said defines as an orientalist construction because it is an arbitrary and unrealistic division of the world into "civilizations" that are not based in reality, fact, or even geographical boundaries, but myth and fiction. In fact, Huntington and Said gave lectures critiquing each other's ideas. At the University of Massachusetts at Amherst in 1996, Edward Said gave a lecture entitled "The Myth of the Clash of Civilizations." Here he argued that an "Islamic" civilization does not exist, but was rather created by neoconservative academics, like Huntington, to justify extraction of resources from Arab countries. Muslims globally make up distinct cultures and beliefs. They speak different languages, have various political interests, and even practice Islam or do not practice Islam in various ways. Yet, Huntington's division of the world into spatial locations, religious beliefs, continents, and even one nation-state (Japan) was not dismissed as ridiculous or baseless, but instead appeared in the way US foreign policy was instituted after the September 11th attacks. The GWOT relied on the construction of a Muslim terrorist who comes from the Islamic world. It was not important that the terrorists who committed the violent attacks on 9/11 did not come from the two countries against which the United States engaged in a military strike, Afghanistan and Iraq.

Scholars have since built on Said's concept of orientalism, situating it within the current context. "Neo-orientalism" or 21st-century orientalism (Kerboua 2016: 8), for example, emerged after the events of 9/11, but reproduces essentialized ideas of Islam and Muslims similar to those evident in Said's original concept of orientalism, yet specifically focusing on Islam. Using discourses of the GWOT, neo-orientalism produces a binary logic that not only defines Islam as terroristic and Muslims as terrorists or potential terrorists but conflates Islam with fundamentalism to the point that the two are rendered indistinguishable. The focus on terrorism and fundamentalism essentializes the difference of Muslims and Islam with western and non-western citizenries and nation-states who are socially, politically, and militarily concerned and engaged with the GWOT. However, rather than simply focusing on the element of *western* patriotism and democracy as opposed to Islamic or Arab totalitarianism, neo-orientalism focuses more on the negative dimensions of Islamic theology and Muslim lifestyles, rendering these as incompatible with nation-states' visions and values. In the United States and the United Kingdom, freedom, equality, and democracy are perceived to be antithetical to Islam and its adherents. In non-western nations such as China and India, neo-orientalist logics pose values of secularism, ethnonationalism, and unity as being threatened by the presence of Muslim subjects and Islam within state borders. Consequently, even though it emerges from western sociopolitical discourse, neo-orientalism offers non-western nations the language, political discourse, and mass-mediated narratives that reify an orientalist binary of us vs. them that is uniquely attuned to and influenced by the politics of the GWOT. Co-opting these neo-orientalist logics facilitates the GWOT's global racial project of racializing Muslims by attaching specific meanings of terrorism, fundamentalism, and danger to Muslims and Islam, which then shape public sentiments, conceptions, and state policies that locate Muslims as outside of each nation-state's national imaginary.

One of the major contributions of neo-orientalism is the attention to gender. According to the neo-orientalist logics

Introduction 11

of the GWOT, Muslim men are to be perceived as terrorists or potential terrorists, national security threats, suicide bombers, and illegal immigrants, while Muslim women are to be perceived as passive victims, oppressed by Muslim men, and as cultural threats – who, by the virtue of being women and potential mothers, may inculcate within their children Islamic belief systems thought to be antithetical to each nation-state's specific values (Mishra 2007; Cainkar 2009). It is this logic that drives forced marriages for Uyghur Muslim women to non-Muslim Han men in China and how the rhetoric of "saving" the women of Afghanistan from the Taliban was popularized when the United States invaded Afghanistan, which will be further expanded on later in this book. Thus, the terrorist justifies borders, surveillance tools and technologies, and prisons while Muslim women who need saving or are viewed as cultural threats justifies policing intimate relations. These gendered and racialized meanings are manifestly evident in the discourse used to create and validate state and federal policies in each of the countries examined in this book.

Orientalism and concepts like neo-orientalism are not without their flaws. Sexual orientation is mostly absent, with the exception of Ghassan Moussawi (2020), who broadens the concept of orientalism to incorporate sexuality in his study of LGBTQ people in Beirut. Said's concept of orientalism has also been critiqued for being narrow in its focus of specific European countries and leaving little room for resistance in the way it was conceptualized (Lowe 1991; Kumar 2021). Furthermore, neither concept engages with the concept of race. Kumar (2021) advances orientalism by showing how institutional orientalism was a racial project that began in the 19th century that was tied to capitalist imperialism. "The ability to colonize Muslim lands and to deny rights to the colonized created the conditions for modern anti-Muslim racism . . . the necessary and sufficient conditions for the production of Muslims as a race in its modern form were present only in the nineteenth century in the era of capitalist modernity" (pg. 46). Most of the focus on orientalism, neo-orientalism, and institutional orientalism has been on the relationship of Europe or the United States to Muslim majority countries via colonialism or capitalist imperialism. We move this argument forward in new directions by showing how the construct of Muslim men as terrorists and Muslim women as in need of saving are racial constructions resulting in the erection of racialized securitization globally in both western and non-western societies. Orientalist notions of Muslims as monolithic, misogynist, and a threat have served European colonialism in the 19th century, and the United States in the 21st century in their military operations in Iraq and Afghanistan, but are also being used in countries like India and China to control their population via hyper-nationalism. The racialization of Muslims does not only serve white supremacy but is also serving nationalist supremacies as well.

The Racialization of Muslims

In order to understand racialization, we have first to acknowledge that race is not a static concept but shifts within nations over time and is also not recognized by every nation-state. In the United States, race has been universally understood as being about phenotype, with skin tone and pigmentation being the main characteristics that determine one's experiences with racism. However, there are other factors, like cultural attributes, that race someone (Naber 2007; Cainkar 2009; Selod and Embrick 2013; Garner and Selod 2015; Love 2017; Aziz 2021; Kumar 2021). Cultural markers in addition to biological ones play a huge role in how someone is read as raced, resulting in their encounters with discrimination and racism. Cultural racism describes the process by which cultures mark someone as inherently inferior (Bonilla-Silva 2006). Our argument however is not that phenotypes no longer matter, as they certainly do, particularly in European countries and the United States. Biological racism never went away, as many scholars have argued, it is just no longer the only way someone is raced (Bonilla-Silva 2006; Omi and Winant 2015). The resurgence

Introduction

of genomics is an example of how biological and scientific racism have always been a part of our epistemologies (Roberts 2011; Benjamin 2013; Williams 2013). But Muslim encounters and experiences with racism are often dismissed across the globe because beliefs about what has to do with race and what does not have to do with race are often connected to antiquated notions of biological difference.

Currently, there are many scholars who use race theory to frame the Muslim experience since 9/11. Some have argued that Muslims are a new race (Rana 2011). Others have noted that Muslim experiences with race must be understood within the context of empire (Kumar 2020; Kazi 2021). Naber and Rana (2019) argue that anti-Muslim racism should be examined within the history of imperialism and colonialism, highlighting the global nature of racism. This global recognition of racism enables movement building against imperial racism (Naber and Rana 2019). Aziz (2021) provides various types of racial Muslims that have been created as a result of a long history of racism within the United States and particularly after 9/11. We add to this burgeoning critical race scholarship on Muslims by using the theoretical concept of racialization to explain how Muslims are encountering racism today within a global context. Racialization is not static, but constantly shifting because it reflects the structures of the era within which it is captured or studied.

Racialization is a concept that allows for an understanding of how groups of people are read and understood in racial terms. For our work, racialization enables us to think about how a religious identity acquires racial meaning without relying only on phenotypical or biological factors, like skin tone, which allows for its use in countries that do not acknowledge racial classifications. To use it, we first need to examine the definitions of this term. In their seminal book *Racial Formation in the United States* (2015) Omi and Winant argue that racial formations are tied to specific historic and sociopolitical contexts. For example, to understand how African Americans experience racism, we have to continuously examine the political and social context of the era within which the racism occurs. As we stated above, racial

14 A Global Racial Enemy

experiences shift over time. Racialization allows us to capture the fluid nature of racism. Omi and Winant define racialization as "the extension of racial meaning to a previously racially unclassified relationship, social practice, or group" (Omi and Winant 2015: 111). We appreciate this definition as a starting point; however, it is limited because it still relies on phenotype, something we see in scholarship that centers on Europe and the United States. They state, "we provide a concept of racialization to emphasize how the phenomic, the corporeal dimensions of human bodies, acquires meaning in social life" (Omi and Winant 2015: 109). While phenomic and corporeal dimensions are important, they do not capture the entire scope of experiences with racism.

Weiner (2012) writes that racialization is the process of ranking groups of people on a hierarchy that can shift depending on the sociopolitical context. This definition does not rest on phenotype but includes cultural traits as well. For us, racial hierarchies as a way to think theoretically about racism (Bonilla-Silva 2004; Weiner 2012; Treitler 2013) also has limitations. Racial hierarchies can ignore the nuances of the lived experiences of racialization, especially as the hierarchies are often based on a limited number of measures, such as socioeconomic status, rather than incorporating everyday experiences with racism. For us, racialization does not necessarily mean that groups are acquiring a new racial classification or becoming a race, but that they are encountering racism and racist structures. These structures shift in response to what is going on in society. Nevertheless, Weiner (2012) provides several empirics and indicators of racialization that we find useful in this book, which include citizenship laws, state control, and criminalization.

We use instead Selod's (2018) definition of racialization: "the process by which bodies become racial in their lived realities because of biological and/or cultural traits as a result of the intersection and cooperation between ideologies, policies, laws, and social interactions, resulting in the denial of equal treatment in society" (pg. 23). In the twenty years since the GWOT began, the institutionalization of counterterrorism policies has expanded and grown globally. For

Introduction 15

this to occur, Muslims have been continuously racialized as a threat. But this construction shifts over time and space; thus, we must constantly examine and re-examine what these constructions are and how they operate. As we have moved further away from 9/11, we are able to see how the racialization of Muslims has actually become more widespread because policies imbued with racial stereotypes of Muslims have been embedded into our society. It is how we allow horrific human rights abuses to occur in the name of national security – because that threat is seen as so evil and dangerous that any means necessary are supported to thwart terrorism.

The process of racialization allows for an understanding of how other identities such as sexuality, gender, language, and religion intersect and can also be understood racially (Garner and Selod 2015). For example, in India Muslim men's sexuality has been racialized as hypersexual and therefore viewed as in need of policing and surveillance (Puar 2009; Puri 2016). Racializing Muslim men as hypersexual justifies policing and surveillance of them because they are seen as a threat to women – because of their gender and racialized religious identity (Puar 2009; Puri 2016). Another example of how racialization captures intersections like gender, race, and religion is in airport experiences. Because airplanes were used in the September 11th terrorist attacks, security practices in airports have greatly shifted. The Transportation and Security Administration (TSA) was created in the United States to deal with security at the borders. But airport security and the TSA have been accused of racially profiling passengers, specifically Muslims (Selod 2018). Since 9/11, Muslim men and women, particularly those that visibly appear Muslim because of their religious attire, like the hijab, or men who don beards, have been removed from flights because of their religious identity. For example, Eaman Shebley, who wears the hijab, and her family were removed from a United Airlines flight in 2016 simply because she asked for a child harness for her toddler (Mohammad 2016). Muslims did not encounter these experiences on airplanes before 9/11 like they have since. Racialization allows us to see how Muslim women who wear the hijab are viewed as a threat in airports and on airplanes

16 A Global Racial Enemy

and are thus subjected to profiling due to the institutionalization of security practices in airports.

Race, Ethnicity, and Communalism in the United States, the United Kingdom, China, and India

In order to apply racialization to the four different contexts we examine in this book, we first turn to the ways that each country thinks about race. In the United States, race is not a fixed category, but one that has shifted and changed over time. The creation and erasure of racial categories has been documented by the Pew Research Center. An interactive chart shows how racial classifications changed over time on the US Census (Brown 2020). The 1790 Census lists "free white males/free white females," "all other free persons," and "slave" as the three racial classifications. On the 1860 Census "Mulatto" and "Indian" are listed as racial classifications. Between 1920 and 1940, "Hindu" is listed as a racial classification on the US Census, which was used to capture Asian Indians. One might wonder why a religious classification was used to denote a racial classification. Ian Haney Lopez answers this question in his book *White by Law* (2006), where he shows how the courts used a religious identity for South Asians and Arabs as the justification for denying them access to citizenship. At this time, one had to be white in order to become a naturalized citizen. The courts determined that one could not reasonably be white if one were Hindu, because the cultural values associated with this religion were too distinct from those of a European Christian identity, which defined whiteness. In the early to mid-20th century several Asian Indian men attempted to gain citizenship by challenging the notion that they were not white in the courts. The courts ruled their religion situated them as not white, thus the failure to attain citizenship and the racialization of religion is reflected in the racial classification of Hindu on the census. Currently, Arabs are racially classified as white in the US Census, something that is being contested by Arab advocacy groups because many have argued they do

Introduction 17

not experience the privileges of whiteness due to skin tone and/or religious identity, like being Muslim (Maghbouleh 2020). Although whiteness is a racial classification that has been constant on the US Census, who has been included and excluded has changed over time.

The UK differs from the United States in terms of racial classification. The 1976 Race Relations Act gave rise to the classifications that would later be expressed in the census. It made discrimination on racial grounds illegal, and defined "racial grounds" as: color, race, nationality, or ethnic or national origins. However, there was no official racial classification in the UK until the 1991 Census. Unofficially, public policy discussions of "colored" immigration from the late 1940s referred to postcolonial migration from Anglophone colonies and former colonies principally in the Indian subcontinent, the Caribbean, and Africa. The term used in the census since 1991 is "ethnic" rather than "racial," although the classification uses color, country, region, and continent of origin. In 1991 respondents were asked to choose between: White, Black-Caribbean, Black-African, Black-Other (write in), Indian, Pakistani, Bangladeshi, Chinese, and any other ethnic group (write in). The three subsequent censuses have seen an expansion of the number of groups identified within the classification with the introduction of the category "Mixed," as well as groups vying successfully (Irish, Arab, Traveller) and unsuccessfully (Latin Americans) for inclusion. Some organized groups of Hindus, Sikhs, and Muslims wanted religious affiliation to be included in the census (the question had been asked once, in the 1851 Census, in England) because they felt that country of origin and the umbrella category of "British Asian" were not specific enough to their identity. The religious affiliation question was introduced into the census in 2001 as a result of the lobbying undertaken by these three religious based groups. For the 2021 Census, people first identify with one of the five "high-level" categories: Black, Asian, White, Mixed, Other, then choose the nineteen subcategories within these five, and are able to further expand their answers to a total of 287 options. Thus, while the UK uses ethnicity over race in its census, what it shares with the United States is that it is ever shifting. These fluid racial and ethnic categories reflect the changing social and political climate. It also reveals whiteness is a constant racial classification, like in the United States.

India does not have the ethnic and racial classifications that exist in the United States and the UK. The context of colonialism played a significant role in the othering of groups of people. After the British rule in India ended, Pakistan was created as a Muslim country, with India being majority Hindu. At this time, there was an intense rise in nationalism. The right-wing Hindu extremist group, the Rashtriya Swayamsevak Sangh (RSS), were making associations between an "Indian" nationalist identity and a "Hindu" one in the early 1920s, perpetuating the idea that Hindus shared a "common blood" (Bharucha 2003). Scientific racism was a global phenomenon in the 1920s, so it should not be surprising that India was also engaging with it. The difference is they were applying it to religious difference. A nationalist Indian identity and who was allowed to claim it was prominent during the period of independence from the British colonial rule and the creation of Hindu (India) and Muslim (Pakistan) nations (Bharucha 2003). Religion was deeply tied to how the state viewed and treated its citizens, while race on the other hand was viewed as a colonial project that was about phenotypical differences (Puri 2016). Thus, communalism, defined as group connections to their religious communities that interfere with their patriotic duties, is the way discrimination and prejudice in India are framed (Puri 2016). Communalism masks power dynamics by the dominant groups and the human rights abuses that occur as a result. Cháirez-Garza et al. (2022) contend that racialization allows for a more expansive understanding of the ways that racial differences are experienced in India. Puri (2016) also argues that racialization is a useful analytical tool to understand the treatment of Indian Muslims by allowing one to think beyond just phenotypes as a way to understand individuals in racial terms. As she states, "race and racializations are wrought from cultural and historical regimes

Introduction 19

of classification that rationalize forms of inequalities on the basis of natural, extracultural difference" (Puri 2016: 86).

China does not collect racial data, but surveys ethnicity. In 1963 the first census was conducted in China, with the last being in 2020. Han Chinese account for over 91 percent of the population with fifty-five recognized ethnic minorities making up 8 percent. The reasons for surveying ethnicity in China was due to the passage of the 1953 Election Law, which promised minority representation in the Nation's People Congress (Maurer-Fazio and Hasmath 2015). The government did not have an accurate account of how many ethnic groups were in China and decided to survey the population. An initial survey, which relied on self-identification, produced over 400 ethnic groups. Because of the large number, the Chinese Communist Party (CCP) put together a team to categorize the population into smaller ethnic minority groups. The group went to various regions around China to create a taxonomy based on several factors, like language, religion, and social history (Maurer-Fazio and Hasmath 2015). The state reduced the number of ethnic minorities from 400 to thirty-nine in the 1953 Census and to sixteen in the 1965 Census. Thus, ethnic minorities in China are determined by the state, which is tied to who gets representation in the government.

For each of these countries, racialization provides the language to describe how Muslims acquire racial meanings and experience racism because they are marked as threats to security and a national identity. The ways that each country conceptualizes race, ethnicity, and communalism can make invisible Muslim encounters with racism. For example, in the context of the United States, people argue that Muslims cannot experience racism because they encounter religious discrimination, which is an entirely different phenomenon. We interrupt this logic by showing how racialization allows us to understand Muslim experiences as racial, even in societies that do not classify their population by race. Racialization is about how groups of people are marked in specific ways that justify discriminatory practice against them by the state and its citizens.

The Global Racialization of Muslims: 21st-Century Racism

We use the term "global racialization" to interrogate how security and surveillance practices rely on the construction of Muslims as a threat to national security and a national identity via cultural practices in the United States, the United Kingdom, China, and India. Others have argued that racism should be understood within a global context as there have been calls to think globally about race. Many race scholars argue that racism must be understood in relation to colonialism (Mills 1997; Weiner 2012). While race and racisms in the United States and the UK are often framed in relation to white supremacy because it has been rooted in European colonial histories, in countries like India, scholars argue that race, racism, and racialization should be understood both within the context of European colonialism as well as outside of it (Loomba 2009; Puri 2016; Ejiofor 2023). In other words, Europe did not invent racism as it had always existed prior to colonialism (Loomba 2009; Ejiofor 2023). European colonialism enables us to understand the relationship of racism to white supremacy in some countries like the United States and the UK, but it limits our ability to understand how racism operates in spaces where white domination is not the ultimate goal, like China and India. Global racialization of Muslims allows us to think about how racial constructions of Muslims as a threat to either the nation-state or the culture of a society exist both to uphold white supremacy in some contexts and to uphold religious or national supremacy in others.

One of the ways that we see how the racialization of Muslims is a global phenomenon is through the expansion of the surveillance industrial complex in the name of security from terrorism. Simone Browne (2015) argues in her book *Dark Matters: On the Surveillance of Blackness*, that blackness has been a central target for surveillance in the United States, dating back to slavery. Her work centers the role of race in surveillance, highlighting the various technologies that have been created historically

Introduction 21

to surveil Black people, along with the tools created to counter this surveillance. It extended to both African Muslim slaves as well as Black Muslims in the middle of the 20th century. Thus, surveillance societies have always been a characteristic of the United States because of the way the state targeted African Americans. The September 11th terrorist attacks justified the expansion of the United States' surveillance capabilities with regard to both its citizens and non-citizens. In the name of preventing another terrorist attack, surveillance systems and new technologies were deployed via federal laws and policies. For example, the Uniting and Strengthening America by Providing Appropriate Tools Required to Intercept and Obstruct Terrorism (USA PATRIOT Act), which was passed in 2001, gave the United States government expansive surveillance powers that it did not have before in order to combat terrorism. While these systems of surveillance that targeted African Americans have always been in place, the scope for their application became much larger in the War on Terror. Surveillance technologies, like body scanners at airports and facial recognition tools, are utilized globally in the name of security, and reflect the investment in new technologies for surveillance. In the first few years after 9/11 airports used metal detectors for security. But the government invested in newer technologies, like body scanners, to prevent another terrorist attack (Selod 2018). The United States is not the only country to invest in advanced surveillance technologies. China's use of these surveillance tools has far surpassed that of any other country, inciting an international outcry because of its authoritarian implementation. An example of its reach are the reports of a facial recognition tool that can identify Uyghur Muslims and create a "Uyghur alarm" that alerts authorities to their movement, which can result in their imprisonment (Harwell and Dou 2020). As countries advocate for population control in the name of security in the Global War on Terror, the market for advanced surveillance tools is growing.

But while the justification of surveillance tools and technologies is to deter terrorism, their use goes beyond their intended target. China and the United States both use facial recognition to surveil civil unrest and protests. In the United States, they are also used to securitize borders and police undocumented migrants via biometric surveillance technologies. These technologies are also used to address climate change. Climate security is the catchphrase that captures how climate change is being dealt with via the securitization of borders to prevent migration due to climate disasters (Miller 2019). In other words, the threat of terrorism and the racialization of Muslims globally may initiate the advancement of surveillance tools, but these tools are not limited in their scope and have an impact on other racialized populations.

We do not argue that 9/11 or the GWOT created Muslims as a threat, but it has become institutionalized via counter-terrorism policies, citizenship laws and policies, and the idea of who does and does not belong within a nation-state's polity. Within the context of the GWOT, security is an inherent racial project because it targets bodies, the racialized Muslims, that are perceived to be a threat to the safety of the nation. We show how a global racialized Muslim identity serves a rising global surveillance industry through the construction of a Muslim as a terrorist. The "Muslim threat" is not just a physical threat, but also a cultural one. From the manufacturers of surveillance technologies and military equipment to the companies managing detention centers, there are multiple entities who profit from anti-Muslim racialization that rests on the assumptions of Muslims as people that need to be watched, monitored, and detained for a nation to be secure. Thus, for the purposes of this book, we argue that the marking of Muslims as a threat to national security and cultural values, which has triggered their surveillance, detention, and denial of citizenship, is a global racial project that we call *global Muslim racialization*.

In order to identify how the racialization of Muslims is a global phenomenon, we provide examples from four distinct contexts to show how Muslim racialization transcends borders. The United States and the UK provide examples of what many race scholars have shown: the ways in which immigrant groups are racialized in the service of white

Introduction

supremacy and a perpetuation of empire and colonialism. The inclusion of India and China allows us to show how the objectives of racism are similar, to dehumanize groups of people for the purposes of power, but they are done in the name of nationalism. In other words, race, a social construct, may be constructed differently in India from the United States due to the sociopolitical histories of each country, but this does not mean that the racisms in each nation are completely disconnected from one another. The ways that Uyghur Muslims experience racialization in China differ from Muslims in the United States, but there are similarities in the ideological construction of Muslims as a threat to society. A Muslim identity erects a system of racialized surveillance instituted in all of the countries we examine. The history of Uyghur Muslims is one of separatism and independence from an oppressive state, compared to Muslims in the United States, who encompass a variety of ethnicities and races and histories of migration. Muslims in the United States migrated for a multitude of reasons, from the forced migration of Africans via slavery, Iranians seeking political asylum, Pakistani and Indian Muslims searching for better economic opportunities, to current examples of Syrian, Iraqi, and Afghan refugees escaping military invasions and interventions by the United States. While Muslim men in China, India, the United States, and the UK are distinct from one another culturally, they have all been labeled as a potential threat to national security because of their religious identity, and consequently encounter similar types of subjugation like surveillance in their respective countries, because of each state's engagement in the Global War on Terror. In addition to showing how the racialization of Muslims is global, in the next section we also show how this is deeply gendered.

Gendered Racializations: Muslim Men as Terrorists and Muslim Women as Cultural Threats in the GWOT

The construct of the terrorist is one of the ways we see Muslim men racialized as dangerous and violent. Ahmed, the clock boy, is a perfect example of this racialization at play. In 2015, Ahmed Mohamed, a fourteen-year-old student at MacArthur High School in Irving, Texas was arrested on suspicion of terrorist activities. The young student of Sudanese descent was an aspiring engineer, who brought a clock he built to impress his teachers. Instead, one of his teachers accused him of making a bomb, leading to his arrest. Ahmed was released and the case received national attention, getting Ahmed invitations to the White House and talk shows (Glenza and Woolf 2015). The incident also reveals how a Muslim identity marks men and young boys as potential terrorists and threats to security.

How we got to a place where a kid like Ahmed could legitimately be accused of bringing a bomb to school requires some examination. Lisa Stampnitzky studies the history of terrorism in her book *Disciplining Terror: How Experts Invented "Terrorism"* (2013). As the title suggests, terrorism as a field of study was invented. She shows how the term insurgency was once used to describe acts of violence committed in service of political goals. Insurgents were seen as individuals who had deeper motivations for the attacks that scholars and state agents felt were important to understand. However, over time, the term terrorism became the way that these acts of violence were framed. According to Stampnitzky (2013), an entire field of studies on terrorism was created that framed terrorism as an act of violence without a motive. The terrorist was constructed as an irrational and violent criminal, devoid of any motivations, which justifies violence against those marked as a terrorist. But the terrorist is not just irrational, the terrorist is also a Muslim – explaining how a young Muslim boy could be stereotyped as a potential terrorist and his clock mistaken for a bomb.

Deepa Kumar has coined the term "terrorcraft" to explain how the concept of the "terrorist" is a term that racializes Muslims (Kumar 2020). "Terrorcraft is a process. It consists of evolving state policies and ideologies. The security state is an essential actor in the creation of a racialised terrorist subject through practices of racial profiling. Terrorcraft incorporates 'statecraft' and the security practices that inform racialization" (Kumar 2020: 37). Thus, the terrorist, which is a racialized construction, justifies the growth of the surveillance industrial complex that targets racialized bodies, aka Muslims.

Junaid Rana (2016) articulates the ways in which the association of terror with Muslims fuels the terrorist industrial complex:

> the impact of the terror-industrial complex is far more extreme than a representational mistake based in the fearmongering of Islam and Muslims. Rather, it is the larger systems of structural violence that are normalized through the workings of concepts such as race and permanent war that create an unprecedented flexibility in the workings of social domination and capital accumulation. As an ideological structure it is present in a range of security and biopolitical technologies, including, for example, policing, health care, social services, and the framing of criminality and illegality in the detention and deportation regime. (pg. 114)

This "terror-industrial complex" that Rana describes fuels a security apparatus. The detention and surveillance of Uyghurs is one example of this terrorist industrial complex. China's president, Xi Jinping, gave speeches critiquing how England put human rights above security concerns, after the London Bridge stabbings of five people, two fatally, in 2019. The stabbings were carried out by Usman Khan, who had been recently released from prison, where he was serving time for plotting a terrorist attack. Khan was seen as rehabilitated, which is why he was released. President Xi critiqued the UK for its liberal approach that valued civil liberties, arguing that it had led to the attacks, and advocated for his hard line on terrorism, including his policy of rounding up Uyghur Muslims and putting them in detention centers in China (Ramzy and Buckley 2019).

The Chinese government has placed over 1 million Uyghur Muslims in internment camps. The Chinese state argued that these detention centers were necessary to entice Uyghur

Muslims away from radical terrorist ideologies, which make them a threat to the state. According to a *New York Times* article that exposed leaked Chinese documents about the detention of and crackdown on Uyghur Muslims, "Mr. Xi urged the party to emulate aspects of America's 'war on terror' after the Sept. 11 attacks" in response to a violent attack committed by a Uyghur Muslim (Ramzy and Buckley 2019). The GWOT gave the Chinese a reason to detain and surveil Uyghur Muslims by characterizing them as terrorists and threats to national security. Although the struggle of Uyghurs is characterized by a history of separatism, the ability to mark one as a terrorist erases the political context for any violence one may enact. China is an extreme example of how the label of terrorist strips one of any humanity and consequently justifies draconian punishments (Stampnitzky 2013). We find that it is Muslim men who are marked as the threat to nation-states and framed as the potential terrorist. This does not mean that women are not imprisoned in China or have not been targeted as a terrorist, but the overwhelming construction of the terrorist is a Muslim man and they are the ones who are more likely to be detained and imprisoned.

While Muslim men are racialized as terrorist, justifying security in the GWOT, Muslim men and women are both racialized as threats to the nation via cultural transgressions, with Muslim women being surveilled and policed in unique ways. In each of the countries we examine, Muslims are painted as outsiders who do not belong, with Muslim women being framed as carriers of cultural attributes that are viewed as threats to the nation-state. In the United States, the UK, India, and China assimilationist frames are used to explain the failures of Muslims. These sentiments rely on the myth that Muslims are newcomers, thus making invisible the long history Muslims have had in each of these countries, as we show in the next chapter.

Muslims are framed not only as invaders, but also as corrupting the values of the nation. Anti-immigration sentiments are not just held by white populist movements in the United States and Europe but are also growing in places like China and India, where their Muslim populations are treated as an unwanted foreign presence. The detention camps in China, referred to by the state as "re-education" camps, are used to rid Uyghur Muslims of their cultural distinctions. In these camps, the CCP forces people to learn Mandarin in an attempt to rid them of any Uyghur culture. Speaking Uyghur, a different language from the national one, is criminalized because the act is seen as rejecting loyalty to the nation. In India, citizenship laws that exclude Muslim immigrants are done so under the ideology that they are unassimilable into the nation. In the United States, right-wing groups instill fear that Muslims are taking over the country via their propaganda. Muslims are portrayed through nationalism and ethnonationalist populisms as cultural threats to the nation.

In addition to the policing of cultural traits and attributes, intimate relationships have also been subjected to state control. We show in the chapters that follow that in China, Uyghur Muslim women have been forced into marriages with Han men in order to prevent the growth of Muslim families. Uyghur Muslim women have had contraceptive devices put into them without their consent and subjected to forced sterilization. Their bodies have literally been policed and violated in the name of controlling a Muslim population in China (Fallert 2021). Love Jihad laws in the state of Uttar Pradesh in India make it illegal for Muslims to marry outside of their religion, which has resulted in the arrests of Muslim men (Sharma and Khan 2021). The fact that the law is named "jihad," a term associated with terrorism, is indicative of how the fight against terrorism is now being waged in intimate spaces. We provide more detailed examples of all of this in the chapters that follow, but the point is to show how the GWOT has triggered policies that surveil and police intimate relationships, which highlights the gendered nature of the global racialization of Muslims.

Gendered racialization of Muslim men as violent and Muslim women as threats to culture has been used to push through a more expansive counterterrorism surveillance and security apparatus globally (Selod 2019). Muslim men and Muslim women experience the impact of global racialization differentially, which we demonstrate in this book. We show

28   A Global Racial Enemy

in the chapters that follow how Muslim women's racialization is experienced via the policing of cultural attributes, forced sterilization, imprisonment, miscegenation laws, and finally forced marriages. These constructs of Muslim men and women are not new, as we explained earlier, but they are shared across borders and used to achieve various objectives of each state. By using the United States, the UK, China, and India as case studies, we examine how the global racialization of Muslims transcends geographical boundaries, highlighting that this racial project can no longer be described as the "West vs. the Rest."

Outline of Book

In chapter 1, we identify the relationship of Muslims to the nation-state of the United States, the UK, China, and India. We show how Muslims are not new migrants to any of these nations but have had a long history in them. The relationship of Muslims to the nation, via struggles for visibility, citizenship, and independence, plays a major role in the identity of each nation and the current global racialization of Muslims.

In chapter 2 we look at the role of the media and social media in current representations of Muslims in each country. This chapter identifies how the ideological construction of Muslims via their representation has similarities and differences globally. The social construction of Muslims as a terrorist and threat to society is why there has been very little public outcry about the human rights abuses that Muslims encounter globally. We highlight how policies are justified when the dehumanization via the racialization of Muslims is so prevalent in the media.

In chapter 3 we examine the relationship of ethnonationalism and nationalism to the global racialization of Muslims. Here we uncover how anti-immigrant and anti-Muslim sentiments have worked together to contribute to the rise in nationalism that is xenophobic and racist. The increasing popularity of anti-Muslim sentiments played a role in the election of authoritarian leaders who campaigned on vilifying a Muslim population.

In chapter 4 we examine some of the counterterrorism policies that have been implemented in the United States, the UK, China, and India. We reveal the connections between security practices globally. Part of this is due to the charge by the United Nations to its members to partake in combating terrorism after 9/11. While there are many differences in the types of laws and policies that have been put in place and the impact they have had on Muslims in each nation, it is important to show there are also connections between them. Counterterrorism is a global strategy and does not occur in a vacuum.

We conclude the book by reflecting on how, in the 21st century, the global racialization of Muslims is one of many types of global racism. We highlight how the racialization of Muslims has a much larger reach, beyond Muslim populations. We also show how people are resisting this racialization in each nation, putting a spotlight on how acts of oppression are always met with acts of resistance, regardless of how small or large they are. We ask readers to think about how racism does not occur in a vacuum within one nation-state, but is often intertwined with foreign policy, militarization, colonialism, settler colonialism, and capitalism.

–1–
Muslim Histories: Contextualizing the Global War on Terror

In 2018, Liverpool Football Club fans created several chants about their favorite player, Mohammed Salah. Referred to as the "Egyptian King," Mohammed Salah is considered one of the greatest footballers of his time. Born and raised in Egypt, he made his mark in England on various teams. At a time when a rise in anti-Muslim sentiments could be seen via Brexit and the rise in nationalist right-wing groups, like the English Defence League, many were surprised at how Liverpool football fans created several chants revering Salah. One of them was set to the 1990s British rock band Dodgy's song *Good Enough*.

> *If he's good enough for you, he's good enough for me.*
> *If he scores another few, then I'll be Muslim too.*
> *If he's good enough for you, he's good enough for me.*
> *Sitting in the mosque, that's where I wanna be!*
> *Mo Salah-la-la-la, la-la-la-la-la-la-la.*

Another was set to *You Are My Sunshine*, with the following lyrics:

> *Mohamed Salah, a gift from Allah.*
> *He came from Roma to Liverpool.*

He's always scoring, it's almost boring.
So please don't take Mohamed away.

Media outlets praised such chants and in one study, researchers argue that Salah's popularity aided in reducing anti-Muslim sentiments expressed by Liverpool fans, noting that there were fewer anti-Muslim incidents, such as hate crimes, in the neighborhood where Liverpool plays (Alrababa'h et al. 2019).

While this mostly appears to be a positive story and can be used to argue that anti-Muslim racism must be on the decline, there is something else happening with these chants. These chants become attention worthy because of the overt racism encountered by footballers who are not white or who are Muslim. When white football fans chant that they would "sit in a mosque" or "would be a Muslim too" it is a shocking statement, revealing that underneath these seemingly positive statements lies an intense hatred toward Muslims. Sitting in a mosque is treated as an extreme act a football fan is willing to do if their favorite footballer continues to score goals for the team. It should come as no surprise that at the same time, anti-Muslim chants were also yelled at Salah by fans of opposing teams. Fans of the Chelsea football team were recorded chanting "Mohamed Salah is a bomber!" at one of his games (Rathborn 2019). Both the positive and the negative chants showcase that Muslims are not truly viewed as members of the nation but are outsiders within. Whether they are tolerated or not is dependent, in this case, on a footballer's exceptionalism.

Muslims have a long history in each of the countries chronicled in this book. We chose countries with distinct histories to elucidate how, although the setting is unique, Muslim racialization within the context of the 21st century relies on similar racialized constructions of Muslims as a terrorist and cultural threat to society. One of the ways that anti-Muslim racism is expressed in the 21st century is to erase the histories and relationships of Muslims to each nation-state. Muslims are treated and framed as if they are a unique threat or invader in each state, justifying the draconian laws

32   A Global Racial Enemy

and policies that target them. This narrative that Muslims are invaders ignores how Muslims have a long and complicated relationship to the nation-state and have been a part of its construction. In this chapter we explore Muslim histories of migration, colonialism, settler colonialism, and slavery in the United Kingdom, the United States, India, and China that date back centuries.

United Kingdom

Islam is currently the second largest religion in the United Kingdom, accounting for 6.5 percent of the population, vis-à-vis 46 percent who identify as Christian, and 37 percent who state 'No Religion' on the 2021 Census (Office for National Statistics [ONS] 2022). While Muslims have been in Britain since the 16th century, when North African and Turkish slaves were liberated from captured Spanish Armada ships, the UK's contemporary Muslim demographic landscape has been shaped primarily by Britain's interactions with Muslim powers since the 16th century, its empire, and its military intervention in Arab nations throughout the latter 20th and early 21st centuries.

Although much of Christian Europe harbored hostile views of Muslim societies, which found expression in and fueled the Crusades (11th to 13th centuries), the expansion of the British Empire from the 16th century led to more tolerant interactions between the British and Muslim populations in Asia and North Africa. During the reign of King Henry VIII (1509–47), England cultivated closer relationships in trade and diplomacy with the Ottoman Empire and other nations. This yielded resources and enabled familiarity with Islam and Muslims. The activities of the East India Company (which controlled trade between the British Empire and the Indian provinces) in the 17th and 18th centuries led to the recruiting of Muslim seamen, known as *lascars* (Visram 1986; Sherwood 1991), from the Indian subcontinent and the Arabian Peninsula, as well as from Somalia and Malaysia. However, the poor working conditions and cruelty experienced by many of these sailors and merchants led to many choosing to give up the service and settle in port towns and cities like London, Liverpool, Cardiff, South Shields, and Hull (Fryer 1986; Knott 2018). Many of these new immigrants developed their own communities, married locals, raised families, and continued to practice Islamic traditions. With the formal colonization of India by the British Empire in 1858, these migrants were later joined by Indian and Arab students at universities in England and Scotland, and by the 20th century, there was a small but growing Muslim presence in Britain (Gilliat-Ray 2010).

The establishment of the British Raj was a key point in British–Muslim relations. Interactions between British travelers, aristocrats, merchants, artists, and India's Muslim elite facilitated by empire led to the development of writing, art, and scholarship based in orientalist thought, and also to a number of intermarriages and conversions of British men to Islam (Pugh 2019). Although many of these new Muslims decided to stay in India, others came back to England with their wives and children, supplementing the new population of Muslims in Britain. One of the earliest recorded mosques in Britain was founded in Woking, Surrey in 1889 to accommodate the needs of Indian Muslim students and British converts. Other mosques were built over the next few decades (Saleem 2018).

Through the 19th and into the early 20th century, nationalist groups with a variety of religious, cultural, and social backgrounds were active within empire, from India to Ireland. Two examples of Muslim subjects' resistance are in Afghanistan and India. Afghan resistance pushed the invading British army out of Afghanistan twice, in the 1838–42 war and again in 1878–81. In India, in response to the British Raj partition of Bengal along religious lines in 1905, Muslims formed the All-Indian Muslim League, calling for a separate state.

During both World Wars, there was a slow but steady flow of Muslim settlers into Britain – many of whom had fought for the British. However, large-scale immigration of Muslims to Britain occurred principally after the Second World War, with thousands of migrants arriving from the Indian subcontinent (La Barbera 2014; Ansari 2018). The British economy was to be rebuilt and there were large labor shortages. Britain, like other imperial powers, recruited in their colonies and former colonies (Miles and Phizacklea 1984). While single men made up the majority of these earlier migrants (Rex and Moore 1967), they were later joined by their relatives, settling in Bradford, Birmingham, and London, which now boast some of the UK's largest Muslim populations, and other industrial towns in the North of England. As of the 2021 Census, 15 percent of the capital's population were Muslim (ONS 2022), comprising almost 40 percent of the residents of the Borough of Tower Hamlets (in the East End), a longstanding settlement area for Bengalis. Bradford (ONS 2021a) and Birmingham's (ONS 2021b) figures were 30.5 percent and 30 percent respectively. As the population of immigrants from South Asia, the Caribbean, Africa, and Asia grew in the years after the Second World War, and Britain's empire declined during the decolonization process, British society became increasingly preoccupied with issues of identity preservation.

One of the urgent problems facing British governments in the postwar period was how to manage public attitudes about migration while implementing a form of pluralism that enabled a continued supply of labor to enter the country (Elshayyal 2019). Substantial concerns about the social, political, and cultural implications of having growing immigrant communities in the UK were voiced both in popular culture, and at a political level particularly, but not exclusively, by small far-right parties and elements of the Conservative Party (Barker 1981). Pressure was exerted on the postwar governments to restrict what was referred to at the time as "Colored" immigration, i.e., from the Caribbean, Africa, and the Indian subcontinent. However, leaders of both governing parties, Labour and the Conservatives, were hesitant to take action for fear of "antagonizing the Commonwealth and partly because they recognized the economic value of immigrant workers" (Pugh 2019: 219). In the late 1950s, however, a slight downturn in the economy resulted in a reduced need for labor. Thus, the government decided to enact the Commonwealth Immigrants Act in 1962 and restrict further immigration. While the Act was intended to restrict immigration, it provoked a spike of new immigrants seeking to enter the country prior to the implementation of the Act. Pugh (2019: 220) notes that the result of the Act was an increase in Muslim Pakistani immigrants in particular: "between 1955 and 1960 there were only 17,000 immigrants from Pakistan, but during the 18 months prior to the 1962 Act some 50,000 arrived." Not only were many of these immigrants from small rural towns, but upon arrival they were also heavily exploited as labor and faced racial discrimination in British society. With a uniquely visible change in the demographic, concentrated in a relatively small number of urban centers, there were renewed concerns of identity politics in the British political sphere. Amendments to immigration rules were made again later in the 1960s, with the aim of reducing migratory flows from former colonies in the category of "colored" immigration.

In 1964, Conservative Party leaders made immigration a major political issue and this consequently contributed to their advantage in the parliamentary elections of that year. Virulent anti-immigrant propaganda gained a foothold in British politics and came to the fore in April 1968 when Health Minister Enoch Powell delivered his "Rivers of Blood" speech. Ironically, although Powell had encouraged the immigration of doctors from South Asia and nurses from the Caribbean, moves that helped to staff the developing National Health Service, his speech was deeply inflammatory. Not only did he criticize mass immigration but he "repeated unsubstantiated anecdotes, prophesized violence and advocated voluntary repatriation" (Pugh 2019: 220). Powell's speech also drew clear lines around Britishness, implying that it was for whites only (Pugh 2019: 220).

While Powell was soon fired by Tory leader Edward Heath, this speech left a mark on British politics and public sentiment, with right-wing extremist parties emboldened, and racist opinions being openly voiced in the following years. Widespread anti-Muslim and anti-immigrant racism led to an increase in the number of attacks on Blacks and Asians, and right-wing nationalist parties and groups such as the National Front (1970s and 1980s), and later, the British National Party (1990s) and the English Defence League (2010s) organizing marches in Muslim districts to intimidate Muslim immigrants. From the 1970s, these tactics not only spurred increased racist violence but also led to the deaths of Asian immigrants such as Tosir Ali and Altab Ali, stabbed in the East End of London in 1970 and 1978 respectively. The latter's death provoked marches and protests against racist killings (Pugh 2019). Resistance took local forms, with people organizing around their residential areas under a pan-continental identity, like the Asian Youth Movements (Ramamurthy 2013), or national fora, like the Pakistani Welfare Association (Ashe et al. 2016). It is noteworthy that civil society (as opposed to religious) organizations identifying explicitly as Muslim were few until later in the history of anti-racist struggles.

During the 1970s, anti-racist activities had operated with a political understanding of "Black" that included all people of color alongside national, local, and pan-continental identities. By the early 1980s, however, this generic approach was being overridden by the specifics of the struggle (Modood 1994). Muslim activists in London, Birmingham, and Northern towns had begun to adopt a stance which reflected two changes (Allen 2013): first, the development of a British Muslim identity specific to the generation born to postwar migrants, and who had grown up in Britain; and second, the shift in forms of racism from one based exclusively on physical appearance to one that incorporated and highlighted ideas about culture irrevocably separating groups of people, i.e., a "cultural" form, or "new racism" (Barker 1981). The significance of this was that British Muslims generally began to identify with religious affiliation as much as or more than political blackness and felt the umbrella of the latter did not completely address the racism they faced. Activists such as Fuad Nahdi (director of Muslim community media) and organizations such as Action Committee on Islamic Affairs

Muslim Histories

37

and the Muslim Council of Britain began to facilitate debate on how to resist specifically anti-Muslim racism, and a kind of handbook, Kalim Siddiqui's *The Muslim Manifesto: A Strategy for Survival*, was published in 1990.

The "Rushdie Affair" (1989–90) placed Muslims at the center of the national conversation about belonging. *The Satanic Verses* (1988) by Salman Rushdie, a British author, generated an international dispute about blasphemy, religion, and a writer's rights to expression. In Bolton and Bradford, two towns in the North of England, rallies against the book, which protesters claimed was blasphemous, ended with copies of the book being burned. In February 1989, the Iranian Ayatollah Khomeini issued a fatwa against Rushdie and anyone involved with the book. Rushdie spent the next nine years under police protection and the UK froze diplomatic relations with Iran. The key element of this in the British context is that the Rushdie Affair seemed to encapsulate the distinctions between western democracy's relationship with religion, on the one side, and Islam's relationship with politics on the other. This affair enabled Islam to be tied in the public mind to extremism, and the figure of the Ayatollah used as a symbol in the media of fundamentalism. Pnina Werbner (2005) points out that one of the ways in which Islam is imagined is explicitly as a medieval religious inquisition that squeezes out democratic secular society seen as the fruit of the Enlightenment. Such tropes are still very much present in British and indeed European representations of Islam.

After the 7/7 attacks in 2005, a series of four bombings on London's transport system by Islamist terrorists, the debates on multiculturalism changed rapidly, with a new emphasis on the putative failure of Muslims to integrate into British society. The focus became security due to the rise of political Islamist movements in Iran, Iraq, Libya, Yemen, and Syria, the discourse surrounding Anglo-American pro-Israeli policy, and military interventionism of British and American powers in Middle Eastern and North African affairs (Pugh 2019), which triggered refugee flows from theaters of war into Europe. Moreover, several terrorist attacks that occurred including 7/7, the murder of soldier Lee Rigby in Woolwich

38   A Global Racial Enemy

(2013), Westminster Bridge (2017), and Borough Market (2017), coupled with the anti-immigrant sentiments expressed during the period leading up to and after the referendum on Britain's membership of the European Union in 2016 (Brexit), produced a spiral of attacks on mosques and individuals. A survey of British mosques in summer 2021 revealed 42 percent reporting an attack in the twelve months prior to the survey (MEND and Muslim Census 2022). Official statistics on reported attacks on people have been rising since 2012, with over 3,000 attacks per year reported (Home Office 2022); attacks on Muslims accounted for 40–50 percent of the category of "religiously motivated" attacks. This figure reached 3,500 in 2018 (Home Office, 2019), and stood at 3,400 in 2022 (Home Office 2022).

Finally, recent decades have seen the development of a more complex Muslim demography, with growing communities from North Africa and the Middle East, supplemented by refugees from Iraq, Syria, Iran, and Somalia, as well as Bosnia and smaller West African communities. Some British Muslims like Nadiya Hussain (winner of the highly popular *Great British Bake Off*); comedy writer and creator of the sitcom *Citizen Khan*, Adil Ray; and successful Olympic athlete Mo Farah have become mainstream television personalities. Moreover, several Muslims in British politics have now held senior office, including Baroness Sayeeda Warsi (former Minister of Faith and Communities and former Co-Chair of the Conservative Party), Sadiq Khan (Labour Mayor of London), and Sajid Javid (former Conservative Chancellor of the Exchequer). Such representation has certainly begun to challenge the notion that the "Muslim" identity is incompatible with a "British" one.

Yet despite the various successes that British Muslims have historically had politically, culturally, and otherwise, anti-Muslim racism is still alive and well in the United Kingdom at all levels in society, particularly in politics and particular social circles (Jones and Unsworth 2022). Indeed, Warsi, Javid, and Nusrat Ghani MP have all complained formally about Islamophobia in the Conservative Party, for example. A number of civil society groups and Muslim not-for-profits have been involved in countering such negative opinions and resisting the stereotypical views of Muslims that have developed (see concluding chapter). Jones and Unsworth's (2022) survey, carried out in 2021, found that the British public are three times as likely to hold prejudiced views of Islam than of other religions. The survey found that 23.2 percent of social groups ABC1 (i.e., the middle classes) held negative views of Muslims, compared to 18.2 percent of groups C2D (defined as skilled labor) and E (defined as unskilled labor). Overall, 25.9 percent of people had "negative" feelings towards Muslims, with 9.9 percent stating "very negative" feelings. Moreover, 36 percent of people interviewed agreed with the statement, "Islam threatens the British way of life." As our following chapters show, the UK's contemporary relationship with Muslims has been carefully constructed under the framework of the Global War on Terror, resulting in their dehumanization and racialization even as they hold British citizenship.

United States

Forced migration and Islam in the United States

Muslims first came to the United States via slavery. The relationship of Muslims to the nation-state is deeply tied to race, ethnicity, and nation of origin. The Atlantic slave trade brought with it North and West African Muslims as enslaved people (Jackson 2005; GhaneaBassiri 2010; Diouf 2013). Islam's presence is often ignored in the African diasporas particularly in the United States (Diouf 2013). According to Diouf (2013) there are several documented cases of an enslaved Muslim presence in the United States, such as Omar Ibn Said, who left behind testimonies in Arabic (Diouf 2013). But much of this history has yet to be explored due to a lack of documented evidence.

What *has* been written during the time of slavery is illuminating because it highlights how for some African Muslims, Islam played a major role in their experiences in the United States. Diouf (2013) reveals the ways enslaved Muslims negotiated their racial identity with slaveholders at the time. Enslaved Muslims sought their freedom by disassociating with blackness and creating an association with Arabness, highlighting their "Arab" identity over their Black one because of the way that African enslaved people were racialized. Because of the emphasis on reading the Quran, which was in Arabic, many of the enslaved African Muslims were able to read and write in Arabic (GhaneaBassiri 2010; Diouf 2013). Strengthening this association with an Arab identity, which included notions of literacy, was done in the hope that it would distinguish them enough from Africans and consequently result in better treatment. "These enslaved Muslims, then, emerged from elites of West African societies, and thus it is not surprising that they elevated themselves over other black Africans" (GhaneaBassiri 2010: 23). The negative attitudes towards African non-Muslims that were brought to the United States also reflected the conflicts that existed between them back home, with the system of slavery intensifying any tensions between Muslim and non-Muslim enslaved people. Thus, religion has always intersected with race in unique ways in the United States.

Slavery also shows how Islam in the United States is a part of its history, not a recent 20th-century phenomenon due to migration. Christianity and slavery were deeply intertwined, which explains why there is so little documentation left behind by enslaved Muslims because Islam was forced into invisibility via slavery.

It was essential that the new land become Christian as quickly as possible, because evangelization was a large part of the justification for the enslavement of Africans. Moreover . . . the fight against the possible spread of Islam had been an intense preoccupation in the Spanish colonies since the beginning of the sixteenth century. All the conditions were thus present for a rapid disappearance of Islam, or even for its nonemergence. (Diouf 2013: 71)

Thus, the creation of a Christian nation was tied to the erasure of other religions, including Islam when it was introduced via slavery. The conflicts between Islam and Christianity were not new, but rather represented the long history of religious tensions as a result of wars in Europe with Muslim majority countries like the Ottoman Empire. Animosity toward Islam was not a novel sentiment, but one that was brought to America via colonization and empire.

Islam's influence on African Americans can also be seen in the significant role it has had on ideologies around resistance. Scholars note that because of the high literacy of enslaved Muslims, this helped to inspire freedom and rebellious movements (Diouf 2013). This was also seen later in the 20th century via the emergence and rise of the Nation of Islam (Jackson 2005; Diouf 2013; McCloud 2014). The Nation of Islam tied African Americans to their history of Islam via slavery. Noble Drew Ali of the Moorish Science Temple and Elijah Muhammad of the Nation of Islam gained followers by using parts of the theology of Islam to strengthen an African American identity. In contrast to Southern Christianity that many African Americans practiced, Ali and Muhammad presented an alternative religion to those that they viewed as perpetuating assimilationist theologies of fitting into a white supremacist landscape. Instead, they encouraged focusing on one's own community and their needs rather than relying on a structure that was built on their oppression. African Americans who followed the Nation of Islam refrained from drinking and eating pork and the Quran was used to encourage a theology that centered blackness, appealing to a population that had been brutalized by remnants of slavery and the existing Jim Crow policies (GhaneaBassiri 2010). The Nation of Islam, influenced by individuals like Marcus Garvey, promoted a sense of pride in one's racial and religious identity and encouraged self-autonomy rather than relying on a racialized social structure meant to oppress Black men and women. The success of this group is probably best reflected in the fact that in the 1940s there is a record of FBI surveillance of the Nation because they were seen as a threat to the existing racial order (GhaneaBassiri 2010; Browne 2015; Husain

42 A Global Racial Enemy

2021a). Current counterterrorism and surveillance practices stem from this history of surveilling enslaved people, radicals, activists, and intellectuals, including enslaved Muslims and members of the Nation of Islam (Browne 2015). Thus, Islam has always been a target of the state and its security practices.

South Asian and Arab migration to the United States

The presence of Arab and South Asian Muslims in the United States also dates back to the 19th century. Their migration to the United States in the late 1800s and early 1900s reflects the same reasons as other migrants at this time. It was in search for better opportunities, as the United States was seen as a beacon of prosperity. Part of the success in many industries and the rise in capitalism was the direct result of slavery. However, migrants who came of their own free will also contributed to the rise in industries as they were the cheap labor that resulted in their prosperity.

> The establishment's groping for a cohesive national identity and social order through such universalizing concepts as race, religion, and progress in the nineteenth and early twentieth centuries concealed the actual workings of American industry, commerce, culture, government, and science, most of which were advanced by the diligence and ingenuity not only of white native-born Protestants, but also of immigrants and natives who were not considered white (Irish Catholics, Eastern European Jews, African American Baptists, and others) who made up the mass of American workers, thinkers, and entrepreneurs. (GhaneaBassiri 2010: 135)

Roughly 10–15 percent of the immigrants who came to the United States between 1890 and 1920 seeking better opportunities were Muslims. The smaller percentage reflects the anti-immigration policies at the time that prevented a large number of Muslims from entering the United States. Exploitative and cheap labor has always been a key component to the economic prosperity of the United States.

Many of the Syrians who initially migrated to the United States made claims of escaping an oppressive Ottoman regime; however scholars note that this claim may have been exaggerated to facilitate their migration because it appealed to the stereotypes of Ottomans in the United States (GhaneaBassiri 2010). Migration from Syria to the US was also inspired by American missionaries that were already in the region, revealing how an American presence in the Levant already existed (Gualtieri 2009; GhaneaBassiri 2010). The Syrians who initially came were peddlers of goods and eventually opened up small businesses. Compared to Syrians, other immigrant Muslims who came to the United States at the time worked as day laborers. For example, Bosnian Muslims who migrated at the beginning of the 20th century were mostly uneducated and came to make money and then return to Bosnia. They worked in construction, helped to build the subway in Chicago, and labored in the copper mines in Montana (GhaneaBassiri 2010).

South Asian Muslims, including Indians and Bengalis, also made their way to the United States during this time. Many worked as peddlers, but some found themselves laboring in the agricultural industry and lumber mills (GhaneaBassiri 2010; Bald 2013). Along with other Asian groups, South Asian Muslims experienced high levels of discrimination that were tied to economic insecurities. The Bellingham riots of 1907 reflect the hostility of white American laborers toward immigrant labor. A group of 400–500 white men violently attacked South Asian laborers working in a lumber mill in Bellingham, Washington, to drive them out of the city. The mob broke windows, beat up the migrants in the street, and attacked their homes in order to intimidate and scare the South Asian Indian migrant workers, which led to them leaving Bellingham. While the majority of the men were Sikhs, Muslims were represented as well. But what this history reveals is that there has been a South Asian and Arab Muslim presence in the United States that dates back to the early 20th century. They contributed to the growth of certain industries because of their exploited labor, thus they have been a part of the economic growth and development as well.

44 A Global Racial Enemy

This event is just one example of the violence South Asians have historically endured in the United States. Bald (2013) notes that there were Bengali Muslim workers living in Harlem alongside an African American population because of the racism and segregation they experienced elsewhere from white Americans. Because of the prejudice Muslims encountered, many downplayed their religious identity and as a result there is no accurate count of how many Muslims were in the United States in the 19th and early 20th centuries. Many Arabs, including Syrians, who wanted to become naturalized citizens were told their religious identity as Muslim prevented them from accessing whiteness, which was a criterion for citizenship at the time (Lopez 2006; Gualtieri 2009). South Asian Indians were also denied the ability to become naturalized citizens because Hindus were not viewed as white in the US courts (Lopez 2006). The racialization of Hinduism can be seen in the 1920, 1930, and 1940 US Census, where Hindu is listed as a racial classification (Pew Research Center 2020). Religion, race, and citizenship were deeply entwined because of the history of the racialization of religion (Bayoumi 2006; Garner and Selod 2015).

These anti-Muslim sentiments can be seen in immigration policies as well. Although most of the exclusionary immigration laws and policies at the time targeted Chinese migrants, like the Chinese Exclusionary Act of 1885, they also impacted Muslim migration from South Asian and Arab countries. The Immigration Act of 1881 barred Muslim migration by adding a provision that banned anyone who practiced polygamy or who admitted to believing in the practice of polygamy (GhaneaBassiri 2010). Because polygamy is written into Islamic doctrine, this act reveals how Muslims were also a target for exclusion from migrating to the United States. It was not until the Immigration and Nationality Act of 1965 that Muslim migration increased dramatically into the United States. And while the motivations for migration varied – some came to escape political instability while others were pulled toward professional opportunities – this time period saw a growth in a diverse Muslim population.

This immigration policy came after the passage of the Civil Rights Act of 1964, which highlighted the racism structured into American society, including in its policies that were exclusionary to immigrants of color. It also reflected the United States' shifting relationships with Muslim majority countries after the Second World War. This policy did not include all migrants but had in it provisions about the type of immigrant that was desirable, resulting in professionals having an easier time migrating rather than the low wage laborers of the previous decades (Love 2017). As a result, there is a large Arab and South Asian Muslim population living in the United States today, many of whom came with resources and were therefore able to build Islamic schools and mosques. In the decades since this policy passed, Muslim migrants have continued to come for a variety of reasons. Some have fled political persecution, like the Iranians who fled after the Islamic Revolution of 1979, while Pakistani and Indian physicians were drawn to the opportunities offered to them in the United States.

Since September 11th immigration policies have been altered, with the goal of tightening the borders and protecting the state from another terrorist attack, resulting in a decline in refugees and asylum seekers entering the United States. Increased scrutiny was applied to visa application to catch fraudulent activity and prevent terrorists from crossing the border. While this policy reduced overall refugee migration, according to an Institute for Social Policy and Understanding (ISPU) report, Muslim refugees were not exclusively impacted (Counihan 2007). It was nonimmigrant Muslims traveling to the United States for business and tourist visas from the Gulf countries, like Saudi Arabia, Oman, and Kuwait, that were impacted the most by strict immigration policies. But it was under the Trump administration that Muslim immigration was drastically changed. According to the CATO Institute, the Trump administration cut the number of Muslim refugees by 91 percent and Muslim immigration by 30 percent.

According to data from the U.S. Department of State – which records the religions of refugees – Muslim refugees peaked at 38,555 in fiscal year (FY) 2016, fell to 22,629 in FY 2017, and reached just 3,312 in FY 2018 – a 91 percent decline from 2016 to 2018. Refugees of other faiths have also seen their numbers cut, though not to the same extent as Muslims. (Bier 2018)

The fact that Trump did this is not surprising because while campaigning for the 2016 presidential election, he made promises of banning and registering Muslims. Shortly after he won the election, he signed Executive Order 13769, which decreased the number of refugees permitted into the United States, temporarily suspended the US Refugee Admissions Program, and prevented entry of migrants from countries that did not meet the vetting standards of the United States immigration laws for potential terrorists. These countries were all Muslim majority, which included Syria, Iraq, Iran, Sudan, Somalia, Yemen, and Libya, explaining why it was referred to as the "Muslim" ban. Trump revised the ban several times after lower courts blocked two of his executive orders and presidential proclamation. A revised version of the ban was upheld by the Supreme Court in *Trump* v. *Hawaii*, with the assenting justices clarifying the role of the president to prevent migration in the name of national security. It also upheld the association of Muslims with terrorism, a social construction that continues to racialize Muslims living in the United States.

Muslims are not new migrants to the United States. As we have shown, their history is one that dates back to slavery. By examining this history, we show that Muslims have always been racialized in the United States. It is apparent in how enslaved African Muslims were forced to hide their religion, in how anti-immigration laws and policies banned Muslims for their religious practices from coming to the United States, in the barriers to citizenship based on the association of Christianity with whiteness, and in the current ban of Muslims from migrating to the United States because of their association with terrorism. We must not ignore that early Muslim migration, whether forced or voluntary, provided

Muslim Histories 47

free and cheap labor which contributed to the economic prosperity of their colonizers. Muslims have always been a part of the construction of the United States as a prosperous and racialized nation.

India

Although India is currently characterized by interethnic and interreligious conflict, prior to British colonization of the subcontinent, Hindus, Muslims, Christians, and other religious groups lived in relative harmony for centuries (Brown 1949). There was already a small Muslim presence in Sindh in the 8th century AD; however Islam came to the Indian subcontinent in the 10th century when the Ghaznavids – a Turkic tribe – conquered modern-day Punjab (Brown 1949). By the late 12th century, Muslims established the Delhi Sultanate and expanded Muslim-governed territory by conquering much of Southern India. In 1526, Babar, a descendant of Turkic-Mongol conqueror Timur, founded what came to be known as the Mughal Empire. Ruling from 1526 to 1857, emperors of the Mughal Empire extended Islamic rule over much of the Indian subcontinent, with Babar's grandson Akbar innovating relationships with Hindu and Muslim rulers through political marriages, provincial governance, and social, cultural, and political institutions that drew on political and religious ideologies emerging from Islamic and Indic traditions (Michael Fisher 2015). The strategic decisions of Mughal emperors not only solidified the establishment of the Mughal Empire throughout the subcontinent, but also garnered the acceptance of Mughal sovereignty by Muslim and non-Muslim Indian subjects. Under Mughal rule, the number of Muslims in the Indian subcontinent grew, and India became a pluralistic society with political unity. However, with the death of Mughal emperor Aurangzeb in 1707, the empire crumbled, giving way to British conquest and colonization in the mid-18th century.

Although Britain was one of the many European powers present in India, the rule of the British Raj in India began

48   A Global Racial Enemy

in 1757, when Britain defeated the Mughal governor of Bengal in the Battle of Plassey. Throughout the mid-19th century, the British Raj targeted Hindu and Muslim powers through various military excursions, eventually conquering the subcontinent by collapsing the Mughal Empire and defeating the Hindu Maratha Confederacy which had been contesting the Mughal rule since the 1700s. Notably, the biggest blow to the subcontinent's existing interreligious harmony was the partition of the province of Bengal in 1905. British viceroy Lord Curzon used religious and communal conflict as a tool to partition Bengal into a Muslim majority province of Eastern Bengal and Assam, and a Hindu majority province of West Bengal.

The partition of Bengal was an attempt on the part of Curzon to pander to Bengal's Muslims who were experiencing animosity from emerging Hindu political and communal groups (Ludden 2002). Since the Census of 1857, Muslim fears had been growing as the number of Hindu political mobilizations and representation in leadership positions increased (Brown 1949). For example, the Arya Samaj, an emergent Hindu reform movement of the 1870s, organized the reconversion of Muslims to Hinduism and popularized the cow protection movement which later led to various anti-cow-killing riots throughout the nation (similar to today's Indian cow vigilante justice, see pp. 128–9). The partition of Bengal was also critical in sowing seeds of division among Indians in that it would lead to the loss of capital. The strongest opponents to the partition were elite Hindus and Hindu landowners in Eastern Bengal and Assam who faced the loss of rents from Muslim majority renters in the region. In picking up the cause of the Hindu elite, Hindu nationalist groups began to lead violent protests against the British, arguing that the partition was a policy of "divide and conquer." Soon, violent protests and anti-Muslim hostility erupted around the country, furthering communal divides on the basis of religious difference (Ludden 2002).

While initially against the partition because it threatened Hindu–Muslim solidarity in Bengal, India's Muslim elite later saw the partition as an opportunity to form their own organization along communal lines. In 1906, they created the All-Indian Muslim League. In anticipation of the British Raj quelling the protests with possible reforms that would favor the Hindu majority, the Muslim League demanded separate electorates from the British Raj. With rising nationalist tensions and communal divides now in full display, the new viceroy Lord Minto passed the Indian Councils Act of 1909, which gave Indians limited roles in central and provincial legislatures and secured a separate electorate for the Muslim community in accordance with the Muslim League's demands. The partition of Bengal was later rescinded in 1911 when King George V was crowned the Emperor of India; however, by that time, not only had communal relations between Hindus and Muslims soured but calls for the self-government of India coincided with more protests and revolutionary violence, causing great concern to the British Raj.

The events of the First World War drastically weakened the power of the British over the Indian subcontinent. Facing immense pressure from the Indian public for self-governance, the British Raj was forced to reconsider its approaches toward political reform. In December of 1916, a historic agreement was reached between the All-Indian Muslim League and Indian National Congress in Lucknow. Known as the Lucknow Pact, this agreement marked a significant moment of Hindu–Muslim solidarity, with both parties making unified demands of the British, some of which included increasing the number of elected seats on councils, protecting minorities in provinces, and granting all provinces autonomy. The affirmation of the Lucknow Pact gravely threatened British rule, and while the British did grant more legislative power to Indians, they restricted Indian political leadership by limiting the number of eligible voters and ensuring that rural and special interest seats remained under British control.

In 1919, an event known as the Amritsar massacre marked the beginning of the end of British rule in India. In Amritsar, crowds had gathered to peacefully protest against the arrest of pro-independence activists. In response to this unrest, British Brigadier General Dyer commanded fifty British Indian army

50 A Global Racial Enemy

soldiers to open fire on the crowd, leaving hundreds dead, and over a thousand injured. Following the massacre, beginning in 1920, numerous campaigns of non-cooperation and civil disobedience led by Mahatma Gandhi, Jawaharlal Nehru, and members of the Indian National Congress Party gained momentum over the years, calling for independence from British rule. The outbreak of the Second World War in 1939 further eroded British powers in India and strengthened calls for Indian independence from both Muslims and Hindus.

During this time, the Muslim League grew rapidly and became well positioned to make its own demands for a separate state. This demand arose in the face of the Indian National Congress' campaign for freedom which was framed under the slogan of Indian Nationhood. This slogan advocated for a secular state, a United India that was undivided along religious lines (Rahman 2017). However, under the leadership of Muhammad Ali Jinnah, the Muslim League posited that the Indian National Congress distinctly represented the interests of the Hindu majority and would be unable to truly champion its goals for secularism and parliamentary democracy. Thus, in 1940, the Muslim League passed the Lahore Resolution, which demanded that "areas in which the Muslims are numerically in majority as in the North-Western and Eastern zones of India should be grouped to constitute independent states in which the constituent units shall be autonomous and sovereign" (Ambedkar 1945: n.p.). The Lahore Resolution and the political struggle of the Muslim League had two critical dimensions:

first, restoration of Muslim political power in the Subcontinent, at least in that part of it where Muslims are in the majority and as such could enjoy authority to run their own affairs; and secondly, the establishment of a state for Muslims of the Indian Subcontinent where they would be able to practice their religion, promote their culture and civilization, and build a society based on their ideals, values, principles and aspirations. This was the only way to capture political and economic opportunities denied to them under British rule and would have remained denied to them in a political system ruled by the Hindu majority. (Khurshid 2006: 367)

Indian Muslims, and especially the Muslim League, had felt they would be excluded from the newly formed Congress governments and the Congress' goals for a secular state (Dhulipala 2021). Consequently, only a two-state solution as proposed by the Lahore Resolution would lead to long-term sustained harmony between Muslims and Hindus. The Congress strongly disagreed and opposed having separate religious states; however on August 16, 1946, negotiations between the Congress and the Muslim League led to Jinnah demanding a Muslim homeland in British India. The next day, communal riots broke out across the nation, and in the eyes of the British rulers, a partition was imminent. In September of 1946, Jawaharlal Nehru was instituted as United India's prime minister under a Congress-led interim government.

Now that Britain had lost legitimacy throughout the subcontinent, India's last viceroy, Lord Mountbatten, announced Britain's intention to end its rule in India, transfer power to the Congress-led government, and institute a partition by June of 1948. However, due to the increasing communal violence, Lord Mountbatten rushed the plan for independence, and in June 1947, representatives of Congress, the Muslim League, the Dalit community, and the Sikh community met to partition the country along religious lines, creating what is now contemporary India and Pakistan (and Bangladesh). On August 14, 1947, the Dominion of Pakistan was created, and on August 15, the Dominion of India was created, with Jinnah serving as Pakistan's Governor-General and Nehru assuming the position of Prime Minister of India.

Secularism and religious minorities in the new dominion of India

When the Constitution of India was drafted, a number of its articles provided for the equality of all citizens and guaranteed them the right to "freely profess, practice, and propagate religion" (Daniel 2016: 181). During the drafting of the Constitution, the Constituent Assembly had nuanced debates over the rights of religious minorities in an independent India. Choudhary (2021) notes that there were five competing visions present during the assembly: "the social-democratic vision of Nehru, the Ambedkarite thrust [i.e., vision of Dr. Ambedkar], Gandhi's anti-modernist communitarianism, the explicitly socialist position and . . . the Hindutva ideology" (n.p.). These competing visions teased out the contradictory goals of defining the new state as explicitly secular, while practicing secularism in a context of strife with communal hostility, and where a majority of the population is affiliated with a religion or set of religious beliefs. Thus, defining the nation's legal and sociocultural positions on its religious minorities remained one of the more significant challenges of the Constituent Assembly in the nation's early years.

Since India is Hindu majority with sizeable populations of religious minorities, there are obvious challenges to the practicalities of it operating as a secular state. Not only have religious minorities historically complained of incidents of mistreatment by the public and the state, but the religious majority have also questioned the institution of special provisions for religious minorities in the Constitution (Rahman 2017). For example, the issue of cow slaughter was a critical component of the Constituent Assembly's efforts to navigate this terrain. While Article 44 in the Constitution states, "The State shall endeavor to secure for citizens a uniform civil code throughout the territory of India," Article 48 provides protection for the sanctity of cows and prohibition of the slaughter of cows. Even as a secular state, this provision favored the Hindu majority's religious and cultural practices while placing restrictions on the practices of Muslims and other religious minorities. Rahman (2017) argues that cases like these have shown the tenuous relationship that the Indian state shares with its goals of secularism. More specifically, India has long been a "predominantly Hindu and fundamentally religious society [that] has its own flavor of secularism" (pg. 35). This "flavor" favors the Hindu majority due to their representational proportionality in the populace, but it has also provided differential protections to religious minorities in an effort to remain "secular."

The vacillation between India's goals for secularism, legal pluralism, and context-specificity have arguably rendered India's religious minorities, and especially Indian Muslims, particularly vulnerable. The contradictory nature of the Constitution and its attempts at social cohesion have made room for religious and nationalist groups to interpret secularism in a specific context (Rahman 2017). In particular, since the 1980s, Hindutva ideologies have been promoted under the guise of India's secularism. Hindutva is a modern political ideology that advocates for Hindu supremacy and endeavors to transform India into an ethnoreligious nation through the political, cultural, and institutional suppression of non-Hindu religious and ethnic minorities. Populism and nationalism mobilized via anti-religious sentiments deliberately exclude Hindus and Hinduism as targets, and focus instead on othering Islam, Christianity, and other minoritized religions within the Indian state. For example, the Bharatiya Janata Party's (BJP) mobilization of Hindutva ideologies in the 1990s problematized secularism, by arguing that it was "a tool for minority appeasement" and needed to be properly put into practice through the "equal treatment" of religious minorities (Choudhary 2021). At the same time, the BJP's vision of social cohesion under secularism only sees the formation of the Hindu Rashtra (Hindu State) through the communalization of the majority community and exclusion of religious minorities as the solution to India's problem of secularism (Kausar 2006). Thus, it is rather unsurprising that over the decades and within this context, the BJP's stance on Indian politics has taken an anti-secular approach.

Despite the long history that Muslims have shared in India, it is within a context marked by British colonialism, purposefully crafted communal divisions, secularism, and Hindutva ideologies that ethnonationalism and anti-Muslim racism come to shape the experiences of Indian Muslims today.

China

The Huaisheng mosque, also known as the Lighthouse mosque, is considered one of the oldest mosques in China. Built in the 7th century AD, the mosque reveals how Muslims have lived in China since the inception of Islam itself. The mosque is located in the city of Guangzhou in the eastern part of the country, a port that has seen an influx of traders for centuries. Arab traders were some of the first to come to Guangzhou, bringing with them Muslim traders and travelers after the rise of Islam in 620 AD (Su 2017). The Chinese authorities wanted to contain a foreign population and their political influence, requiring them to reside in a separate area of the city known as *fanfang*, translated as "foreign quarters" (Su 2017). The structure of the *fanfang*, where it was separated from the rest of the city by river channels, kept the Chinese population away from any external influence and also created a space where Muslim traders could live in China and practice their religion and maintain their cultural distinction (Su 2017). Muslims were able to attend the mosque, including the Huaisheng mosque, and pray without any interference from the Chinese state. In the 17th century, under the Ming and Ting dynasties, restrictions were put on maritime trade to consolidate control in China, which prevented Muslim migration into China (Su 2017). While migration was limited, during this era Muslim intermarriage with Han Chinese was encouraged, which had been previously banned, and more mosques were built in the country (Su 2017). A Chinese Muslim identity began to develop over time, although Muslims continued to be treated as a minority population.

In the Xinjiang region of China (Xinjiang is the name given to the region by the Chinese regime, whereas some Uyghur separatists refer to the area as East Turkestan or Uyghuristan), the Muslim population has a very different history than those residing in Guangzhou or other parts of China. Scholars note that this history is one of colonialism versus migration (Chung 2002; Roberts 2020). Roberts

Muslim Histories

(2020) identified two colonial relationships that Uyghur Muslims have endured. The first is that of a frontier colony, which "is held at arm's-length from the colonial metropole," and the other is settler colonialism, whereby the region "is absorbed into the colonial polity and settled by the dominant colonizing population" (pg. 25). The shifting of these two types of colonialism had been dependent on who was ruling in China at the time. Thus, even though the Uyghur region and its population have been under the rule of the Chinese state since the Qing dynasty incorporated it into the Chinese polity in the late 19th century, Uyghur Muslims have had vastly different experiences over time depending on the regime they were ruled by.

> In the history of modern China, the Uyghur homeland has largely been constructed as a frontier colony where the local population was able to remain demographically dominant, at least in the Uyghur heartland of the southern Tarim Basin, and the Chinese state retained control of governance and resource extraction while seeking to establish and maintain Han dominance in the region's north, including its capital of Urumqi. Arguably, with the creation of the PRC, the state sought to absorb the entirety of the Uyghur region and its indigenous population into a larger 'socialist nation-state,' but it was largely ineffective in this goal for the first thirty years of communist rule, especially in the southern Tarim Basin. (Roberts 2020: 25)

Although the history of Muslims in China is long and diverse, we focus on the relationship of the Chinese state and Uyghur Muslims because we show throughout this book how the Global War on Terror has had a distinct impact on the state's policies toward Uyghur Muslims. The Qing dynasty initially conquered the Uyghur region in the late 18th century but did not completely absorb it into its empire (Roberts 2020). While the Qing dynasty held military posts within the region, they were not heavily invested in it. Roberts (2020) notes that Uyghur rebellions during the time were not met with a strong military response from the Qing dynasty and they eventually withdrew. Prior to this time a Uyghur identity was also not a unified one as there was a mix of Muslim and Turkic people residing in the area. It was not until later that a unified nationalist identity began to form in relation to more oppressive regimes. One of the reasons for instituting a harsher rule was to protect the area from outside influences, something that the region has always had, because it borders countries like Pakistan, India, Kyrgyzstan, and Mongolia. The Qing dynasty eventually reconquered the region in the late 19th century, this time making it part of the empire. It was at this point in time that the Uyghur region became a part of the Chinese polity and was given the name Xinjiang by the Qing dynasty. The governing structure put in place in Xinjiang was led by a Han population.

Under the Qing dynasty, the Muslim population was put under pressure to assimilate into Han culture and the Uyghur population was encouraged to learn Mandarin as it was the national language of the Qing dynasty (Roberts 2020). An education program was also set up targeting Muslim children to ensure they would learn Chinese culture and to promote the ideology of the Qing empire. The goal was to detach them from their Muslim and Turkic identities to inculcate loyalty to the imperialist government and to prevent nationalist or resistant movements from developing. Under the Qing dynasty of the late 19th century, a colonial structure was set up in the Uyghur region reminiscent of European colonies. It was one where the empire ruled from a distance via cultural domination and inserted its polity structure in the region. Nevertheless, while a Uyghur population lived under colonial rule, they were still able to "practice their religion unfettered, spoke their native languages, had their own informal means of self-governance, practiced agriculture, and traded" (Roberts 2020: 32). This would change in the 20th century after the collapse of the Qing dynasty.

In 1911, the Xinhai Revolution overthrew the Qing dynasty, replacing it with the Republic of China. The Republic of China maintained control over Xinjiang, ruling it from afar with a Han population governing in the region.

Muslim Histories 57

While some Han rulers were more authoritarian than others, Roberts (2020) notes that one Han leader in particular, Yang Zengxin, was careful in how he controlled Uyghur lives out of fear of external influences. Lenin's anti-colonial ideologies and Muslim reformist ideologies from abroad resonated with a rising Uyghur nationalist population. Thus, the Han polity was careful not to push the population to revolt, preventing external countries from coming to their aid. Even still, there was a Uyghur nationalist identity brewing at this time. The term Uyghur reflects a nationalist identity that was created in opposition to a Chinese colonialist regime.

> The national designation of 'Uyghur' was established by Uyghur Bolshevik sympathizers, in what is today Kazakhstan, during the first years of Soviet rule and recognized by the USSR in the 1920s (Boaz 2002). Of particular concern to Yang was that this nascent nation's ideology was based in Leninist anti-imperialist revolution and celebrated the history of Uyghur resistance to Chinese rule as the centerpiece of its historiography. (Roberts 2020: 34)

In the 1920s and the 1940s, the tensions between an oppressive Han regime and resistance by Uyghurs ebbed and flowed. In the 1940s, with the help of the Soviet Union, Uyghur rebels were able to establish the Second East Turkestan Republic (ETR), providing them with autonomous rule in the area for a short time between 1944 and 1945. This ended as the Chinese Communist Party (CCP) ascended to power in Beijing. For a few years the CCP allowed Uyghurs to participate in government and maintain their cultural distinction and ties to the Soviet Union. In 1949 chairman of the CCP, Mao Zedong, formally established the People's Republic of China (PRC), which would replace the Republic of China as the governing body in 1971. In 1955 the Xinjiang Uyghur Autonomous Region (XUAR) was created to provide some autonomy to Uyghurs, even though it was in theory only and not in true governance. But the approach to the XUAR began to shift as the CCP

58 A Global Racial Enemy

sought to eliminate differences in society, resulting in more oppression of the Uyghur population by trying to suppress their cultural difference and rid any Soviet influences in the area (Roberts 2020). The Cultural Revolution, which sought to eliminate capitalist and traditional influences in China, brought an attack on Uyghur lifestyles and culture, including Islam. "In their all-out attack on vestiges of the old society and 'decadent' customs, the Red Guards made these minority areas, where the greatest attachment to religion and to things traditional remained, a major focus of attack" (Dreyer 1968: 101). Additionally, the PRC sent more Han migrants to the area to resettle it, displacing Uyghurs. Thus, Uyghur Muslims experienced attempts to erase their cultural identity as well as displacing them from the land, resulting in armed resistance and attacks by Uyghur rebels. In the early 1980s, after the Cultural Revolution ended, the PRC once again allowed for some ethnic autonomy in the Uyghur region. Uyghur language, schools, and mosques were reinstituted, bringing back what some refer to as the "golden period" of Uyghur culture (Roberts 2020). But this was also short lived, as the PRC's desire to make the region a part of the Chinese state shifted this policy of accommodation to one of intense security and surveillance.

The 1990s brought increased security on any dissent within the Uyghur population, resulting in more resistance and violence including the bombing of buses in the city of Urumqi. The suppression of Uyghurs consisted of cutting off ties with outside influences, including Central Asia. The government's desire to control the region because of its resources and a fear of the influences of the bordering nations justified the continued oppression of Uyghur Muslims. As we show in the following chapters in this book, current policies toward Uyghurs are seen as necessary in the Global War on Terror, as they are now marked as a terrorist threat because of their religious identity, erasing this history of colonialism. Currently, under settler colonialism the Uyghur population is undergoing displacement and erasure by being placed in "re-education camps" and the women forced into marriages with Han men. As we show in this book, the global

Muslim Histories 59

racialization of Muslims as a threat to both national security and culture has enabled this to happen.

The history of Uyghurs in China and the region reflect how the state has always had a complicated and racialized view of Muslims. Religious and cultural difference have historically been seen as a threat to the Chinese nation-state and national identity, one that the state has tried to cultivate through various tactics. The Chinese state has fluctuated between accommodation and suppression of minority populations, but one thing that is clear is that although Islam has been present since the 7th century, Muslims have been racialized throughout their history in China. Like the UK, the United States, and India, religion has played a significant role in the justification of segregating people, controlling their land, and extricating their resources. In many ways, what is happening in China today with Uyghur Muslims is not entirely new, but it is framed as a new problem that China now has to contend with because of the Global War on Terror. The GWOT has enabled states to pursue their materialistic and military agendas without consequence, because national security takes precedence over human rights. It also has the ability to blur the true motivations for oppression, because the goal of racialization is to obscure the humanity of those whose resources the state plans to extract. The ever-evolving relationship of Muslims with the nation-state in China is one of migration and trade, segregation, colonialism, and settler colonialism.

Conclusion

In this chapter we highlight the relationship of Muslims to the United Kingdom, the United States, India, and China in order to contextualize the shifts that have occurred as a result of the GWOT, which we expand on later in this book. The large presence of Muslims in the UK is tied to its history with India, via colonialism, but they first appeared, even if in small numbers, via the Atlantic slave trade. This relocated large Arab and African Muslim populations across the globe, including to the United States. Muslims came to India via the conquest by Turkic tribes. The first Muslim migration to China occurred due to migrants coming to trade from Arab countries. Arab trade brought Muslims to India and China and the expansion of the Ottoman Empire was not contained to one region. While Muslim experiences in each country are somewhat unique, they also variously overlap because of the ways in which trade and slavery was a global phenomenon.

In the chapters that follow, we explore how the Global War on Terror has been used in each of these nations to justify the continued oppression of Muslims within their borders. The GWOT was a global charge to secure the world from terrorism. Each nation has taken on this command for various reasons. In the UK, the GWOT initiated increased surveillance practices and discriminatory policies against a Muslim population within its borders. The United States has witnessed an expansive surveillance state with the passage of the USA PATRIOT Act and increased funding for policing and security. We show how it is not just Muslims that have been impacted by these counterterrorism policies, but it has militarized local police departments and put billions of dollars into securing the borders, targeting a large Latin American population as well. In India, the history of Muslim and Hindu tensions and violence has been ongoing, but the GWOT has justified increased violence and denial of citizenship to Muslims, who have existed in the country for centuries. While in China, the desire to secure the Uyghur region via settler colonialism is being realized as a counterterrorism strategy.

We show how the GWOT in each country relies on a similar construction of Muslims as a threat to national security. It is in this construction of a Muslim threat, both culturally and physically, that we are bearing witness to the global racialization of Muslims. The GWOT obfuscates the real motivations behind Muslim detention, surveillance, and violence in each nation. These true motivations necessitate examination as they force us to call into question the racialization of Muslims. We see the institutionalization of racism against Muslims in each country we highlight, through its laws, policies, and media representations. The global racialization of Muslims is not a unilateral process, but instead it is also responsible for the ways the state is constructed or reconstituted in novel ways. Nationalism and populism are on the rise. States that are labeled as authoritarian seem similar to those that have been labeled as democratic as both invest heavily in security, policing, and surveillance because of the GWOT. The chapters that follow highlight the global racialization of Muslims in media representations, the rise in nationalism and populism, and counterterrorism policies in the United Kingdom, the United States, India, and China.

–2–
The Media and the Racialization of Muslims: Constructing a Global Threat

The stories that we are told have a profound impact on how we think about ourselves and how we choose to treat others. When expressed through literature, music, television, film, news, and social media, these stories create and attach meanings to others' bodies as well as our own, become part of our social understanding, and guide our interactions with one another. In shaping these stories, the media make a reality *real*, which is why racial projects invest heavily in using media to construct a racial problem.

Consider, for example, how the negative depictions of Black Americans in minstrel shows in the 19th and 20th centuries normalized and legitimized white supremacy. Similarly, the Nazis' Ministry of Public Enlightenment and Propaganda headed by Joseph Goebbels was responsible for disseminating antisemitic radio broadcasts as part of the state's efforts to facilitate the intellectual mobilization of Adolf Hitler's ethnoreligious and ethnonationalist agendas. These broadcasts, in addition to Goebbels' control of German film, theater, and the press, were profoundly successful in radicalizing the German public and getting them to rally behind the Nazi state's ideologies, policies, and military strategies throughout the 1930s and 1940s. Similarly, films produced by the United States' War

Relocation Authority in the early 1940s, such as *A Challenge to Democracy* (1944) and *Japanese Relocation* (1943), were successful in inculcating among the American public the association of ethnonationalist meanings of disloyalty with Japanese Americans, thus justifying the internment of Japanese Americans as an issue of national security. There are numerous other examples throughout history where the media have played a critical role in facilitating other global racial projects by spreading ideas and information to influence people's opinions, worldviews, and perceptions of racialized populations. Thus, the media not only shape the nature of racial projects, but they also reify existing racisms and sociopolitical ideologies in the contexts within which such projects form.

The Muslim racial project is no different. In the Global War on Terror, the media have yet again facilitated the formation of a racial project that takes the shape of a "Muslim problem." As a historical project that spans decades before 9/11, the Muslim racial project is characterized by and made real through biased representations of Muslims and Islam (Shaheen 2003; Kumar 2020). For example, in reviewing Hollywood's representations of Muslims since the early 1900s, Evelyn Alsultany (2022) and Jack Shaheen (2003) both show that Muslims and Islam are portrayed as anti-western, anti-democracy, foreign, dangerous, and oppressive. As such, when rendered as unassimilable in western spaces, Muslims and Islam are viewed by the public and state as fundamentally anti-American and undeserving of civil rights (Selod 2018; Islam 2020). Similarly, in non-western nations such as India and China, Muslims are portrayed in political rhetoric and news media as anti-nationalist, in that their affiliation with Islam is posed as a threat to the nation's values of harmony and secularism (Zajączkowska 2021). Perceived as prone to divisiveness – whether along the lines of ethnicity, religion, or nationality – Muslims are racialized as fundamentally threatening, and thus deserving of punitive measures by the state. In India, this has taken the shape of the stripping away of civil rights and citizenship of Indian Muslims, whereas in China, punitive measures against

Uyghur Muslims take the form of internment camps, state surveillance, and ethnic cleansing.

Not only are these representations racial in nature, but they are also deeply gendered. Muslim men are represented in the media as violent, dangerous, and terroristic, with their Muslim identity marking them as a threat to non-Muslims, the West, the nation, and women (Muslim or otherwise). In emphasizing the danger that Muslim masculinity poses in the GWOT, media representations of Muslim men justify the need for the state to surveil them and their bodies, and react punitively toward those it suspects through deportation, incarceration, and even elimination (Hilal 2022). The sexuality of Muslim men as it intersects with their masculinity and supposed propensity to violence is also rendered in media as inherently threatening to the nation-state and public. In India, the BJP's conspiracy theory of Love Jihad constructs and reifies conceptions and narratives of Muslim men as hypersexual, oppressive, and misogynistic toward Hindu and Muslim women (Zajączkowska 2021; Bolsover 2022). While this conspiracy has foundations in historical Indian traditions tied to casteism and communalism, in the GWOT, it utilizes the white supremacist logics of the Great Replacement Theory to presuppose that Muslim men are falling in love with and converting Hindu women in an organized effort to change the religious demography of India, dominate the nation through demographic growth, and create a stronger fundamentalist foothold within the nation. By focusing on Muslim men's sexuality in a gendered and racialized way, the BJP is able to use the media to define the male Muslim subject subversively and overtly as threatening to women and the state's sociopolitical agenda to remain majority Hindu. Consequently, the BJP utilizes already existing logics of the GWOT to determine the limits of the Muslim male subject's relationship with the state.

As for Muslim women, in addition to being portrayed as vulnerable victims of Muslim men and a patriarchal Islam, they are portrayed as cultural transgressors and reproducers of potential terrorists (Cainkar 2009; Abu-Lughod 2013). The intersection of their gender, Muslim identity and

The Media and the Racialization of Muslims 65

faith paradoxically poses Muslim women as dangerous and vulnerable in the GWOT, centering their intimate lives and their bodies as the necessary foci of state surveillance. In *The Monstrous and the Vulnerable: Framing British Jihadi Brides*, Leonie Jackson (2021) shows how infamous British "jihadi brides" including Shamima Begum, Sally Jones, and others were framed in British news media as either vulnerable victims of the violent Islamic State or as monstrous mothers who had transgressed expectations of good motherhood. Jackson argues that the framing of Muslim women in this way not only emphasizes their role as mothers or potential mothers to Muslims, but also justifies why the state must intervene and surveil Muslim women's intimate lives and biology. It is this framing that is used to justify the Chinese state's policies on the sterilization of Uyghur Muslim women, and forced marriage to Han cadres.

As a result of the racial logics of the GWOT, as well as historical constructions of Muslims and Islam, there are common threads underlying gendered and racialized representations of the Muslim subject. However, how the media frame and represent Muslim subjects within these contexts is uniquely shaped by differing ideologies of ethnonationalism, populism, and anti-Muslim racism specific to the contexts in which they are created. With nation-states utilizing various mass media forms to disseminate their ideologies and the Muslim racial project, global populations now hold conceptions of Muslims that tend to emerge from and reify securitization frameworks which assume that Muslims – regardless of gender – pose a threat to national security. Consequently, in the GWOT, the public's perceptions of Muslims, the media's sociocultural narratives, and governmental administrations have worked in conjunction to create a powerful sense of urgency for nation-states to address the global and domestic "Muslim problem" by instituting anti-Muslim policies and practices within and across their borders.

But how does this occur? More specifically, how is the Muslim problem framed within the contexts of the United States, United Kingdom, India, and China? What are the

66   A Global Racial Enemy

similarities and differences of the constructed Muslim in each context, and why are Muslims framed in this way? Furthermore, what are the implications of such framing for Muslim citizens within each context?

This chapter offers insight on how various media forms within these four contexts work to shape the Muslim racial project according to ethnonationalist, populist, and anti-Muslim racist frameworks. We examine anti-Muslim popular film, television series, news media coverage of global and national events, as well as social media posts to illustrate the ways in which a "terrorism genre" constructs a gendered Muslim problem that is unique to the politics of each context. This analysis illustrates that there is an ideological consensus of the GWOT consistent across all four contexts that attaches meanings of danger and threat to the Muslim body. However, the gendered frame by which Muslim men are constructed and surveilled for the threat of ideological or physical violence they pose operates differently from how Muslim women are constructed and surveilled for the threat they pose. Such media coverage works effectively to dehumanize Muslim men and women, thereby justifying each nation-state's anti-Muslim ideologies and legislative reaction to its constructed Muslim problem. In centering how Muslims and Islam have come to be constructed in our global imaginary through the media, we are better able to account for how the media serve as a critical tool in the Muslim global racialization project.

United States

Although anti-Muslim portrayals were common in US films, television, and news stories before 9/11, there has been an astounding increase in the number and frequency of both biased and seemingly positive representations of Islam and Muslims in US media in the last two decades (Baker et al. 2013; Alsultany 2022). On the one hand, Hollywood has capitalized on the affective experience and tragic sensationalism of 9/11 to produce films that reify binary logics of patriot vs. terrorist, Good Muslim vs. Bad Muslim, democracy vs. dictatorship, and freedom vs. tyranny (Mamdani 2004; Alsultany 2013). On the other hand, Hollywood and the American entertainment industry have also capitalized on the need to respond to the increasing anti-Muslim hostility during and after the Trump administration by creating more diverse and inclusive representations of Muslim Americans in television shows like *Ramy, Mo, Ms. Marvel,* and *Shahs of Sunset* (Alsultany 2022). News channels have remained consistent in their representation, choosing to conflate stories of Islam and Muslims with religious fundamentalism and extremism (Falah 2005), highlight the oppression of Muslim women by Islam and Muslim men in foreign lands (Jiwani 2005), and emphasize an apparent danger that Muslim Americans and the Islamic world pose to those within America's borders. With social media now dominating the public sphere as a space of mass-mediated discourse, we are witnessing an increasing number of ethnonationalist white supremacist anti-Muslim groups active on Facebook, as well as the circulation of Islamophobic material and posts by anti-Muslim groups and organizations through various social media platforms and sites like Twitter, Reddit, and 4chan (Muslim Advocates 2020). As such, there have been a number of ways by which various media forms contribute to the Muslim racial project through shaping Muslim representation.

The power of these mass-mediated representations in facilitating anti-Muslim racism lies in their efforts to reproduce ethnonationalist populist ideologies characteristic in United States politics and public sentiment. In essence, these representations affirm the idea that the cultural Other exists in the United States in the form of the Muslim (regardless of whether the Muslim is an American citizen or foreign born), and they also ossify ties between Islam and religious fundamentalism. In structuring representations of Muslims and Islam in this way, these representations accomplish one thing very effectively: they perpetuate the question of Muslim-American loyalty to the United States, and decide that Muslims and Islam are wholly un-American.

68   A Global Racial Enemy

Film and television

American film and television are riddled with racialized images of Muslims. Jack Shaheen's work *Reel Bad Arabs: How Hollywood Vilifies a People* (2001) remains to date the most comprehensive analysis of Hollywood's manipulation of the image of Arabs (and Muslims) in film. Shaheen analyzed over 900 Hollywood films that were produced between 1896 and 2001 and found that a majority of them were negative in their portrayal of Arabs, often demeaning the group by centering them in storylines that characterized them as savage, terroristic, threatening, brutal, and greedy. Additionally, since Arabs and Muslims are conflated in the American imaginary (despite the two being very distinct in actuality), the two groups tend to be represented in a similar fashion. Thus, a monolithic Arab-Muslim Other comes into being on-screen and is perceived to have an inherent association with an Islamic world that has actual or fictional geopolitical borders, usually represented in the form of the Middle East. The blurring of these categories emphasizes an essential foreignness of the Arab-Muslim character and Islamic faith, which then locates both further outside of the imaginary of who or what is or can be "American."

While Shaheen's work regrettably did not include an analysis of film portrayals after 2001, his findings on biased representations in pre-9/11 Hollywood films remain applicable to post-9/11 representations of Arabs in Hollywood (Alsultany 2012). Many of these representations tend to appear in military and war films like *Jarhead* (2005), *Munich* (2005), *Syriana* (2005), *United 93* (2006), *The Kingdom* (2007), *The Hurt Locker* (2008), *Special Forces* (2011), *Act of Valor* (2012), *Zero Dark Thirty* (2012), *Lone Survivor* (2013), *American Sniper* (2014), and *The Wall* (2017). In these films, Islam and Muslims feature as cinematic identities framed by both the geopolitical conditions and binary logics of patriot vs. terrorist in the War on Terror. The framing of these identities serves a critical purpose, which is to garner public support for the state's anti-Muslim policies and military strategies in the Middle East. In fact, after 9/11 the federal government

The Media and the Racialization of Muslims   69

enlisted the "film and television industry in shaping images of America and of terrorism in ways that would assist and promote U.S. foreign policy" (Prince 2009: 80).

Not only did government interest influence Hollywood's preoccupation with the War on Terror, but the industry itself is motivated by the profit driven by public interest in shaping, perpetuating, and consuming narratives of American patriotism, freedom, and liberation (Labidi 2021). These narratives are powerfully evoked through negative representation of the Arab-Muslim character and his or her ideologies, which are framed as antitheses to American values. Take the military film *American Sniper* (2014), for example. Directed by Clint Eastwood, *American Sniper* is a biopic of US Navy Seal sniper Chris Kyle that follows his personal and professional life as a marksman during and after the Iraq War. Kyle is shown to regularly refer to Iraqis as "savages," using this term to refer not only to militants, but to Iraqis as a whole. The film does not explicitly problematize his racism and dehumanization of Muslim Iraqis, but instead purposefully mitigates it through his character development throughout the film. For example, there are numerous scenes whereby Iraqi families are systematically decimated by Kyle and American troops. While this violence is treated with little empathy, viewers are made to feel compassion for Kyle through storylines that focus on his relationship with his family and the struggles of veterans adjusting to life after war. Understandably, the film illustrates the post-traumatic stress, psychological toll, and personal struggles that veterans face; however, it dangerously glorifies the War on Terror in ways that condemn Muslims as a fanatical group prone to violence and a danger to the United States. Moreover, these representations are deeply gendered. Even though women and children do not feature prominently in the film, the first of Kyle's kills on-screen are a mother and child, who are shown to attack US Marines with an anti-tank grenade. While a majority of Kyle's kills are Iraqi and Muslim men who are portrayed as physical threats to the US military, his interactions with Iraqi and Muslim women (and children) portray them as potential threats with terroristic tendencies. It is precisely this framing that binds meanings of terrorism

70 A Global Racial Enemy

and danger to Muslim men, and meanings of "producers of terrorists" to Muslim women in the GWOT.

Not all films are as straightforwardly racist in their anti-Muslim portrayals as *American Sniper*. There have been a number of seemingly positive or sympathetic portrayals of Muslims, where they appeared as patriotic citizens or as victims of post-9/11 hate crimes (Alsultany 2013). Television shows such as *Homeland* (2011–20) and *24* (2001–10) and films such as *Body of Lies* (2008) and *The War Within* (2006) tend to construct narratives that "flip the enemy." This narrative leads the viewer to believe that a Muslim is plotting to commit an act of violence or terrorism, but eventually reveals that either the Muslim was innocent all along or was part of a larger terrorist network that does not have ties to Islam. For example, in the second season of *24*, the non-Muslim protagonist spends the first half of the season subverting a nuclear attack that is supposedly being undertaken by a Middle Eastern terrorist network. However, the season ends with viewers discovering that the attack itself was motivated by European and American businessmen who sought to benefit from an increase in oil prices when the United States waged war on the Middle East (Alsultany 2013). Alsultany argues that these problematic narratives ought not to be commended for being pro-Muslim or anti-racist, rather, "positive representations of Arabs and Muslims have helped form a new kind of racism, one that projects antiracism and multiculturalism on the surface but simultaneously produces the logics and affects necessary to legitimize racist policies and practices" (2013: 162). This liberal form of racism is based on Mamdani's (2004) conception of the Good/Bad Muslim paradigm, where Good Muslims are those patriotic American or European Muslim citizens who participate in the GWOT by surveilling and reporting on Bad Muslims (usually portrayed as Muslims in foreign countries or immigrant Muslims).

An example of the Good/Bad Muslim paradigm in film is *Traitor* (2008). Don Cheadle portrays the male character of Samir Horn, an Arabic speaking, Sudanese American Muslim who viewers are led to believe is part of a terrorist organization, until it is later revealed that he is a veteran of the US Army Special Forces. It is fairly evident that the film's suspense hinges on viewers' suspicion of Horn being a terrorist since it is unclear until halfway through the film whose side Horn is truly on. Viewers are shown that Horn infiltrates the terrorist organization Al-Nathir in order to thwart their terroristic efforts, while also contributing to the organization by using his skills as an engineer. His contributions to Al-Nathir lead to the successful bombing of a US consulate in France, which Horn is shown to deeply regret. The film ends with Horn successfully thwarting Al-Nathir by killing all of its members, and is shown to be offered a career with the FBI in recognition of his heroic efforts.

By basing its storyline on the gendered and racialized logics of the GWOT, *Traitor* reifies the connection between Muslim masculinity and terrorism, utilizes the flip-the-enemy narrative, and also portrays Horn as the archetype for the Good Muslim, which is made clear through his decisions, patriotism, military career, and devotion to his faith (Labidi 2021). This film also puts into perspective Mamdani's characterization of the Good/Bad Muslim, which posits that unless proven to be "good," a Muslim is to be presumed "bad." For Cheadle's character, it is only through his actions that Horn can prove to the United States government (which suspects that he has been radicalized) that he is a patriotic citizen willing to surveil, thwart, and kill Bad Muslims. The media's reliance on rigidly framing Muslims along the Good/Bad Muslim paradigm erases the complexity and nuance that exist in the actual lived experience and formation of the Muslim subject, and confines them within frameworks of state suspicion and a proneness to terrorism. Thus, films create a commonsense logic about Muslims and Islam, which is internalized by the public and assists in justifying and garnering public support for Islamophobic and racist policies created by the US nation-state (Alsultany 2013).

News

In addition to American film, news media have had a profound impact on facilitating anti-Muslim racism since

72   A Global Racial Enemy

9/11. Network evening news in the four years following the attacks as compared to the four years prior are reported to have had a decline in the coverage of domestic issues including crime and law enforcement (by 47 percent), science and technology (by 50 percent), and alcohol, tobacco, and drugs (by 66 percent) (Pew Research Center 2006). In lieu of domestic issues, the number of minutes devoted to the coverage of terrorism rose by 135 percent and coverage of foreign policy rose by 102 percent. The rise in this coverage had a deep impact on the American public, with 82 percent of Americans who were polled in 2001 saying that they favored military action in order to retaliate against those responsible for the terrorist attacks (Hartig and Doherty 2021). Consequently, the United States government was not only able to garner the trust of a majority of the American public (60 percent), but it was successfully able to invade Afghanistan and institutionalize many national security policies that specifically targeted Muslims in America and abroad (Hartig and Doherty 2021). Accounting for the role and impact of the news in eliciting public support and trust illustrates the power of news media in shaping public opinion and perceptions of Muslims.

News coverage of Muslims is certainly nuanced due to ever-evolving sociopolitical contexts, but much like film it tends to frame Muslims and Islam in predictable ways. A study conducted by Samaie and Malmir (2017) on news stories covering Islam and Muslims produced by *CNN*, *Newsweek*, and the *New York Times* shows that not only is the biased representation of Islam and its association with terrorism and conflict abundantly evident in the news media, but "radicalism" and "Islamic extremism" were the two most frequent issues discussed in news stories related to Islam and Muslims. A swath of other studies support and confirm this finding, suggesting that Muslims and their faith are portrayed as a dangerous problem with which the United States must contend (Abbas 2001; Jackson 2010; Baker et al. 2013; Steiner 2015; Brown et al. 2015).

It is noteworthy too that the media representations of Muslims are heavily gendered. While news coverage of

Muslim men emphasizes their connections – or suspicions of – to terrorist networks, Muslim women are framed through the lens of oppression – especially by Muslim men and patriarchal Islam. Rochelle Terman's (2017) computational text analysis of US news media shows that stories in the *New York Times* and *Washington Post* tend to prominently feature Muslim women's conditions in Muslim majority nations with notably poor records of women's rights. However, even when covering Muslim "countries with relatively good records of women's rights" news media were found to deliberately feature content that emphasizes systemic gender inequalities (2017: 490). In choosing to highlight these stories, news media seek to affirm a bias that Muslim majority countries – as a result of their association with Islam – are more likely to oppress Muslim women. Furthermore, Terman finds that the "oppressed Muslim woman" news story also tends to be framed in contrast with coverage of non-Muslim women residing in countries where women's rights are respected. It is precisely in creating this opposition – that Islam uniquely oppresses women, while America exhibits exceptional gender equality – that the news media assign racialized and gendered meanings to the global Muslim racial project.

Similar narratives are constructed in print media. Falah (2005) shows that print media use images of Muslim women in two major ways: as a passive victim, or as a political agent. For example, stories of Muslim women's oppression in far-off lands are accompanied by images of hijab-wearing or burqa-clad women, who may not even be connected to the story being told (Falah 2005; Jiwani 2005). These images, Falah argues, are not aimed to evoke sympathy from viewers, but rather feelings of "self-righteousness and/or moral revulsion" (2005: 305) which reify negative perceptions of Islam and a savior complex within the western subject. In contrast, when portrayed as political subjects, Muslim women take the form of suicide bombers (especially in the case of Palestinians) or as participants at political demonstrations, showing that "women (yet again) appear to be brainwashed to support evil regimes" (2005: 314–15). Through both these gendered

74 A Global Racial Enemy

frames, negative emotions are evoked, as is the perception that Islam and Muslims are essentially foreign and oppressive toward women.

As for the portrayal of Muslims within the borders of the United States, the US news media either fail to distinguish between Muslim Americans and non-American Muslims, or seek to confine the perception of the Muslim American subject within the Good/Bad Muslim paradigm. This is particularly evident in contemporary news stories covering two of the most well-known Muslim Americans in the United States, Congresswomen Ilhan Omar and Rashida Tlaib. News coverage of their elections and subsequent political careers by right-wing and conservative news channels such as *Fox News* has been relentlessly anti-Muslim, positing that Omar and Tlaib are un-American, and even *anti-*American due to their religious affiliation. An analysis of local news coverage of Omar and Tlaib in the 2018 mid-term elections shows that for both politicians, their faith (rather than their gender or race) became the key focus of anti-Muslim coverage. Omar's election campaign and career were especially framed through negative stereotypical frames of Islam, and this is likely due to her presenting as visibly Muslim through her hijab (Bashri 2019). The coverage of Omar was framed in the intersection of her religion and gender, with Omar receiving more media mentions of her faith as compared to Tlaib.

Similarly, the focus on Omar's faith and her refugee background has also been used by mainstream right-wing and conservative networks to emphasize her anti-Americanness and supposed intention to "replace the constitution and implement sharia law" (Omar 2021). Both Omar and Tlaib have also been the target of online anti-Muslim vitriol from anti-Muslim social media hate groups who allege the politicians' hatred for America and advocate for their deportation (Speakman and Bagasra 2022). Working in tandem, news networks and hate groups on social media work to fearmonger and create narratives of everyday and public Muslim figures that reject the possibility that a Muslim identity can coexist fully with an American one (Islam 2020).

The Media and the Racialization of Muslims 75

Social media

Due to the rise of hate groups (anti-Muslim and otherwise) on Twitter, Facebook, Instagram, and Reddit, these platforms have instituted policies and procedures that filter out or remove groups and posts that spread anti-Muslim hatred. Anti-Muslim hate groups have flocked to alternative online spaces more conducive to racist Muslim discourse, such as online messaging boards 4chan and 8kun, which are used to circulate Islamophobic misinformation and material produced by anti-Muslim websites like Jihad Watch (created by propagandist Robert Spencer), The Atlas Shrugs (created by social media personality Pamela Geller), and Stop Islamization of America (co-founded by both Spencer and Geller). In a study that uses a network analysis of anti-Muslim groups on Facebook, Megan Squire finds that anti-Muslim hate groups serve as the ideological center for members who subscribe to several other ideological categories of far-right extremism, such as anti-immigrant, anti-government, antisemitic, neo-Confederate, neo-Nazi, and white supremacist ideologies (Squire 2018). These findings show that anti-Muslim racism serves as a common ground and *acceptable* form of racism in online spaces because of how it is framed as being necessary for saving America from Muslims and Islam (as is evident by the Facebook group "Pro-Islamophobia Saves Lives!!"). Thus, when located in securitization frameworks and ethnonationalist ideologies, anti-Muslim racism comes to be justified – regardless of whether it is undertaken by the public or the state.

United Kingdom

Like the United States, the United Kingdom's Muslim question is shaped by the GWOT, but the contemporary British version of the Muslim problem is influenced primarily by ethnonationalist populist ideologies that were mobilized during and after Brexit. The America First and Britain First campaigns in the United States and the United Kingdom respectively share the same ethnonationalist frameworks in which immigrants, Muslims, and Islam are positioned as threatening identities to the nation. In the UK, these frameworks are characterized in the media "by highly divisive rhetoric and sensationalist appeals to racial and national sentiment" that conflate issues of immigration, a supposed refugee crisis, and Islamic terrorism in order to create resentment toward Muslims and minority ethnic groups (Trades Union Congress [TUC] 2016: 3). Of course, these frameworks are also gendered. As expected, British (and immigrant) Muslim men are posed as threatening to UK's national security, thus necessitating their surveillance through programs like PREVENT. However, Muslim women are framed as cultural threats and problema-tized in relation to frameworks of British multiculturalism, with their intimate lives, religious and cultural clothing, and gender relations surveilled by the British public and state. In spite of the enduring history that Muslims share with Britain, the gendered and racialized British Muslim problem has been carefully constructed through anti-Muslim rhetoric that renders British and immigrant Muslims as fundamentally outside of the British imaginary.

Film and television

British films share many of the same orientalist and anti-Muslim gendered tropes evident in Hollywood. While the narrative focus on the GWOT and the villainization of Muslim characters remains standard in both UK and US cinema, the difference between the two lies mainly in UK cinema's representation of British multiculturalism. Unlike in the United States where the represented Muslim is an Arab, it is usually Pakistanis who represent "Islam" in Britain. Films such as *Love + Hate* (2005), *Yasmin* (2004), *Mischief Night* (2006), and *Four Lions* (2010) reaffirm cultural construc-tions of difference, and construct Pakistani Muslims as undesirable citizens in racialized, gendered, and classed ways. Specifically, Pakistani men are framed as being prone to Islamic fundamentalism, which is presented in films through their adherence to religious practice, attendance in mosques, and patriarchal cultural traditions. Pakistani Muslims are also represented in film and news media as being a drain on state resources, which is framed through stories of their chronic impoverishment, reliance on welfare, and their working-class status – which, in the context of Brexit, is also posed problematically through the narrative of "immigrants stealing our jobs." However, extending beyond Pakistanis, as a group Muslims in the UK tend to be confined to the usual storylines of terrorism, securitization, and fundamentalist violence.

Take the film *Mischief Night* (2006). The storyline of this film focuses generally on cultural tensions between Pakistanis and a white residential community in an impoverished Leeds estate. The film depicts the story of a working-class second-generation Pakistani family that struggles to navigate British multiculturalism in gendered ways. For example, one element of the film's storyline attends to the oldest daughter's resistance to arranged marriage, while another focuses on the oldest son's communication issues with his Pakistani wife, who is portrayed as having a high sex drive. Although these gendered storylines may seem fairly innocuous, we would do well to remember how orientalist representations of Muslim women hypersexualize and exoticize them and their intimate lives (Shaheen 2001). Furthermore, under the framework of the GWOT, the focus on Muslim women's intimate lives as being structured and constrained by patriarchal cultural and religious traditions also tends to be problematized and rendered in conflict to western notions of female empowerment and agency in determining their gender relations (Abu-Lughod 2013).

The film also predictably tackles religious extremism and the threat of Muslim masculinity. In addition to featuring male characters that are jihadi extremists, the film focuses on the theme of Muslim radicalization through the South Asian character "Eye Patch Imam." This religious leader is shown to beat children, thus representing an inherent propensity toward violence, and to preach fundamentalist Islam to his congregants, which results in him losing the support of the more liberal Muslims at his mosque. However, his story ends with him and his supporters taking over the mosque by force and continuing to teach his fundamentalist viewpoints on Islam. While one might appreciate *Mischief Night* for portraying Muslims in different ways – as fundamentalists, liberal Muslims, empowered women, and compassionate men – producing films in the context of the GWOT necessitates that a Muslim storyline exhibit some connection to terrorism or fundamentalism, whether this connection is maintained through Muslim masculinity or Muslim womanhood (Alsultany 2022). For example, the film *Yasmin* (2004) features a young Pakistani woman whose husband is arrested on charges of suspected terrorism. Although the character Yasmin is shown to be a "modern" working woman who has adapted to British cultural norms, her association to Islam – personally (even though she is portrayed as not particularly practicing) and through her husband – is framed as the reason for why she must navigate issues of British securitization, law enforcement, and anti-Muslim racism. The British media's reliance on the Muslim-as-terrorist or potential-terrorist trope confines Muslim men and women to frameworks of the GWOT while privileging ideas of their inevitable Otherness in the global Muslim racial project (Bolognani et al. 2011).

Similarly, British television series also reify terrorist narratives. In recent years, no British television series has received as much criticism for its Islamophobia as Netflix's production of *Bodyguard* (2018), starring Richard Madden and Keeley Hawes. This thriller series excels not only in terms of its global popularity, but also in terms of its negative representation of Muslim women and focus on the oppression experienced in their intimate lives. For example, one of the protagonists of *Bodyguard* is Nadia, a hijab-wearing Muslim woman to whom viewers are first introduced by her "hiding in the toilet of a busy train, about to detonate a vest she is wearing packed with bombs" (Nazeer 2018). In addition to representing Nadia as a terrorist, *Bodyguard* has her take form of the trope "oppressed Muslim woman," by revealing over the course of the series that she is "actually a victim who looks frightened and vulnerable" and requires the white savior of the series to step in and save her (Nazeer 2018). Not only are we starkly reminded of the white savior trope in this narrative, but creating the specific dynamic of a brown Muslim woman who needs saving by a white man also reminds us of Lila Abu-Lughod's (2013) book *Do Muslim Women Need Saving?* Abu-Lughod argues that in messages of the media and human rights groups, the cultural icon of the Muslim woman is given meanings of vulnerability and victimhood, which have been used to justify foreign and military interference in matters of the Muslim world. In analyzing the GWOT's gendered use of Muslim womanhood, Abu-Lughod problematizes the western trope of rescuing Muslim women from Islam and patriarchal Muslim men, and argues for understanding the lived experiences of ordinary Muslim women within their various contexts.

Bodyguard attempts to add complexity to Nadia's lived experience – however the way in which it does so is arguably absurd. Despite displaying Nadia as a victimized Muslim woman, the series goes on to show that after failing her initial attack, she decides to help the actual villain of the series commit terrorist assassination plots in the US. The villain is revealed to be a white man by the name of Luke Aikens, who is a member of an organized crime syndicate and enlists Nadia to use her skills as a bombmaker to carry out his plans. Thus, even though Nadia-the-oppressed-but-suspected-terrorist is portrayed as unable to carry out her own terror attack, it is ultimately her hatred for the British government and commitment to "jihadi" plans that become her defining characteristics, and serve as the narrative crux of *Bodyguard*'s overall plot.

Within the Brexit context, this storyline is incredibly dangerous. In addition to problematizing Muslim women as oppressed and as terrorists, narratives like these reify ideas of Muslim disloyalty to the nation. Ironically, when series writer Jed Mercurio was asked about these stereotypes, he claimed that "he had upset the stereotype apple cart by making Nadia the master bomber and exploding (excuse the pun) the oppressed Muslim woman myth" (Islamic Human Rights Commission 2018). Unfortunately for Mercurio, this

80 A Global Racial Enemy

attempt does nothing but confine Muslim women, Muslims, and Islam to the same problematic and racist discourse that Muslims have been critiquing for more than the past two decades (Alsultany 2022). It is thus no surprise that Muslims face a significant challenge in trying to resist and break out of the confines of the GWOT's narrative discourse.

News

Beyond films and television, UK news media coverage of national and global events involving Muslims is typically framed through anti-Muslim discourse, securitization frameworks, and ethnonationalist ideologies unique to the UK. For example, news coverage of 9/11, the 2005 London bombings (7/7), and the coverage of the political discourse of Brexit have been found to present Muslims as fundamentally not-British, unable to integrate within British multiculturalism, and threatening to the safety and security of Britain due to their global social connections outside of the UK (Poole 2006; Moore et al. 2008).

While news coverage by right-wing and conservative networks frames these events in ways that invoke ethnonationalist ideologies and dehumanize and distrust Muslims, liberal and politically neutral news networks rely on the already-established frameworks of the GWOT that create an affective power of fear of Muslim populations. For example, Ameli et al. (2007) conducted a two-week content analysis of four news networks (BBC, ITV, C4, and BBC2's *Newsnight*) after the 2005 London bombings and found that the networks "used basic discourses of fear, incompatibility, difference, loyalty and trust in presenting arguments about why these men [i.e., the perpetrators of the bombings] were choosing to give up their 'normal' lives and sacrifice everything in such a manner" (pg. 29). When the bombings were found to have been carried out by British citizens, news networks then constructed narratives of radicalization that portrayed "the young men as having had a normal upbringing, education, job, family and living ordinary lives, until their (re)discovery of Islam, [consequently] the reports focused on Islam as being the main factor that had led them away from this normality into something extreme and sinister" (pg. 29). Radicalization narratives that center Muslim masculinity lead audiences to come to a number of anti-Muslim conclusions: first, they create the notion of the "enemy within"; second, they illustrate that any Muslim – British citizen or otherwise – has the potential to become the enemy; and third, international dimensions of an Islamic terrorism are deemed the core factor that motivates the socially acceptable and possibly integrated moderate or liberal Muslim to commit acts of terror against the United Kingdom (Centre for Media Monitoring [CfMM] 2021). Consequently, in each of these conclusions, the (usually male) British Muslim is confined to the discourse of disloyalty and treated as deserving of the state and public's suspicion due to their faith's inherent inclinations to extremism, and indifference to British values and traditions.

Similar anti-Muslim animosity was identifiable in the coverage of the EU referendum of 2016 (CfMM 2021; Haji et al. 2021). The hostile anti-Muslim and anti-immigrant political climate following Brexit was cultivated mainly by Conservative administrations who mobilize the media to legitimate racist ideas, scapegoat migrants, and link migration and illegal migration to Muslims (Poole and Williamson 2023). Migrants from Middle Eastern, Asian, and African Muslim majority countries have been portrayed as freeloaders and undeserving welfare recipients, who – when not unemployed – occupy jobs that rightfully belong to British-born citizens (Balch 2016). Similarly, Poole and Williamson's (2023) study on news media frames of Muslims during the COVID pandemic illustrates that Brexit political discourse in conservative media mobilized an intersection of anti-Muslim racism and anti-immigrant discourse to blame Muslims for the spread of the virus. Their analysis of four newspapers, *The Daily Mail*, *The Mirror*, *The Telegraph*, and *The Sun*, finds that there was a disproportionate focus on Muslims in which their supposed failure to observe COVID regulations due to religious rituals and cultural traditions was deemed threatening to public health and believed to have added a strain on the nation's health services.

82 A Global Racial Enemy

Other news stories problematize immigrant and Muslim cultures for encouraging immoral and "abnormal" behaviors and traditions not based in British values. Muslim schools tend to be a particular focus in this regard. Poole (2002) notes that newspapers such as *The Times* frame the allegedly inferior values, morals, and traditions associated with the Muslim identity as the reasons why British schooling is superior to Muslim schooling (see also Jaspal and Cinnirella 2010). In defining Muslim values, traditions, and morals as abnormal, news outlets constitute a means of denigrating Muslims as Other and construct an ethnonationalist dynamic of difference that presumes and defines Britishness – in particular, the norms and values of a constructed white British culture – as *normal* (CfMM 2021). Thus, immigrant and British Muslims are carefully constructed as deviants who must be located outside the ethnonationalist conception of who qualifies as British.

Cyber-attacks on Muslims

We can see the same kinds of anti-Muslim rhetoric and framing in cyber-hate crimes targeting Muslims in the UK. Launched in February 2012, the UK-based project Tell MAMA (Measuring Anti-Muslim Attacks) documents anti-Muslim incidents in England to provide evidence for, and counter online and offline anti-Muslim hate crimes. In 2013, Tell MAMA produced its first annual report, which found that 632 anti-Muslim hate incidents were reported from March 2012 to March 2013, with 58 percent of those incidents targeting Muslim women, and 74 percent of them occurring online (Tell MAMA 2013). The report also found that 70 percent of online incidents reported were linked to those affiliated with the far-right, including (but not limited to) the English Defence League (EDL) and the British National Party (BNP). These groups and their ideological supporters have been found to promote material from anti-Muslim websites such as American Islamophobe Robert Spencer's Jihad Watch, illustrating the global nature of anti-Muslim racism in online spaces, especially during and after the Trump administration's rise to power and the passing of the EU referendum in 2016 (Copsey et al. 2013).

Brexit's impact on online anti-Muslim racism is well documented (Awan 2016; Evolvi 2018; Tell MAMA 2018a, 2019; Civila et al. 2020). In her study of tweets posted after Brexit in 2016, Giulia Evolvi (2018) finds that internet-based views of Islam reflected the political narratives espoused by those campaigning for Brexit, with stories centering mainly on "the need of stopping an alleged 'Muslim invasion' that would threaten U.K. identity" (pg. 4). These tweets did not indicate criticism of individual Muslims, rather they expressed hatred for Islam as a whole, and were focused mainly on dehumanizing Muslims, describing Islam as "monolithic, violent, and unable to adapt to western values," and advocating for Muslim exclusion from British society (pg. 10). Evolvi's analysis also shows that in Brexit-themed tweets, Muslims were not only blamed for supporting the Remain position in the EU referendum, but this accusation was framed "not as a genuine political ideology, but rather as part of a general hostility against the West" (pg. 8). These findings clearly illustrate the impact that already-existing ethnonationalist political discourses as well as anti-immigrant and anti-Muslim attitudes have had on the nature of online anti-Muslim hate during and after the EU referendum. Furthermore, this online hate facilitates the support for radical right populism, stricter policies on immigration, and policies aimed at curtailing multiculturalism in the UK, which continue to drastically shape British politics and the everyday experiences of Muslims in the UK.

Although online anti-Muslim racism does not *necessarily* lead to offline hate incidents, there is strong evidence that "online Islamophobia is likely to incite religious hatred and xenophobia leading to real world crimes and a rise in political extremism" (Oboler 2016: 56). Studies have shown that anti-Muslim hate online often involves threats of offline action (Awan 2014; Awan and Zempi 2015; Tell MAMA 2018a). Tell MAMA, which as described above is a national project that collects data on anti-Muslim incidents, put out an annual report for incidents in 2017 that illustrates a 30 percent increase in the number of offline anti-Muslim incidents and a 16.3 percent increase in the number of online anti-Muslim incidents as compared to 2016 (Tell MAMA 2018a). The offline incidents of anti-Muslim racism come in the form of physical attacks (usually targeting Muslim women due to their visibility via the hijab), vandalism, and verbal threats. Reports show that the perpetrators are predominantly white males (Tell MAMA 2018a). Tell MAMA notes that the upward trends in both online and offline incidents ought to be viewed as part of a wider trend in their data sets, where major trigger events (such as terror attacks) are usually followed by an increase in reports of anti-Muslim racism. This is supported by Awan and Zempi's (2015) report on anti-Muslim hate crime in the UK, which finds that "the prevalence and severity of online and offline anti-Muslim hate crimes are influenced by 'trigger' events of local, national and international significance" (pg. 4). Consequently, online threats of potential offline violence incite fear within Muslims who are the targets of such threats, causing victims of Islamophobia to feel as if they are "under siege" (Awan and Zempi 2015: 28). Beyond having negative psychological, emotional, and physical effects on British Muslims, these fears also have the potential to negatively affect their relationship with the UK and their inclination to participate in British politics as democratic citizens.

China

The Chinese state's control of almost all of China's media outlets has allowed for the state to carefully create and disseminate anti-Muslim racism in ways that advance its nationalist agenda. State-facilitated representations of nationalism in film and news media are framed to otherize Uyghurs and justify the creation of the surveillance state, while exacerbating the cultural and ethnic genocide of Uyghur Muslims in the name of nationalism. Even in social media posts propagandizing populism, Uyghur Muslims are presented as an ethnic threat to Chinese culture, national identity,

The Media and the Racialization of Muslims 85

and national security through the binary of us vs. them. Unlike the western binary of us vs. them, which is based in classic orientalist notions of the West vs. the East/Other and has evolved over time, the mobilization of the us vs. them binary in Chinese media is framed through nationalist and populist narratives that posit Islam and Uyghur Muslims as categories to be excluded from the national imaginary. Uyghur Muslims are targeted, surveilled, and incarcerated for markers of cultural (and biological) difference from the Han majority, with Uyghur women surveilled for their reproductive capacities and sterilized to prevent the birth of more Uyghur Muslims. The Chinese state's gendered approach to the systematic incarceration and genocide of Uyghur Muslims necessitates that its media take a targeted gendered approach to constructing its Muslim problem.

Film

Unfortunately, due to state censorship and regulation of media, there is a dearth of film or television that acknowledges or addresses the existence of Uyghur Muslims in China. However, in recent years the global and public outrage over the genocide and incarceration of Uyghur Muslims has led the PRC to produce Chinese films that not only promote its nationalist ideologies, but center Uyghurs in narratives that either erase their mistreatment by the state, or justify the need for its anti-Muslim and anti-Uyghur policies.

There are relatively few Uyghur-focused popular culture films produced after 9/11. Two films worthy of note are *The Wings of Songs* (2021) and *Kunlun Brothers* (2019). Both films were directed by Uyghur comedian Abdukerim Abliz and produced in the Tiansham film studio, which functions primarily as a state-sponsored studio producing ethnic minority-themed films (Frangville 2020). Despite being located in the Xinjiang region, the Tiansham film studio is run primarily by Han employees and is also funded by the Chinese state, which has affected the nature of the studio's output and resulted in the production of nationalist propaganda films (Frangville 2020). For example, the film *The Wings of Songs* (2021) was commissioned by the Xinjiang regional propaganda department and is a musical that follows three men from different ethnic groups (including Uyghurs) who traverse the Xinjiang region to gather musical inspiration. The film clearly emphasizes the PRC's nationalist agenda in that its plot centers ideas of social cohesion and ethnic unity shown through friendships between Kazakhs, Uyghurs, and Han peoples in the region. One of the central themes in the film is the spectacular beauty and range of the Xinjiang landscape. In spite of its seemingly idyllic focus on ethnic unity and the geographic beauty of Xinjiang, the film omits any references to, and images of Islam, Islamic cultures, Muslim identities, or belief systems. No mosques or women in hijabs are seen in the film, nor are any state surveillance technologies such as Xinjiang's concentration camps, border control, security cameras, or cadres. This purposeful omission seems to convey the state's intention to promote harmony through aspirations of nationalism, which is portrayed as possible only through the omission, erasure, and eradication of Islam and Muslim identity from the lives of Uyghurs.

Similarly, ethnic unity is centered as a plot point in *Kunlun Brothers* (2019); however this time unity takes the form of a relationship shared between a Uyghur family and a Han cadre. The cadres of the Chinese Communist Party (CCP) comprise of trained personnel who are employed by the CCP and fulfill a wide range of civil service roles in various organizations across China, including the military. The film follows the unfortunate events of a villager in Xinjiang who is mistaken for a jade thief but is later exonerated with the benevolent help of the cadre visiting a homestay owned by the villager's family. Since the cadre program was initiated in 2017, the Chinese state has been producing propaganda that portrays the program as a necessary and unifying mechanism through which Uyghur Muslims can "pair up and become family" with Han cadres. Through a storyline that highlights the social and material benefits of developing relations with Han cadres in their intimate lives, *Kunlun Brothers* seems to be encouraging Uyghurs to accept and welcome the state's cadre program. However, while *Kunlun Brothers* emphasizes the benefits of the Chinese state's paternalism and benevolence in the lives of Uyghurs, it avoids any mention of the purpose that cadres serve in Xinjiang: to surveil and prevent the practice of Islam and to force compliance to the rule of law in Xinjiang. Thus, even though the cadre program exists to fight three dangerous forces in Xinjiang (extremism, separatism, and terrorism) media depictions of cadres are framed positively, paternalistically, and for the benefit of Uyghurs in Chinese propaganda film.

News

The cadre program and other forms of state-initiated anti-Muslim practices and policies have been similarly framed in Chinese news media. Much like film production, the news media in China are also regulated and surveilled by the state. Since alternative sources of media are regulated, censored, and inaccessible to the general public, state news media play a key role in forming the Chinese public's perceptions of Uyghur Muslims. When covering stories on Muslims and Islam (whether national or international) news coverage focuses on stories about religious extremists, refugee crises, terrorist acts, conflict and civil unrest in Arab countries, and the West's struggles with curtailing the Muslim problem in the GWOT (Luqiu and Yang 2018; Ye 2019; Abbas 2021). While county-, city-, and provincial-level networks are only allowed to cover domestic news stories due to state regulation, central-level media, such as the *Xinhua News Agency*, *CCTV*, and the *People's Daily*, are permitted to cover international news and events (Luqiu and Yang 2018). This monopoly, in addition to stringent state regulation over output, has led to biased domestic and international news coverage concerning Islam and Muslims.

For the most part, Chinese news stories had largely elided any mention of Muslims until the Xinjiang riot of 2009. In their analysis of ten years of Chinese state news media reports on Uyghur Muslims and Islam, Luqiu and Yang (2018) found that not only are Muslims portrayed negatively in state news media, but this negative view has worsened over time, resulting in dire consequences experienced by Uyghurs and other Chinese Muslims. For example, after the Xinjiang riots between Han and Uyghurs in 2009 and the mass stabbings at Kunming railway station in 2014, the "official rhetoric for reporting domestic terrorist attacks, which emphasized the necessity of ruling with an iron hand in Xinjiang, also constructed a link between global antiterrorist efforts and local politics" (Luqiu and Yang 2018: 603). Here, there are two things worthy of note to our analysis. First, the framing of these events justifies a distinct conflation of Uyghurs and Islam with domestic terrorism. For example, the Chinese government's coverage of the Xinjiang riot and Kunming attack referred to all forms of ethnic protest and domestic separatism in Xinjiang as "terrorism." The use of language created commonsense logic that justified why anti-Muslim and anti-Uyghur policies were put in place by the state (Chung 2002; Hillman 2016). Second, the reporting of these domestic terror attacks, as well as any coverage of Muslims or Islam in world events, follows frameworks that parallel those evident in western discourses of the GWOT. According to Luqiu and Yang (2018), not only do Chinese news networks derive their coverage from western news agencies such as the *Associated Press*, but the anti-Muslim agendas of western nations influence the narrative of Chinese state-run news networks and facilitate the justification of the Chinese government's own anti-Muslim domestic and international policies. This is precisely why the Muslim racial project must be understood as a global phenomenon.

Along with the GWOT's framework, the Chinese state's news media also co-opt western binaries of us vs. them in its coverage of Islam and Uyghur Muslims. News stories are overwhelmingly negative and framed in nationalist discourses that portray "Chinese Muslims as belonging to the Muslim world, rather than being their fellow citizens" (Luqiu and Yang 2018: 603). This idea of belonging uses a binary of Sinicization vs. Arabization, which assumes that Uyghur Muslims are not only disloyal to the Chinese nation, but are inherently "spiritually Arab" and thus could never *be*

Chinese (Miao 2020). In supposing that Muslims are inherently not-like-us and are therefore unassimilable, Chinese nationalist ideologies emphasize the untrustworthiness of, and danger posed to China by Uyghur Muslims. As such, the only solution believed to be acceptable to the state and the Chinese public is the Sinicization or eradication of Uyghur Muslims, both of which the state is contemporarily and systematically undertaking (Miao 2020).

While the negative framing of Uyghur Muslims is evident in state news representations, there is also "positive" propaganda about Islam being published by the PRC's state media. Positive propaganda takes the shape of news stories that focus on the benevolence of the state's paternalism toward ethnic minorities, and the benefit that Uyghur Muslims reap through governmental policies. In an analysis of ideological representations of Chinese Muslims in the newspaper *China Daily*, Ye (2019) finds that the government portrays itself as having a paternalistic relationship with Uyghur Muslims, who benefit from the government's subsidies for improvement in education, programs in Mandarin language proficiency, and family planning (mainly through the cadre program). While posed as policies that benefit Uyghur Muslims, these "improvements" are in fact nationalist programs and surveillance policies aimed at erasing ethnic markers that differentiate Uyghur Muslims from the Chinese majority. Ironically, these policies are a point of contention for Chinese nationalists online who criticize the government for its paternalism and leniency toward Uyghur Muslims. They advocate instead for stricter policies in the Xinjiang region that are punitive in nature and do not drain the state of its resources (Haiyun Ma 2019).

"Positive" propaganda is also aimed at targeting Uyghur activism within and outside of China's borders. Through its state-run networks, the CCP has consistently produced videos that weaponize family members of activists inside and outside of China against them, "forcing them [family members] to read scripts in videos spread internationally that condemn their activist family members" (Abbas 2021: 6). In these videos, family members denounce activists and accuse them

90 A Global Racial Enemy

of spreading disinformation about the reality of Xinjiang and the treatment of Uyghurs by the state. An independent review of 3,000 of these videos by the *New York Times* and *ProPublica* finds that "these videos share far too much consistency to be true first-person unfettered narratives," illustrating the state's involvement in spreading anti-Uyghur propaganda through coercion of Uyghurs (Abbas 2021: 9). The surveillance of the intimate lives of Uyghur families, and the abuse they experience through state coercion are the outcome of the state's systematic anti-Muslim human rights abuses. Disseminating content that ignores or seeks to erase evidence of Uyghur genocide illustrates China's attempts to influence national and global opinions on the genocide of Uyghurs at the hands of the Chinese state.

Social media

State-led nationalism and anti-Muslim discourse are increasingly supported and enhanced by Chinese populism on social media. Populist nationalists and Chinese netizens are not only amplifying the state's anti-Muslim propaganda through a growing network of activists, but are also creating propaganda by spreading rumors, misinformation, and fabricated news stories that paint domestic and international Muslims and the Islamic faith as threatening to the Chinese national identity. The largest Chinese social media site, Weibo, is particularly representative of Chinese populist nationalism. Populated by Chinese "cyber-warriors" who "post a steady stream of news stories and opinion articles with an avowedly anti-Muslim bent," Weibo serves as a major source of anti-Muslim racism and disinformation (Haiyun Ma 2019: 47). The stories and articles on Weibo are accompanied by analyses offered by individuals who are known anti-Muslim activists and radicals in China, including Mei Xinyu, a Ministry of Commerce analyst, and Xi Wuyi, a researcher of Marxism and expert on atheism (Haiyun Ma 2019). These analyses are racist in that they not only mock Muslims and Islam and depict them as being threatening to non-Muslims in China, but work to create fears that Uyghur Muslims are

The Media and the Racialization of Muslims 91

trying to Islamicize the nation through their organizations, activism, and reproductive capacities. Since these sentiments align with those in the PRC's anti-Muslim nationalist agendas, online populist nationalists are not censored by the state authority. In fact, many share critical connections with powerful politicians (as evidenced by Mei Xinyu), allowing for a systematic coordination between the state and online populists. This coordination has only "strengthened the assault against Islam" (Haiyun Ma 2019: 48).

The spread of populist created anti-Muslim propaganda is characterized also by anti-western, anti-foreign, anti-Black, anti-immigrant, and anti-feminist ideologies. In an analysis of the core ideological features of online right-wing Chinese populism, Zhang (2020) finds that "discourse on Chinese social media is combining the claims, vocabulary and style of right-wing populisms in Europe and North America with nationalism and racism in Chinese cyberspace" (pg. 88). In other words, the same anti-immigrant, anti-Black, anti-foreign, and anti-Muslim rhetoric that is mobilized in right-wing, ethnonationalist populisms in the United States and the United Kingdom is also evident in Chinese populist nationalism online. However, added layers of anti-western, anti-feminist, and anti-liberal elitism within the Chinese context support ideas of Chinese hegemony and superiority in a global hierarchy and emphasize the construction of a Chinese nationalist identity that is made to stand in stark contrast to the "declining Western other" (Zhang 2020: 90). Anti-Muslim racism is central to problematizing the current world order. Chinese nationalists online express criticism and contempt for the West's liberal, multicultural, progressive, and reflexive approach toward Muslims and Islam, in terms of dealing with the Muslim problem both regionally and internationally via the GWOT. In suggesting that the United States, the United Kingdom, and other western nations have been too soft in dealing with their Muslim problem, Chinese nationalists are able to bolster the state's nationalist agendas, while also providing support for punitive policies in dealing with China's Muslim problem. That said, these netizens have also co-opted right-wing populisms from the US presidential election of Donald Trump in 2016 and the Syrian refugee crisis in Europe (Zhang 2020), which have facilitated anti-refugee and anti-liberal rhetoric that targets Muslims and non-Muslim Others within China. Thus, when centered in the nexus of these ideologies, anti-Muslim racism in Chinese social media spaces is mobilized as a tool to place the Chinese regime at the top of the "hierarchical imaginary of global racial and civilizational order" (pg. 90), and to facilitate various forms of racial, ethnic, religious, and other discriminations within China's borders.

Netizens also have constructed Muslims as oppressors. Ying Miao's (2020) analysis of posts and articles on a well-known Islamophobic account on Weibo shows that it frames Chinese Muslims and Islam as oppressive *toward* the Han majority. Miao notes that this narrative presumes that the Han people have "been putting up with unreasonable demands of religious affirmative action, and suffering under the state-sanctioned preferential policies for ethnic minorities" (pg. 753). The preferential policies being critiqued include affirmative action policies in civil service and university entrance exams, which Han families claim encourages ethnic fraud. Notably, it is not the Uyghur Muslims who are deemed exploitative in this regard – it is Hui Muslims, another Muslim population in China, who are made to be oppressors of the Han majority because of their preferential treatment. Uyghur Muslims, on the other hand, are framed as both the oppressed and as villains. The oppressed narrative frames Uyghur Muslims as deceived victims who have been brainwashed by Islamic teachings, and who might be brought into the fold of the nation through Sinicization. Contrarily, the villain narrative frames Uyghur Muslims and Chinese academics and politicians with pro-Uyghur sentiments as advocating for terrorism on the behalf of Islam and betraying the interests of the general population. In using anti-liberal elitist discourse co-opted from western media, online populist narratives also suggest that the elite class must not be trusted because it is disloyal to the Chinese nation, and that "any hint of preferential treatment given to minorities [is to be] viewed with extreme suspicion" (Miao 2020: 758). Consequently,

The Media and the Racialization of Muslims 93

criticism of pro-Uyghur individuals and the state's solutions to China's Muslim problem is abundantly evident on Chinese social media, with criticisms of the latter receiving more censorship by the state than the former.

The dynamic that the state and Chinese public share in shaping anti-Muslim discourse along various other ideologies co-opted from the West illustrates the complexity of China's Muslim problem. Couched primarily within a nationalist agenda that is shaped through state-controlled and surveilled media, China's Muslim problem draws on frameworks of the GWOT that dehumanize and demonize Uyghur Muslims, and justify their detention, forced assimilation, and genocide in Xinjiang.

India

India's construction of Muslims as a problem in the media plays into pre-existing tensions of Hindu–Muslim relations. This division is made more pronounced by presenting Muslims as inherently anti-nationalist, as collaborators with terrorists and jihadis – if not terrorists and jihadis themselves – as corrupt and corrupting, and as a threat to Indian democracy and goals for secularism. Consequently, much of the success in the rise of Hindutva ideology in mainstream Indian public discourse can be attributed to nationalist messages in films, in news channels, and on social media.

Film

Despite the historical presence of Muslims in India, there remains a noticeably stark underrepresentation of diverse Muslim characters and storylines in Indian film. Hindi cinema's representation of Muslims has varied drastically according to India's changing sociopolitical contexts over time, however the Muslim-as-Other has remained a consistent depiction on screen (Rai 2003; Chadha and Kavoori 2008; Jain 2011). Films of the 1950s and 1960s reflected the more tolerant secularism of the Nehruvian era, presenting Muslims as members of the respectable upper-class who "lived with their grandeur and idiosyncrasies intact" (Khatun 2016: 42). In the 1970s and early 1980s, the tumultuous politics of Indian society coincided with the beginnings of a systematic marginalization of minorities, which gained momentum in the late 1980s and 1990s, and morphed into the robust Hindu right-wing movement which dominates Indian society today. The representation of Muslims in Hindi cinema during these times reflects the contemporaneous religious and political conflicts in India, with a deplorable Muslim underworld of Mumbai being a predominant feature in cinema in the 1970s and 1980s. Additionally, depictions of the divisiveness of minorities' communal identities and violence of Muslims through riots (which were concurrent with real-world riots that followed the demolition of the Babri Masjid mosque in 1992) were a common theme of mainstream films of the 1980s and 1990s (Khatun 2016). These films illustrate the media's efforts to shape and (re)present ongoing social and political conflicts between India's Hindus and Muslims.

Post-9/11, Indian films took on the securitization rhetoric of the GWOT, with many film plots depicting an ongoing ideological conflict between violent Muslim (and often Pakistani) jihadis and Hindu nationalists. Among the racialized and gendered symbols used to connote the Muslim jihadi on screen are the hijab and burqa for women, and the beard, skullcap, and Aligarh sherwani (long-sleeved outer coat) for men. These symbols are not unique to Hindi cinema but are also predominant in western film representations of the Muslim male or female terrorist. However, in Hindi films, the *Hindu* nationalist is posed as quintessentially Indian – i.e., patriotic, liberatory, and a savior of the marginalized and of women. In presenting the "essence of 'Indianness'" which exists in explicit opposition to the Muslim identity, Hindi cinema builds its own binary of us vs. them and constructs an imagined Muslim problem within the frameworks of nationalism. Consequently, it serves as one of the more critical mediums through which Hindutva ideology can be contemporarily mobilized and disseminated (Rajgopal 2011: 240).

While there are films that portray Muslims as empathetic protagonists, such as *Fanaa* (2006), *My Name is Khan* (2010), *Student of the Year* (2012), and *OMG: Oh My God* (2012), these films still bind Muslims to frameworks and narratives of Islamic terrorism, often implicitly portraying (almost always male) characterizations of the Muslim jihadi through protagonists' social connections. Despite the usefulness of these narratives to Indian messages of nationalism, the positive representations of Muslim protagonists made these films and others targets of censure by the BJP and other right-wing parties. India's Censor Board of Film Certification has faced increasing pressure from these political parties to ban or censor these films for "critiquing or 'hurting' the sentiments of Hindus" since they elicit sympathy for Kashmir or Muslims, despite being bound within frameworks of the GWOT (Khatun 2016: 47). Faced with this pressure, most filmmakers have acquiesced to right-wing agendas and sought to deploy narrative plots that contrast the male Muslim terrorist against "the progressive and secular projection of Hindus" (pg. 48). Literature and media scholar Amit Rai (2003) has argued that in utilizing the rhetoric of the GWOT, Bollywood frames it as a holy war waged by Muslims and Islam against the non-Muslim world. Consequently, the Muslim depicted in Bollywood films operates within this framing, and manifests as the Good Muslim who must prove their loyalty to the Indian nation by warring against other Muslims or Islamic fundamentalists, like in the film *Fanaa*. The danger of the imagined Muslim and the threat that Islam poses to the Indian nation and its goals of pluralism and unity are made to feel so pronounced in Hindi cinema that films can be seen to emphasize the need for "the state [to] adopt its own violent techniques to put down such a threat" (Hirji 2008: 59). It is thus that Hindi cinema creates a fear of Muslims among the Indian public, as well as an illusion of urgency for the state to mobilize its nationalist agendas and take immediate action against resident and immigrant Muslims who are believed to threaten the normative and secular ways of Indian life.

News

Beyond issuing policies on censure, the Indian state does not regulate the media. However, there is an increased involvement of the state in shaping information (and disinformation) about Muslims and Islam through news networks. Prime-time news channels are explicitly racialized and gendered in their anti-Muslim discourse and representation. Onaiza Drabu's (2018) study of Indian media's coverage of two highly racialized and gendered campaigns, Love Jihad and Triple Talaq, illustrates the Indian public and media's contemporary anti-Muslim racial prejudice. While the phenomenon of Love Jihad is described as the "alleged campaigns carried out by Muslim men targeting non-Muslim women for conversion to Islam by feigning love," Triple Talaq is a form of "divorce that has been interpreted by certain Islamic lawmakers and Muslims in India to allow Muslim men to legally divorce their wives by stating the word 'talaq' (Arabic for 'divorce') three times in oral, written or electronic form" (pg. 2). Drabu finds that news channels covering these phenomena "propagate associations between Islam and backwardness, ignorance, and violence" which are mobilized through gendered and racialized tropes. Specifically, these tropes emphasize Indian Muslims as being essentially "anti-national" or "not fully Indian," and are focused on Muslim men's misogyny and oppression of Muslim and Hindu women (pg. 1). Both campaigns are framed to hypersexualize and hypermasculinize Muslim men, posing them as a danger to Hindu and Muslim women, thereby deepening the association of Islam as a patriarchal and misogynistic religion that oppresses women through Muslim men.

Framing these issues along gendered and racialized discourses primes the Indian public on how to think about Muslims and Islam. For example, headlines such as "CAUGHT: ISIS Converting Hindu Girls For 5 Lakh Rupees" in *Times Now*, and "BAN 'Nikah' Sex Racket in Hyderabad" in *Republic TV*, portray Muslim men (and Islam) as sexually, morally, and religiously threatening to Indian society and Hindu women. The former headline on

ISIS also utilizes rhetoric of the GWOT, emphasizing an association between Indian Muslims and global terrorist networks, while also indirectly suggesting that ISIS and Indian Muslims are attempting to Islamicize Indian society. Consequently, the media's coverage of these phenomena exacerbates anti-Muslim racism through frameworks of the GWOT and offers legitimacy to the belief that there is a Muslim problem in India.

Politicians have a unique role to play in stoking anti-Muslim ideologies through news networks. With the BJP in power, politicians espousing nationalist and anti-Muslim ideologies are routinely scheduled to appear and discuss their political viewpoints and agendas on news channels and in segments relegated for political discussions (Drabu 2018). Consequently, India's Muslim problem evolves and is heightened through their disinformation and propaganda on popular Indian news networks. Natalia Zajączkowska's (2021) analysis of 243 instances of disinformation archived by Tattle Civic Technology, a Delhi-based news project, illustrates the role that BJP state actors have played in fueling anti-Muslim racism during the COVID-19 pandemic. Zajączkowska finds that Hindutva-driven anti-Muslim racism facilitated by members of the BJP government takes the shape of "fake news" which has deeply affected the Hindu public's perceptions of Muslims and Islam, especially in relation to the spread of the virus during the pandemic. For example, at the beginning of the pandemic, there was an increase in Islamophobic news headlines with hashtags like #CoronaJihad and #TablighiJamaatVirus, which blamed Muslims for the virus. The BJP politicians' and media's use of these hashtags further facilitated the virality of these news stories on social media, resulting in the creation of more anti-Muslim disinformation and propaganda. Stories and political propaganda on news networks stigmatized Muslims as carriers of the virus, calling for the economic boycott of their goods and services and advocating for their physical separation from other Indian citizens. Fake and manipulated videos "showing Indian Muslims spitting on police and medical services, poisoning food before selling

98   A Global Racial Enemy

it, and ostentatiously ignoring the lockdown guidelines" contributed to the idea that Muslims were responsible for spreading the virus and killing Hindus by passing on the contagion (Zajączkowska 2021: 256). These stories framed Muslims as carriers of disease and facilitators of the genocide of non-Muslim Indians through COVID-19 and constructed Muslims as *bio-terrorists*. Bound once again to frameworks of terrorism, Muslims were believed to be facilitating a new form of jihad uniquely tailored to the pandemic – i.e., "Corona Jihad." New Delhi based political commentator Zainab Sikander states that through this term, "many Hindus say Muslims are deliberately attempting to spread coronavirus to wage a holy war or jihad against the majority Hindus" (cited in Yasir 2020). Since frameworks of the GWOT provide the fertile ground necessary for demonizing Muslims, the co-opting of this term by BJP politicians, chief ministers, and government organizations such as the Press Information Bureau helped to incite more fear and anti-Muslim hate against Indian Muslims, further exacerbating feelings of division and nationalism within the nation.

A similar study by Baharuddin and Baharuddin (2022) found that mainstream Indian media, such as *The Times of India*, *Sabrangindia.in*, and *Theprint.in*, specifically blamed the spread of the pandemic on an Islamic religious congregation held in mid-March 2020 at Nizamuddin Markaz mosque in New Delhi. This congregation was organized by Jamaat-e-Islami, a religious organization that is also located in New Delhi but shares connections with other chapters worldwide. Sharma and Anand (2020) find that mainstream media labeled the congregation as the "Markaz event" and defined it as a coronavirus hotspot, using the number of positive COVID tests as an indication that Jamaat-e-Islami was the single largest source of infection in Delhi. Interestingly, other religious communities who held gatherings at the same time in Uttar Pradesh and Madhya Pradesh were not criticized, blamed, or framed by the media as facilitating the spread of the virus (Sharma and Anand 2020). Moreover, reporters from the independent website Scroll (Daniyal 2020; Jain 2020) argued that the media's framing of the number of

COVID cases among the attendees is biased, since "a large proportion of Tablighi attendees were positives because they were tested, whereas overall testing for the rest of India is low" (Sharma and Anand 2020: 650). In this case, the media's particular focus on Jamaat-e-Islami illustrates how the media took advantage of already-existing anti-Muslim discourses to further problematize India's Muslim problem. Moreover, in ignoring positive COVID cases prevalent in other non-Muslim religious gatherings, the media framed the Markaz event to highlight the threat that Islamic religious organizations pose to the well-being of India's citizens, as opposed to the virus itself. Thus, in a similar manner by which #CoronaJihad was framed as bio-terrorism carried out by Muslims, the campaign of #TablighiJamaatVirus emphasized a connection between Islam, the virus, and Muslims' supposed proclivity toward terrorism, purposefully reifying the danger that India's constructed Muslim problem posed to the nation.

Social media

Social media use by BJP politicians has also played a part in facilitating these anti-Muslim campaigns. Many BJP politicians (including Narendra Modi) have enormous followings on social media, and often use their platforms to spread pro-BJP discourse, Hindutva nationalist ideologies, political propaganda, and misinformation that polarize the Hindu–Muslim divide. The head of the BJP's information technology unit, Amit Malviya, is a known Islamophobe who has been critiqued for spreading propaganda and misinformation to his sizeable following on social media. His social media presence and efforts in spreading fake news have earned him the title "Mr. Misinformation," given to him by the Indian media watchdog News Laundry (Zajączkowska 2021: 252). Malviya and other politicians' social media presence has allowed for "direct leader-to-people connections [and has also facilitated] a personality cult around Modi" in the same way that former US President Donald Trump's presence on Twitter facilitated his rise to power (Bolsover 2022: 1940).

The state's use of social media in mobilizing a nationalist authoritarian populist agenda during the BJP's rise to power in 2014 illustrates the sheer influence that social media have in facilitating India's state-created racial projects. After its rise to power, the BJP has systematically used social media as a tool to polarize the Indian public along religious and caste lines, thereby worsening Hindu–Muslim relations, while gaining public support for their anti-Muslim policies. The BJP has not shied away from acknowledging its use of social media for creating and sharing viral nationalist and anti-Muslim content. Former president of the BJP Amit Shah is quoted as saying to social media volunteers in Kota, "Real or fake, we can make any message go viral . . . It is through social media that we have to form governments at the state and national levels. Keep making messages go viral" (Basu 2019: n.p.). In the hands of the BJP, the effective use of social media as an anti-Muslim and nationalist propaganda tool facilitated the creation of the Indian Muslim problem, as well as proposing ethnonationalist solutions to this problem in the form of anti-Muslim exclusionary policies and violence.

There are a number of instances where social media have been found complicit in furthering the state's anti-Muslim nationalist agenda. In 2020, the Delhi State Assembly found Facebook guilty of "aggravating the Delhi riots, and posited that it should be investigated for every riot since 2014" (Muslim Advocates 2020: 22). Prior to the riots, a number of fake news stories and posts were circulated on Facebook depicting Muslim religious leaders calling for Hindus to be kicked out of Delhi. Enraged by these stories, mobs of Hindu men gathered in Delhi to harass Muslims and these tensions evolved into city-wide anti-Muslim riots and clashes on February 23, 2020, resulting in fifty-three deaths, a majority of whom were Muslim. Facebook was used widely during the riots to disseminate information and glorify violence. In response to both the riots and the Peace and Harmony Committee's findings, Facebook consequently took down a number of anti-Muslim accounts and posts in the months following the event (Muslim Advocates 2020).

Other social media platforms have also come under fire for facilitating anti-Muslim violence in India. In 2018, WhatsApp received formal warnings from the Indian government for being the source through which false rumors of Muslims and other religious or ethnic minorities killing cows, eating beef, or kidnapping children were disseminated (Akram et al. 2021). The widespread sharing of this misinformation in the form of fake news stories and manipulated photos and videos on WhatsApp led to nearly thirty mob lynchings around India, undertaken primarily by Hindu "cow vigilante" groups (Vasudeva and Barkdull 2020). The non-profit data journalism watchdog IndiaSpend found that from 2012 to 2017, seventy-eight cow-related hate crimes were reported across the country, with Muslims comprising 53 percent of the reported injuries and deaths. In 2017 alone, there were thirty-seven reported incidents of cow-related hate crime, with Muslims comprising 86 percent of those killed (Saldanha 2017). Although WhatsApp (and other social media platforms) was not the cause of cow vigilante violence and anti-Muslim hate crimes, its technological interface (e.g., group chat, unlimited number of forward messages) has arguably facilitated the potential for offline violence in much the same way social media have in the United States and United Kingdom (Muslim Advocates 2020).

Since frameworks of the GWOT are *global*, the influence of India's nationalist anti-Muslim agendas on social media has been found to extend beyond the geographical borders of India. Hindutva ideologies and sentiments on the urgency of addressing the Indian Muslim problem can be found espoused among those of the Indian diaspora residing in the US and UK. In an analysis of thirty-nine Twitter accounts of diasporic Indians during the Brexit referendum and Trump's election in 2016, Eviane Leidig (2019) finds that diasporic Indians mobilized Hindutva ideologies and anti-Muslim racism to express pro-Brexit and pro-Trump views. Leidig notes that "diasporic Hindutva becomes a mediator of trans-national ideological manifestations of anti-Muslim anxiety, albeit adapted to local contexts" and allows for diasporic Indians to facilitate a sense of belonging in their local contexts

102   A Global Racial Enemy

while maintaining a connection to their homelands through Hindutva ideologies (2019: 80). There were five noteworthy themes in these Twitter accounts that illustrate the populist radical right discursive politics of Brexit and Trumpism in 2016: immigration, foreign policy, establishment, Islam, and Indian (emphasizing the subtheme: Hindu). In using these right-wing ideologies, with the flavor of the BJP's anti-Muslim rhetoric, diasporic Indian social media users described Muslims as a "cancer," Islam as "a poisonous ideology," and Muslim men as rapists who threaten women, thus extending and applying these Islamophobic assumptions across UK, US, and Indian contexts. The political mobilization of this rhetoric through social media unites Hindutva ideologies with the neo-orientalist anti-Muslim racisms that are particular to the national contexts of the US and UK (Leidig 2019: 86). What is evident is that these themes are fundamentally connected to the underlying discourses of the GWOT that "distinguish a boundary against the Muslim 'other', building on Islamophobic anxiety prevalent in a post-9/11 era" (pg. 77).

Thus, within a post-9/11 context, the imagined non-Muslim diaspora, constructed as "us," encompasses those who identify as radical right populists, populist nationalists, and ethnonationalists who vie for politicized anti-Muslim agendas that target "them": the imagined Muslim diaspora. In being able to operate beyond the limits of nations' geographical boundaries, social media not only facilitate the anti-Muslim sentiment that India, the US, and the UK require to further their respective populisms, but also combine multicultural and transnational identity politics fundamental to the contemporary GWOT.

Conclusion

As this chapter shows, the media's role in facilitating the global racialization of Muslims is abundantly evident. In each context – the United States, United Kingdom, China, and India – the media deliberately produce biased, gendered,

The Media and the Racialization of Muslims 103

and anti-Muslim portrayals of Islam and Muslim men and women to create and reinforce the supposed danger that Muslim subjects and Islam pose to "the nation" and its (non-Muslim) subjects. Through affective mechanisms, media promulgate commonsense "knowledge" that Muslims and Islam are to be feared and excluded from the national imaginary due to their inherent associations with violence and terrorism. Consequently, state governments are provided with the fertile ground they need to propose, institute, and justify their anti-Muslim policies. Uniting these mechanisms, representations, and frameworks is the global Muslim racial problem, which evolves and is shaped according to each nation's ethnonationalist, populist, and racialized context.

Largely due to their proclivity to sensationalize stories for viewership, one can safely say that not much change is to be expected from anti-Muslim portrayals in news and social media posts. Except for notable individuals like Mehdi Hassan, Wajahat Ali, and Ali Velshi, there is a distinct lack of Muslim newscasters and journalists especially in the United States, United Kingdom, and China, which has led to biased, binary, and uninformed storytelling of local and global events that are framed in easy-to-consume frameworks of the GWOT. On social media, there is still an overrepresentation of Islamophobes and anti-Muslim posts that disseminate anti-Muslim content and reify connections between terrorism and Islam through their commentary on local and global events involving Muslims. Unsurprisingly, the sheer abundance of anti-Muslim posters drowns out the voices of Muslims denouncing these events, while also obscuring the positive and diverse representations of Muslim influencers, social media celebrities, and everyday Muslim men and women on social media. As such, it is unlikely we will see any radical changes in the anti-Muslim representations that are plentiful online or in the news.

In popular culture, however, there is some hope for change. Since the US presidential election of 2016 and the rise of anti-immigrant and anti-Muslim sentiments surrounding Brexit in the United Kingdom, there has been significant pushback by those in the British and American entertainment industries for positive representations of Muslims. Film and television industries in India and China do not seem to show the same impetus or call for a change in representations – perhaps this is because current representations serve the public sentiments and politics of these nation-states, or perhaps, in the case of China, state control of the film industry means there is no space for calls for change. Regardless, in the US and UK, the industry's newfound diversity initiatives have also come to include the Muslim identity as a category that falls under diversity. In analyzing Hollywood's diversity initiatives, Alsultany suggests that during and after Trump's administration, Hollywood responded to the anti-Muslim sentiments in politics by expanding its representations of Muslims. Calling this a form of "crisis diversity," Alsultany argues that while diverse representations of Muslims – such as in *Ramy*, *Ms. Marvel*, *Mo*, (and in the UK) *We are Lady Parts*, etc. – are refreshing and increasingly necessary, these representations fall victim to the "diversity compromise" (Alsultany 2022: 75). Alsultany describes this as "when Hollywood producers and writers make a concerted effort to challenge stereotypes but still fall flat in some way, whether big or small" (pg. 75). The diversity compromise usually involves a Muslim character or storyline being given additional characteristics or layers to represent their depth and diversity (such as being LGBTQ+, not wearing the hijab, struggling with their faith or familial expectations, etc.), but is still linked with frameworks of securitization and terrorism, or is attributed orientalist and neo-orientalist meanings of violence, oppression, or exoticism. For example, *Ramy* showcases the lead character's identity crisis as a Muslim American man and highlights his experiences dealing with anti-Muslim hostility from non-Muslims during his childhood and adulthood. While arguments can be made that these representations offer diversity of the Muslim experience, they are few in number and still fall short in providing complex and authentic representations of Muslims and Islam. Instead, they run the risk of reifying the frameworks of the GWOT that do Muslims symbolic and physical harm.

The Media and the Racialization of Muslims   105

Understanding the connections shared between the media and the global Muslim racial project is only one lens through which we can understand how Muslims have been constructed as an identifiable and threatening citizenry. In this chapter, we have offered some examples of ways by which the Muslim racial problem is constructed through media representation, framing, and discourse, thereby facilitating sociopolitical agendas that lead to the racialization, sociopolitical exclusion, and (in some cases) systematic genocide of Muslims within these nations.

–3–
The Global Racialization of Muslims and the Rise in Nationalism and Populism

On January 6, 2021, a mob of mostly white men stormed the US Capitol building as Congress was set to count the electoral votes for the 2020 presidential election. The votes would confirm Joe Biden as the 46th president of the United States. In protest, a group of men gathered to contest the election because they believed it was stolen. The mob walked en masse to the Capitol after attending a rally organized by Donald Trump before he left Washington DC (Blake 2021). Televisions around the world broadcast these (mostly) men, with a few women, breaking windows and entering the Capitol building while chanting for US vice president Mike Pence to be hanged (Pengelly 2021). While reporters and journalists responded to this event with shock, there has been a steady rise in a nativist and exclusionary populism in the United States, something that Trump capitalized on when running for president. But how was this event related to the global racialization of Muslims?

The idea that Muslims are invading or taking over the country is one of many anti-immigrant narratives that fuel right-wing populist movements that have escalated and intensified in the decades since 9/11 in the United States and UK. Nationalist and populist sentiments are growing in many countries. In this chapter we examine how this is tied to the global racialization of Muslims in China, India, the United States, and the UK. While the reasons for the rise in each country differ, there are some similarities in how racialization as an ideological tool has played a role in its popularity. The social construction of Islam as an invader or threat to the nation-state that has been used to justify the Global War on Terror has intensified in each of these countries, resulting in a national identity that has become more exclusionary and more racist.

To be clear, anti-Muslim hostility alone did not cause nationalism or populism in these countries, but rather it is playing a role in fueling their growth. As we have shown, the GWOT, which has resulted in military invasion as well as anti-terrorist policies popping up across the world, has relied on the racialization of Muslims. The ideological construction of Muslims as a threat to the nation results in their exclusion from a national identity. The relationship between anti-Muslim and anti-immigrant sentiments must be understood in relation to the strengthening of national identities globally, not just in Europe or the United States. Nationalism and ethnonationalist populisms produce the type of racism that targets Muslims, which we are witnessing flourish in the 21st century. And while in some countries, like the United States and the UK, this is tied to upholding white supremacy, in countries like China and India, anti-Muslim racism is used to uphold ethnonationalism, where white domination is not the goal. Thus, global racialization of Muslims is a broader racial project that should not just be understood as tied to white supremacy.

Nationalism and Populism: Definitions

A campaign ad by the Alternative for Germany (AfD), a right-wing populist group in Germany, created a stir in 2019. The ad used a 19th-century painting by French artist Jean-Léon Gérôme titled *Slave Market*. The painting, which happens to be the exact same one that Edward Said critiques for being an example of orientalism, depicts Arab men surrounding

108 A Global Racial Enemy

a white woman who is naked and going to be auctioned off. The image in the ad is accompanied by the slogan "So that Europe won't become 'Eurabia!' Europeans vote for AfD" (Grieshaber 2019). The ad perpetuates the idea that Germany is being taken over by immigrants and if this were to continue, white women would suffer this treatment at the hands of these misogynistic and barbaric Arab men. It aims at instilling fear that Muslims are taking over Europe and that Germany should leave the European Union and close its borders. This ad reflects the anxieties in Europe and the United States around Muslims and immigration as well as the rise in populist sentiments.

The rise in nationalism and ethnopopulism was seen as an unexpected response to the opening of borders in the latter part of the 20th century. Some argued that as a result of globalization, borders would loosen, and national identities would become less important (Pelinka 2011). The creation of the European Union exemplifies how, economically, nations stopped operating in silos, but rather became deeply connected to one another. This globalized economy has had a direct impact on the rise of populism in Europe. The viewpoint that jobs are being taken away by immigrants and foreigners and that the people of a country need protection from outsiders, both economically and culturally, represents a rising ethno-nationalist populism. Scholars have argued that Brexit was fueled by this type of nationalism and populism, one that is directly tied to the impact felt by a global economy (Bachmann and Sidaway 2016). Thus, this particular populism is one that is xenophobic, where a national identity is exclusionary in terms of race, ethnicity, and religion.

Similarly, in the United States, there has been a steady increase in populism. Scholars argue there are multiple types of populism in the United States. Bonikowski (2017) defines populism as "a form of politics predicated on the moral vilification of elites and the veneration of ordinary people, who are seen as the sole legitimate source of political power" (pg. S184). This definition enables a critique of the majority of political factions in the country for being elitist and not having the people's interests at heart. This attitude exists in

The Rise in Nationalism and Populism   109

both right-wing and left-wing segments of the population. An example of the left-wing segment can be seen in Bernie Sanders and his supporters (Bonikowski 2017). This group critiques the elite for their economic and capitalist practices. They differ in that they are not scapegoating immigrants as the problem, which has been prevalent in the anti-immigrant and xenophobic flavor of right-wing populism. Thus, ethnonationalist populism is one that is characterized by xenophobia and racism. This type of populism criticizes the state for being corrupt and not having the people's interest in mind; however, it differs in whom the polity includes. Ethnonationalist populism excludes individuals based on race, ethnicity, and religion (Bonikowski 2017).

In contemporary China there is another form of populism that differs from the type that is seen in the United States and UK. Rather than a populism that is responding to a government that is seen as elitist (Bonikowski 2017), some scholars have noted that the form of populism seen in China is an "authoritative populism" (Liu and Shen 2022). This populism is coercive and pushes a narrative of unity between citizens and their government, which is often authoritarian (Mamonova 2019). State propaganda is used to perpetuate this type of populism amongst its citizenry (Liu and Shen 2022). Thus, populism in authoritarian governments is used by the state to get its population to adhere to the interests of the state.

Nationalism is not the same as populism in that it is tied to the political body. Whereas some forms of populism are viewed as a struggle between the people and the elite and others are perpetuated by the state, nationalism is a reverence for the state. Puri (2008) states, "nationalism refers to relatively recent beliefs and practices aimed at creating unified but unique communities within a sovereign territory . . . such forms of community are thought of as nations and sovereign territory is associated with the concept of the state" (pg. 2). According to Puri, nationalism is an "expression of power" (pg. 5). Used by politicians and state leaders, nationalism encourages and incites individuals to act in what is believed to be the best interest of the state. After 9/11, for example, President Bush stated in a speech to the nation "You're either

110   A Global Racial Enemy

with us or against us," invoking a sense of patriotism to the state by telling its citizens where their loyalties must lie in a time of crisis. Similarly, slogans like "United We Stand" that emerged after 9/11 also produce a sense of allegiance to the nation, reflecting how the state can enforce a sense of nationalism. In the UK, the definition of what it means to be British has shifted over time, with some eras encouraging multiculturalism and others treating difference as a threat to the nation. India and China provide examples of how nationalist identities are forcefully promoted by authoritarian states. In all of these examples, Muslims are racialized as invaders of the nation.

In this chapter we identify how the global racialization of Muslims has been used to promote nationalism and populism, perpetuated by both the people and the state. The United States provides examples of rising ethnonationalist populism. To be clear, the state has pushed anti-Muslim rhetoric in order to gain support for their foreign and domestic policies in the Global War on Terror. The rise in nationalism and patriotism is tied to the ways the state has participated in the racialization of Muslims, as we show in this book. It is therefore not surprising to see the emergence of these ethnonationalist populist movements, as they are rooted in countries that have been pushing a patriotism and nationalism in the wake of the terrorist attacks on 9/11. Thus, we have to understand how state-fed nationalism has also nurtured xenophobic populism.

The United States: 9/11 and Patriotism, Nationalism, and the Rise of Ethnonationalist Populism

Patriotism after 9/11 soared in the United States. There are different ways in which an increase in patriotism has been measured since 9/11. One way is by noting an increase in displays of the American flag. Several studies showed that 74–82 percent of Americans bought and displayed flags after 9/11 (Moore, 2003; Skitka 2005). The act of flying the flag in the immediate aftermath of 9/11 revealed an increase in pride and love for one's country (Li and Brewer 2004; Skitka 2005). While one study found that the patriotism was not necessarily characterized by xenophobia or exclusionary attitudes (Skitka 2005), we have seen in the United States a sharp increase in anti-immigrant and anti-Muslim attitudes.

The rhetoric coming out of the state relied on the social construction of Arabs and Muslims as misogynistic, backwards, anti-American, and anti-modern. This rhetoric has shifted in the decades since September 11th. Compared to Trump's speeches about Muslims, Bush's rhetoric was somewhat softer. Bush stated in his speech on the War on Terror that the terrorists hijacked Islam and did not represent Muslims, yet the way in which he described Muslim majority countries was riddled with stereotypes. Bush's language was reflective of Huntington's "clash of civilizations" thesis, which stated that the next major world conflict would be between the West and Islam. When addressing the nation on October 7, 2001, Bush defined the terrorists' motivation as being in opposition to American values and as a result wanted to destroy it (Bush 2001). Bush justified invading Afghanistan, arguing terrorists were trained there, but the terrorists were largely described without a national identity. They were simply characterized as evil and anti-American, justifying the widespread tactics the United States would have to use in order to try to combat terrorism.

> Many will be involved in this effort, from FBI agents to intelligence operatives to the reservists we have called to active duty. . . . The *civilized world* is rallying to America's side. They understand that if this terror goes unpunished, their own cities, their own citizens may be next. Terror, unanswered, can not only bring down buildings, but it can also threaten the stability of legitimate governments. And you know what – we're not going to allow it. (Bush 2001, my emphasis)

Following this address, Bush referred to the Iraqi regime as uncivilized in his State of the Union Address on January 29, 2002.

112 A Global Racial Enemy

> This is a regime that has something to hide from the civilized world. States like these, and their terrorist allies, constitute an axis of evil, arming to threaten the peace of the world. By seeking weapons of mass destruction, these regimes pose a grave and growing danger. They could provide these arms to terrorists, giving them the means to match their hatred. They could attack our allies or attempt to blackmail the United States. In any of these cases, the price of indifference would be catastrophic. (Bush 2002)

This rhetoric of terrorists being evil, uncivilized, and a threat to the nation did not dissipate over time, but only became more intense within a faction of the Republican Party. The characterization of Muslim majority countries as inherently violent and prone to evil solidified the connection of Muslims and particularly Muslim immigrants as potential terrorists, justifying the counterterrorism laws and policies that were put into place hastily after 9/11. Even though Bush stated there were "good" Muslims, this did not temper the backlash and hate crimes Muslims encountered in the United States as a result of this rhetoric (Peek 2011; Selod 2018).

Anti-Muslim activism: The Tea Party, the ground zero controversy, and the birther movement

In 2009, there were several movements that were brewing in the United States. A populist movement was gaining momentum and mobilizing in response to the Obama administration's economic policies. Initially, the Tea Party was made up of white, middle-class men who advocated for lowering taxes and reducing government spending (Williamson et al. 2011). Social programs, like Obama's stimulus package and the Affordable Health Care Act, greatly angered these men. Resistance to social programs that helped those on the margins ignited neoliberal and racialized rhetoric of who deserves government assistance, ignoring the structural barriers put in place in a racialized social system (Bonilla-Silva 2006; Tope et al. 2014). As the movement grew, splinters occurred, with some espousing a more overt nativist and xenophobic tenor. The Tea Party Patriots, Tea Party Nation, and the Southern Tea Party are just a few examples of the various groups that formed who espoused racism against Muslims. A report produced by the Institute for Research and Education on Human Rights (Burghart and Zeskind 2010) examined the various factions of the Tea Party and their associations with anti-immigrant and racist sentiments. The Tea Party Patriots, for example, hosted Pamela Geller at one of their conferences. Geller, known as an Islamophobic activist, led the campaign against the building of an Islamic community center in New York City, Park51, blocks from the World Trade Center. In 2010, Geller founded the American Freedom Defense Institute, also known as Stop Islamization of America. The organization is considered a hate group by the Southern Poverty Law Center because it organizes and promotes anti-Muslim sentiments (Steinback 2011). There was a similar organization in Europe, Stop Islamification of Europe, that merged with Geller's Stop Islamization of America to form an umbrella organization called Stop Islamization of Nations, revealing the global connections between these anti-Muslim organizations. Both groups view Islam as taking over their countries, revealing how racialized notions of Muslims as invaders are a global construct. One of their goals was to prevent the building of mosques in the United States. Resistance to mosques being built was not new, but after the protests against Park51, there was a spike in anti-mosque activities around the country (American Civil Liberties Union [ACLU] 2022). In addition to organizing protests against the building, Geller's organization was responsible for putting up ads that racialized Muslims in New York City's subways. In 2013, her organization paid for dozens of ads to run in the subways that had an image of the World Trade Center burning on September 11th with the following quote said to be from the Quran placed over it: "Soon shall we cast terror into the hearts of the unbelievers" (CBS/APNews 2013). These efforts did not occur in a vacuum, but rather were part of a larger network that promoted the notion that Islam was

114   A Global Racial Enemy

taking over the United States, which aligned with views of right-wing populist organizations, like the Tea Party Patriots.

Another effort that was taking place at the same time was the anti-sharia movement. This one was headed by David Yerushalmi, the co-founder of the American Freedom Law Center and a member of the Center for Security Policy. The anti-sharia bill movement perpetuated the fear that Muslims were taking over the United States and wanted to institute sharia, or Islamic, law within the courts. The anti-sharia bills, formally known as anti-foreign bills, to avoid appearing to discriminate against Islam, sought to ban the use of Islamic laws in civil court cases. In the United States, judges often consult with Islamic law in order to adjudicate Muslim civil cases, such as divorces, to ensure they are done in accordance with their religious practices, a practice that protects religious freedom (Sacirbey 2012). But anti-sharia advocates used one court case to justify banning the use of Islamic, or what they refer to as foreign, laws in determining the outcome. The case, which has been widely referenced, involved a Muslim woman in New Jersey who filed for a restraining order against her husband for physically and sexually assaulting her. The judge ruled in this case that the man did not intend to harm her because he was abiding by his religious practices. The husband found an imam who would testify on his behalf, leading the judge to rule in his favor (Sacirbey 2012). Even though this ruling was overturned, it was used to fuel the anti-sharia bill movement with advocates arguing that Islamic law is barbaric and uncivilized and has no place in American courts. Furthermore, it relied on gendered racialized stereotypes that Muslim men are abusers of women, and that this behavior is permitted in Islamic law. Anti-sharia law activists perpetuated the idea that Muslims were trying to take over the laws in the United States.

While Yerushalmi was one of the original architects of the movement, it was Frank Gaffney, founder of the Center for Security Policy, who wrote the model bill that would be reproduced and introduced in several states by legislators across the country via copycat bills (Gardiner and Olalde 2019). Gaffney has been widely known to push racist theories

The Rise in Nationalism and Populism   115

that radical Muslims are trying to infiltrate and take over the government. His organization worked with another one, ACT for America, that has also been labeled as a hate group by the Southern Poverty Law Center (Shanmugasundaram 2018). ACT for America, headed by Brigitte Gabriel, would campaign for these anti-sharia bills by getting their supporters to show up and support the legislation when they were introduced (Gardiner and Olalde 2019). By 2018, 201 anti-sharia bills had been introduced since 2010 with fourteen states passing them (Shanmugasundaram 2018).

Anti-sharia movements and the protests against mosques reflect a growing vitriolic attitude about Muslims and Islam within a certain segment of the American population. There is no doubt that racism toward Muslims has played a crucial role in mobilizing a far-right ethnonationalist populist movement. According to a *New York Times* article, "A confluence of factors has fueled the anti-Shariah movement, most notably the controversy over the proposed Islamic center near ground zero in New York, concerns about homegrown terrorism and the rise of the Tea Party" (Elliott 2011). Ethnonationalist populists mobilize around nativist and anti-immigrant sentiments, which include the belief that Muslims are one of the threats that is invading the United States and needs to be expunged from American society. This sentiment ignores the long history Muslims have had in the United States and racializes them as outsiders and invaders.

The birther movement is another example of how an ethnonationalist populist movement participates in racializing Muslims. During Barack Obama's campaign for the 2008 presidential election, rumors began circulating that he was not an American citizen because an assistant working for Obama's literary agent made a mistake on his biography, misidentifying his birthplace as being Kenya. The assistant, Miriam Goderich, took responsibility for the error which occurred in 1991, yet the rumor took off when conservative sites like Breitbart published the rumor as fact (Stableford 2012). The birther movement is a prime example of the rejection of a Muslim identity from an American one, racializing Muslims as foreign and inherently incapable of being

116 A Global Racial Enemy

American. This rumor that Obama was not born in the United States and was a Muslim was used in political campaigns to mobilize voters. The speculations were initially supported by both Republicans and Democrats. Hillary Clinton supporters, eager to see her beat Obama in the 2008 primaries, leaked false information about his birthplace in order to push him out of the primaries. While Mitt Romney, the Republican candidate who ran against Obama in 2012, did not openly claim Obama was not born in the United States, he nodded to it at a campaign rally when he told a cheering crowd, "No one's ever asked to see my birth certificate; they know that this is the place that we were born and raised" (Serwer 2020).

Birtherism was a strategic ideological tactic used to garner support from right-wing populists who helped Donald Trump ascend to the White House. Trump pushed the rumor well before he ran for president. His goal was not about proving or disproving whether or not Obama was a citizen, but to push forth an ideology of what America should look like and who should and should not be included within its polity. This notion of a racialized citizenship – in this case being Muslim is equated with not being American – fueled an ethnonationalist populist vision of the United States.

> Birtherism was a statement of values, a way to express allegiance to a particular notion of American identity, one that became the central theme of the Trump campaign itself: To Make America Great Again, to turn back the clock to an era where white political and cultural hegemony was unthreatened by black people, by immigrants, by people of a different faith. By people like Barack Obama. The calls to disavow birtherism missed the point: Trump's entire campaign was birtherism. (Serwer 2020)

Trump's campaign slogan appealed to an ethnonationalist populist vision of America. Making America Great Again was about exclusion of racialized groups, including Muslims. There is no doubt that racist attitudes and racism toward

The Rise in Nationalism and Populism   117

Muslims played an integral part in fueling and mobilizing this movement that consists of various groups that have been organizing and popping up in the United States at an increasing rate since 9/11. It should not be surprising that birtherism took off around the same time as the rise of the Tea Party, protests against mosques, and the anti-sharia movement, which all occurred in the context of an increased nationalism and patriotism within the era of the Global War on Terror. Although Trump eventually admitted that Obama was a citizen, he spent years questioning his citizenship in media outlets like *Fox News*. A 2014 survey conducted by political scientist Alexander Theodoridis found that 53 percent of Republicans believed that Obama was a Muslim, even after he produced his birth certificate and publicly stated he was a Christian (Max Fisher 2015). In the next section we examine the ways Muslims are cast as outsiders by the state in the UK.

The UK as a Federated Nation

How to produce a Muslim problem: Two versions of nationalist populism

The UK is a colonial nation with citizenship laws that have evolved to limit the basis for citizenship from "civic" to "ethnic" since the Second World War (Paul 1997). The UK contains three nations (England, Scotland, and Wales) in one geographical space (Great Britain), plus part of the territory of a nearby nation (Northern Ireland), all in one political space (officially the United Kingdom of Great Britain and Northern Ireland). The national identities claimed there are necessarily complex and multilayered, and the story is more complicated than "British" vs. Others, where others are solely non-British nationals. "British" in the Northern Ireland context signifies an attachment to the continuing existence of Northern Ireland (established in 1921) as opposed to its re-integration into the Republic of Ireland. Identification with individual national identities (English, Scottish, and Welsh), as expressed in opinion polls and surveys, has been increasingly more popular than the umbrella of "British," except for one significant section of the UK population: ethnic minorities of color (Nandi and Platt 2015). The various attempts to measure forms of identification disaggregated by ethnicity since the turn of the 21st century demonstrate a pattern of disproportionate identification with Britishness, particularly strong among those self-identifying as Muslim but also Sikh, Hindu, or African-Caribbean (Elgenius and Garner 2021). This disproportion is the opposite of the patterns of identification with the individual component nations of the UK by people ticking the white UK box (Garner 2015). To imagine that British is a monolithic set of ideas is inaccurate. Even if we assume that the dominant English nationalism is what we actually mean by British in most cases, we need to exercise caution. We begin with this framing because it underscores that the narrative with which we have to engage is highly politicized, and not merely a reflection of commonsense truths.

From the late 1990s, a long period of increasing hostility expressed toward immigrants and minorities was identified in opinion-polling (Crawley 2005). This partly fueled the rise of the far-right British National Party (BNP), and later, the short-lived but highly influential United Kingdom Independence Party (UKIP), which crucially campaigned for a vote on membership of the European Union. Subsequent quantitative analyses of voting patterns in the Brexit vote established statistically significant relationships between negative attitudes toward immigrants and minorities; identification with English rather than British identity; and authoritarian sympathies and voting for Leave (Lord Ashcroft 2016; Swales 2016). An important part of the narrative of that "right populism" (see below) is a critique of the dominant multiculturalism, especially after the 7/7 London bombings in 2005, which was a terrorist attack on London's tube and buses that resulted in the deaths of fifty-six people. Previously, discussions of multiculturalism had revolved around a set of identities, such as white, African-Caribbean, British Asian, etc. However, after 2005, discussions of multiculturalism were mainly

The Rise in Nationalism and Populism   119

subsumed into an argument about whether Muslims are or could be integrated into Britishness, and a subcategory of literature critical of multiculturalism that had already started in the early years of the century intensified (Goodhart 2004; Phillips 2007; Caldwell 2009). After years of stress being placed on Britishness as a multicultural identity under the Blair and Brown governments between 1997 and 2010, a shift occurred under the first Cameron administration, where the policy area of "community cohesion" was abandoned, and the PM moved to flag up a number of perceived crises in British society. One of these crises was the fragmentation of the nation. In Cameron's speech at the Munich security conference in 2011, he outlined "muscular liberalism," which was slated as a more proactive and aggressive version of national liberalism that aimed to eradicate the outcome of old multiculturalism, the so-called parallel lives of Muslims and non-Muslims in Britain.

> Under the doctrine of state multiculturalism, we have encouraged different cultures to live separate lives, apart from each other and apart from the mainstream. We've failed to provide a vision of society to which they feel they want to belong. (Kirkup 2011)

According to this logic, an excess of multiculturalism, which encourages people to think of themselves as part of subgroups rather than of the unfragmented "British" group, is what spawned the British-born London bombers. This core message of multiculturalism having "failed" was also conveyed by the French president and the German, Australian, and Spanish prime ministers in the space of a few months.

Indeed, it is really important to keep in mind that although right-wing nationalist populist parties have made significant contributions to the racialization of Muslims in many countries, most notably the BNP (1999–2005) and UKIP (2010–16) in Britain, mainstream political parties have made decisive and arguably more impactful contributions to hostility toward Muslims (Bale 2018). In the UK, the two main political parties, Conservative and Labour, which have

120 A Global Racial Enemy

governed the UK since 1918, have long been hostile to, or at least ambivalent about, immigration from the Indian subcontinent, Africa, and the Caribbean, and migrants' capacity to integrate into British values. Indeed, Gilroy (1987) observed decades ago that immigration restriction is one of the few cross-party consensus topics.

There are two levels of the discourse on Muslims' failure to integrate. One is the formal political discussion of culture and security, which includes the world of the nationwide PREVENT scheme (Kundnani 2009; Awan 2012; O'Toole et al., 2012; Kundnani 2014), Trojan Horse (see below), and media discourse on the fragmentation of Britain. The other is the more or less global racialization of Muslims via images of veiled women held up as threats to democracy; Muslim men ravaging white women and oppressing Muslim women; and terrorist cells linked in universal jihad against the West. The two levels are interdependent: a putative (monolithic) Islamic culture is understood as producing Good and Bad Muslims. In the formal discourse the Good are seen as the majority, while in the popular discourse, they are seen as a minority or even a mythical fabrication masking a global project of takeover. Each terrorist attack like 7/7, Woolwich (2013), Westminster (2017), London Bridge (2017), and the murder of MP David Amess (2021) generates a revisiting of the central point of the discourse: that Muslims, as a group, do not belong in the country. The longstanding trend of physical attacks on mosques and individuals (particularly women who wear headscarves or more, who experience insults, spitting, and attempts to pull headscarves off), plus cyber-attacks, usually sees a spike in the immediate aftermath of one of these incidents (Tell MAMA, 2018b).

Trojan Horse: The cost of not being seen as a loyal citizen

In 2014 an anonymous letter was sent to Birmingham City Council which seemed to outline a plot to take over schools and radicalize schoolchildren in Birmingham. The letter referred to this plan as "Operation Trojan Horse." Although the council initially took no action, the UK government later

The Rise in Nationalism and Populism 121

responded to the letter by investigating over twenty schools in majority Muslim areas of the city. No plot or evidence of Trojan Horse was discovered, and no charges were brought. However, lengthy school inspections and reports over a period of months resulted in a number of teachers being dismissed from the teaching profession for life. All but one of these bans was overturned later in tribunals. An investigation revealed that individual teachers managed to influence teaching on citizenship and sex education, for example toward particular conservative and gender-biased versions of Islam. However, the key element we need to retain is that an unattributable letter, whose authenticity or claims were never substantiated, became the basis of state intervention and intense media focus precisely because it expressed what many suspect about Islam, that it seeks to "overthrow" non-Islamic values and destroy "British culture" and that this is being done as part of an ongoing organized plot (Holmwood and O'Toole 2018). Muslims were racialized here as invaders.

The Muslim problem (Hajjat and Mohammed 2013) is defined as a failure to integrate combined with a concomitant ongoing threat to overthrow British values and replace them with Islamic ones, hence the allure of Trojan Horse. The overemphasis on culture as way to define Muslims and deny them political agency is a clear outcome of this. However, most of the work on Islam proceeds as if the actors are not embedded in economic situations and gender is only relevant in terms of illustrating the misogyny of Muslim men (Rashid 2014). Moreover, the state has developed an array of mechanisms of control, surveillance, and punishment that are specifically used on Muslims above and beyond what is used on other groups.

The dominant discourse is split into two overlapping elements: (1) Islam is a threat to the West and will never change – all Muslims are bad; and (2) parts of Islam are a threat to the West and the state's role is to encourage the "Good" Muslim. By using a culturalist and security framing of Muslims in Britain, the binaries of good versus bad, loyal versus disloyal, threatening versus unthreatening, for example, are kept as live elements of a relational and oppositional view in which Muslims, unlike people in other

122   A Global Racial Enemy

communities, are interesting or relevant only in connection with the question: can Muslims ever really be British? On one level it does not matter if most Muslims say "yes" unhesitatingly to this question, because they are not the ones who usually ask it. Merely posing the question is a demonstration of power relations exercised by the state and the gatekeepers (Elgenius and Garner 2021) of the nation. Indeed, the question of who belongs to the nation is fundamental to understanding the basis of a racialized Muslim identity in the contemporary world. The version of this question posed in India is what we shall now turn to.

India: Populism, Nationalism, and Hindutva

India's current state-led racialization of Muslims shares a number of elements with those of the other states we focus on in this chapter, yet the context is very different. India is a postcolonial and multicultural state less than eighty years old, and the largest so-called democracy on earth, with more than a billion inhabitants and an electorate of more than 800 million (Philips 2021). Caste is a very significant and longstanding socioeconomic hierarchy alongside which sit other forms of racialized diversity within the country (Michelutti 2020). However, it is important to note that India's 1947 Constitution makes explicit provision for the incorporation of religious and less powerful castes into official institutions (Mandal 2022).

Due to the embedding of its independence movement leadership in the British colonial system, India's political system is modeled on western liberal democracy. This has produced different versions of nationalism (primarily secular and Hindu) that have been hegemonic at different times. The officially secular Indian National Congress (INC), the party that ran the country until the early 21st century, created patterns of support, clientelism, and ideological normalization (Ziegfeld 2021). While they were acknowledged and given access to some resources, minorities were hardly cherished or embraced as key members of the nation. Muslims and

The Rise in Nationalism and Populism 123

Hindus lived in segregated areas and caste profoundly shaped socioeconomic patterns of inequality. Minorities sometimes came into conflict with the state. In 1984, two of Prime Minister Indira Gandhi's Sikh bodyguards retaliated against their government's attack on the Golden Temple in Amritsar by assassinating her. Gandhi's leadership style was also populist and autocratic (Rudolph and Rudolph 1987). She had responded to being found guilty of electoral corruption by establishing a State of Emergency, which suspended democracy in 1975 until 1977, arrested opposition politicians, and afforded power to her close relatives (Prakash 2019).

Indian politics has thus hardly been devoid of populist or majoritarian tendencies. Yet since the Bharatiya Janata Party (the BJP, Indian People's Party) under Narendra Modi took power in 2014, there has been a shift in intensity and focus on the state's engagement with Muslims. Some of these aspects demonstrate continuity rather than a break with the past, while others are innovations; but the result by 2022 is to place Muslims in a particularly vulnerable place, both socially and economically. The BJP, founded in 1980 as part of the reaction to Indira Gandhi's authoritarian leadership, had been in power in coalition before but without the means to establish the kind of populist nationalism that Modi has been able to exploit (Seshia 1998). And exploiting Hindu nationalism means using Muslims as a significant folk devil, as we will see below.

Scholars of Hindutva (Hindu-ness as a political and cultural movement) suggest that there is continuity in its uses between the INC and BJP eras. Hinduism has long been a theme in political campaigning. However, the legal distinction between Hinduism (as a religion) and Hindutva (as a way of life) produced by the landmark 1995 Supreme Court ruling created a space for a Hindutva-propelled politics. Prior to this decision, it would have been illegal to campaign explicitly for Hindu votes, as an appeal to religious identities was considered beyond the pale of democratic secularism. The amalgamation between the Office of the Prime Minister and the cultural and social process of intensifying Hindutva

124 A Global Racial Enemy

that Christophe Jaffrelot calls "saffronization" (Anderson and Jaffrelot 2018) has discursively produced Muslims as the principal threat to the Indian nation. This political and cultural project around which Hindus can bond is characterized by Anderson (2015) as "neo-Hindutva." It is neo-Hindutva that has successfully positioned Muslims not only as a fifth column, but importantly as a group that can be verbally and physically attacked with impunity.

Simple binaries hamper our understanding of how Muslims are racialized, so we need to stress first what our argument does not say. We do not argue that Modi invented "hard" Hindutva or that everything before 2014 was much better for Muslims; or that the various actors involved in Hindu organizations share an idea of what is desirable or acceptable; or that the only logical development of the BJP in power is increased investment of different types of resources in racializing Muslims. Instead, we note that two important elements have emerged as possible and achievable since Modi took power in 2014. First, the 1995 legal loophole taken advantage of to instill Hindutva as an organizing principle has allowed the de facto propulsion of India towards becoming an "ethnic" rather than secular state. Second, the emergence of what Jaffrelot terms "a parallel state" (Anderson and Jaffrelot 2018: 474) of vigilante operations that are enforced in people's private and professional lives is a new orthodoxy. At the other end of this spectrum are Hindu organizations that now have important decision-making power in various areas of public life (education, the legal system, media, etc.).

Modi, the RSS, and Hindutva

The Rashtriya Swayamsevak Sangh (RSS, or National Volunteer Organization) is the largest of the Hindu civil society organizations under the Sangh Parivar (RSS Family) umbrella of Hindu activism. It was established in 1925 and currently has between 5 and 6 million members. There are two principal gurus for the RSS. The first is V.D. Savarkar, whose 1923 pamphlet, *Hindutva*, argues that India is synonymous with Hinduism, and faiths generated from outside India are not part of the nation. The second is M.S. Golwalkar, who was the RSS leader during the Second World War and admired Nazi Germany and the Nazi social movements' importance to nationalism. Golwalkar scrupulously avoided engagement in the anti-colonial movement throughout the 1940s. The RSS is a parallel society of organizations, schools, media, priest training, etc. that advocates for Hinduism to be considered the core of the Indian nation, and the exclusion of contrary perspectives that contest or seek to qualify this claim (Sarkar 2022). It exerts a significant influence over the "family's" political wing, the BJP (Tozawa 2015). It should be noted that this nationalist organization is deeply socially conservative and has never been involved in any anti-colonial, anti-caste, or feminist equality campaign (Sarkar 2022).

From 1998 to 2004, the BJP was in power under its leader, Atal Bihari Vajpayee, who governed with a coalition. The BJP was clearly then a party whose internal power dynamics were balanced in a different way from its present incarnation. A parallel can be drawn between Modi's present-day BJP and Trump's Republican Party. The Modi-led BJP in power is more focused on Modi as a charismatic leader and has the obvious strategy of exacerbating the vulnerability of religious minorities, using them as a normalized focus of anger and othering (deflecting). This can be seen in both internal and external security considerations (especially but not exclusively in Kashmir and Pakistan); and the narratives about nation, hierarchies, and power that the Hindutva organizations relate (Jaffrelot 2015).

For the BJP, Muslims and Christians in particular are "anti-national" by dint of who they are, while a set of ostensibly "national" actors can be categorized as "anti-national" depending on what they do. Political and intellectual opponents of Hindutva are labeled "anti-national" while members of the Scheduled Castes (Dalits) and Scheduled Tribes, the most disadvantaged caste, have been labeled anti-national if they adopt a critical political stance toward the BJP, which is a common occurrence. This bank of "enemies of the nation" sustains BJP's victim narratives (Natrajan 2022).

126   A Global Racial Enemy

Indeed, the Hindutva politics of grievance is essential to understanding the ideological thrust of Muslim racialization. The groups listed above are posited as being treated by the liberal Indian state and media as if they were superior to Hindus. The BJP has been in power as the ruling party since 2014, and has extended its reach into regional government. As of May 2022, it controlled seventeen (twelve outright and five in coalition) of the twenty-eight state governments. In 2018 it had controlled twenty-one, and more than 70 percent of the population. Given the reality of BJP political domination, it is difficult to understand how the grievance actually translates into discrimination *against* Hindus. However, this type of self-serving victim narrative is a key component of the populist right across the world. It generates resentment, bonds supporters, and provides targets for anger.

Hindutva and Muslims

Hindutva is a national cultural project as much as a political one, aimed at changing the norms of India, which has been successful. Researchers discern two elements: "hard" (aggressive, violent, and explicit) and "soft" Hindutva (soft also engaged in by other political parties) (Anderson and Longkumer 2018). Key projects that the BJP has prioritized since taking power include building a temple to the deity Ram on the site of the Babri Masjid mosque (destroyed by Hindu mobs in 1992); revoking Muslim personal law; and revoking Article 370 of the Constitution (which granted special status to Kashmir and Jammu, majority Muslim provinces on the border with Pakistan). Indeed, some commentators began referring to the "second phase" of India's republic beginning in 2014. A Hindu nationalist agenda would become the political norm after the "Nehruvian secularism" of the first fifty years of post-independence Indian politics (Kim 2017; Singh 2019). Muslims are identified as constituting a number of overlapping threats. They are viewed as separatists in the North and Northwest on the border with Pakistan; security threats and terrorists operating from within Pakistan; immigrants in the East, and particularly in Bengal and the states surrounding Bangladesh. They are also seen as fifth columnists masterminding two important campaigns that undermine Hindu and therefore Indian purity: eating and distributing beef and indoctrinating, converting, and "stealing" Hindu women (Gupta 2021).

On the one hand, we have the longstanding but sporadic practice of attacks on Muslim places of worship and districts, which have been politically motivated and, importantly, rendered possible by the collusion of the police. This dates back decades, although there are two highly politically significant such attacks in recent history. First, there was the 1992 destruction of the Babri Masjid mosque in Ayodhya, which resulted in subsequent riots, in which almost 2,000 people, mostly Muslims, were killed (Guha 2007). The official inquiry (Liberhan Ayodhya Commission 2009) blamed Sangh Parivar and senior BJP politicians in Uttar Pradesh for the events. Second, in 2002 there were three days of riots in Gujarat province, which claimed thousands of lives, with the majority being Muslim, which was incited by the burning of a train that killed Hindu pilgrims (Jaffrelot 2003). Attacks continued for three months after the initial riots, with minimal police intervention. Modi was personally implicated in these attacks: as Chief Minister for Gujarat he was responsible for law and order. He was accused of inciting the riot, then ordering police not to intervene, and finally for condoning it and downplaying the outcome in public discourse (Human Rights Watch 2002). A variety of actors claim that the evidence suggests the riots, framed as a response to the murderous attack on a train full of Hindu pilgrims, had actually been planned and organized, with the police even participating in some instances, along with RSS, using electoral lists to better target Muslim properties (Brass 2005).

While Muslims have been residentially segregated since the Partition of India and Pakistan, this trend has been exacerbated under Modi. The economic impacts of India's booming economy in the 21st century have been experienced

128 A Global Racial Enemy

very patchily across the geographical and socio-occupational ladders. Muslims have benefited the least and are actually losing economic ground (Khan 2020; Menon 2022). This material aspect of the racialization of Muslims is usually glossed over in studies that focus exclusively on ideologies and the most obvious elements of Hindutva-based discrimination – three of which we shall now look at briefly: "cow vigilantes," "love jihad", and citizenship laws.

Cow vigilantes

Both Hinduism and Sikhism identify cows as sacred animals and thus prohibit followers from eating beef; however, Muslims eat beef. There have been campaigns since the 1800s, originally led by Sikhs, to protect cows and prevent and punish those who slaughtered, sold, and ate them (Doyle 2016: 249). However, there is no national law against eating or selling beef in India, as it is a secular state. Even though Indira Gandhi resisted calls to ban these activities, individual states can and do outlaw cow smuggling and cow slaughter. There were sporadic campaigns against, and attacks on people suspected of buying, selling, and eating beef through the late 19th century and into the postwar independence period, revealing that the BJP have not invented this as an issue (Ghurye 1968; Yang 1980; Groves 2010; Sengupta 2011). However, since 2014, groups of vigilantes have begun attacking, with relative impunity, people suspected, many who were Muslim, of transporting and/or eating beef. Many of these attacks have been fatal. In the 2010–21 period, eighty-two incidents were officially recorded, leaving forty-three dead and 145 injured, with a spike after the BJP's accession to power in 2014.

In response, Modi expressed anger that Dalits, but not Muslims, had been injured or killed. A controversy sparked by NGO Human Rights Watch then ensued about the BJP's role in inciting and supporting cow vigilantes by not condemning them. Indeed, eight men convicted of such a murder, but out on bail, were actually garlanded by a BJP Member of Parliament, Jayant Singh, in Jharkand in 2018

(Huffington Post 2018). As with the attacks on Muslim neighborhoods, the police and the authorities are accused of indifference, or even actively supporting them. The messages conveyed by these patterns of policing and political response say that there is an unwillingness to intercede in such attacks or punish the perpetrators, revealing who is worthy of protection from the nation-state and who is not.

Love jihad

Another way Muslims are being excluded from a national identity in India is via laws that police their intimate relationships. A conspiracy theory from 2008 suggests that Muslim men are actively strategizing to convert Hindu women by seducing them, marrying them, and thus debilitating the Hindu nation. This theory underpins the so-called "Romeo" squads that police people's intimate relationships. Indeed, the most serious incident, the 2013 Muzzafarnagar riots in the Uttar Pradesh province, actually preceded Modi's accession to power. Currently, vigilantes patrol streets surveilling couples, with the expressed aim of preventing Muslim men from carrying out their "love jihad" against Hindu women. However, it has assumed a different level of power since 2014, when the Adityanath Yogi was made Chief Minister of Uttar Pradesh. Yogi is a Hindu priest who frequently makes bellicose statements about Muslims. He established Uttar Pradesh's Prohibition of Unlawful Conversion of Religion Ordinance, 2020, which made it unlawful to convert for the sake of marriage. According to Dhanak of Humanity, a human rights organization supporting LGBTQ and interfaith marriages in India, interfaith marriages are not common but of them over 40 percent involve Muslim women marrying Hindu men (Biswas 2020).

Banning interfaith marriage dates back to colonial times but is currently resurfacing (Biswas 2020). It is an example of how intimate relations are surveilled because of the racialization of Muslim men. What is new is the concerted effort that the Hindu network has invested in communicating "love jihad" as a live threat through all types of print and visual

130   A Global Racial Enemy

media, including social media. Attempts to control women and make their bodies a symbol of the nation are not specific to 21st-century India, but the amalgamation of power, new media, and the political will to disseminate this narrative are new (Gupta 2021).

Indeed, the message is not only that women but also men should be submissive and unquestioning of patriarchal power. In a Supreme Court test case ruling, the Hadiya case (2018) overrode the Kerala High Court's earlier decision to annul the marriage of a Hindu woman who married a Muslim and return her to her father's care because she had been indoctrinated and kidnapped, which is basically the narrative put forward by the vigilantes and the BJP. Their narrative completely ignored the marriage of Muslim women with Hindu men, insisting that relationships the other way around can only be the result of indoctrination and kidnapping. The racialization of Muslim men as threatening to Hindu women was the basis for the 2020 Ordinance, not Muslim women marrying Hindu men.

These vigilantes serve a purpose for the BJP and Hindutva. The bodies of cows and those of women are pretexts for defending boundaries of the pure Hindu nation (which for the BJP is the same thing as the Indian nation, *Bharat*) against the defiling presence of Muslims (Gupta 2021). Moreover, such discourse and practices sustain division, suspicion, and segregation (Sarkar 2018). It should be reiterated that neither interfaith marriage nor beef sales or consumption are illegal (hence the Uttar Pradesh law above) – so given the lack of police action and political condemnation for involvement in these forms of collective violence, an important political objective of such activities is to demonstrate that Hindu mob law de facto supersedes the law of the land.

Citizenship rules

The Citizenship Amendment Bill 2015 brought an amendment to the 1955 Citizenship Law. The amendment enumerates the religious and cultural background of minorities who are allowed to become citizens after entering the country as refugees. On the list are Pakistan, Afghanistan, and Bangladesh, but refugees from these nations must be Hindu, Sikh, Buddhist, Jain, Parsi, or Christian. Muslims are not on the list. The countries identified are characterized as "Islamist" – which both establishes Islam as a threat and sets up a hierarchy of refugees, according to religion. Non-Muslim refugees are more important than Muslim ones, even if they too are also fleeing persecution by authoritarian states and ethnic cleansing. Furthermore, Muslim refugees from neighboring countries such as Myanmar are not included. This state action indeed inserts itself in a space of de facto ethnic exclusion whereby particular groups are defined by the state as threatening, and therefore undeserving of equal access to formal membership of the nation. It should be noted also that some European countries such as the UK and France have either passed or debated the introduction of legislation allowing the government to strip an individual of their citizenship.

Apart from the ongoing material deprivation and residential segregation of Muslims in India, the process of symbolically locating them outside the nation has become central to the project of the governing party and the vast and complex social movement that supports it, and indeed provides the foot soldiers for the ongoing campaigns of border policing involving threats and physical violence. Muslims are racialized as threats to the nation both physically and culturally, embodying a boundary of Indianness which always is coterminous with Hinduism. Producing Muslims as relational threatening Others is part of a populist-nationalist political project to unite elites and the masses.

China: Settler Colonialism and Uyghur Muslims

Because Uyghur Muslims have had a complicated history with the People's Republic of China (PRC) over the last few decades, there has been a rise in nationalism within the Uyghur population. The majority of Uyghur Muslims reside in the Xinjiang or East Turkestan region of China.

132   A Global Racial Enemy

This region borders eight other nations: Russia, Afghanistan, Pakistan, Mongolia, India, Kazakhstan, Kyrgyzstan, and Tajikistan. The proximity to so many Muslim majority nations has had a significant influence on the religious and ethnic identity formation of Uyghur Muslims (Bhattacharya 2003), making them culturally distinct from majority Han Chinese. They have been treated and viewed as an ethnic minority by the state because of their cultural differences, including religion (Bhattacharya 2003). They are also an ethnic population that has been in conflict with the Chinese state over their ability to rule themselves. This desire for self-autonomy has produced a strong nationalist identity amongst Uyghur Muslims (Bhattacharya 2003), which has been met with increased antagonism and state violence because they have been marked as terrorists.

The relationship of China to the Xinjiang region has fluctuated over time. Roberts (2020) describes the history of this relationship as colonialist. The Uyghur homeland was once viewed as a frontier colony, where the population was able to retain its cultural distinction and remain in the majority, yet the resources and governance were controlled by the Chinese state. It was not until the PRC came into being that this relationship began to be characterized as a form of "settler colonialism" with the movement of Han people into this region and the goal of displacing the population (Roberts 2020). This form of colonialism is ongoing and can be seen in the detention, extreme surveillance, limited mobility, and horrific human rights abuses of the Uyghur Muslims. The political and economic motivations for the Chinese state to occupy this region include the desire to build a New Silk Road, a US $900 billion dollar infrastructure that will go through this region giving China access to better trade with neighboring Asian countries, the Middle East, and Europe (Bruce-Lockhart 2017). Thus, the desire to control the region and resources has resulted in the mass targeting of Uyghur Muslims as a threat to national security, because their religion marks them as a threat (Byler 2022). The GWOT provided the Chinese state with the opportunity to reframe Uyghur Muslims from

The Rise in Nationalism and Populism 133

separatists to terrorists, resulting in their discrimination via counterterrorism polices (as we chronicle in the next chapter).

Gendered racialization of Uyghur Muslims and nationalism

Like India, nationalism in China differs from the UK and the United States due to its unique history with colonialism, which plays a significant role in what types of nationalism are promoted and by who. China's history is a long one, which includes periods of empire and expansion. There have been tensions, including wars, with neighboring countries like Japan, Russia, and Turkey. There have also been ongoing wars over territories, like Hong Kong. Hong Kong was once occupied by China, but later taken over by the British Empire after a military campaign in the middle of the 19th century. It was not until recently that Britain relinquished control of Hong Kong to China, which was given the status of Special Administrative Region (SAR) of China by which the territory was able to maintain control over its judicial, executive, and legislative powers (Tam 2012). But China has been able to seize control via a new anti-terrorism law. In 2020, Hong Kong passed a national security law, known as the Law of the People's Republic of China on Safeguarding National Security in the Hong Kong Special Administrative Region, which criminalized secession, subversion, terrorism, and collusion with a foreign entity (Regan 2020). The history of invasions, wars, and tensions with neighboring countries has influenced the state's nationalistic tone. While this history is important to understand in all its complexities and detail, in this chapter we primarily focus on how the current administration's nationalistic tone has taken on a racist tone toward Muslims.

The PRC was founded in 1949 and ever since has been reimagining China as a new global power, economically and politically (Roberts 2020). This economic growth has been accompanied by an increase in Chinese nationalism. Since the Cold War, state-led nationalism in China has been on the rise. The 1990s saw an increase in

134   A Global Racial Enemy

the Chinese government's efforts to promote patriotism and Chinese nationalism via efforts such as the Patriotic Education Campaign. This campaign included providing patriotic education texts in schools that promoted loyalty to the state among Chinese youth. This state-led patriotism is being defined as an authoritarian form of populism, described earlier in the book (Zhao 2021). For example, since President Xi Jinping rose to power, his administration has been pushing forth state-led populism. One example is his promotion of the slogan of the "China Dream," which encouraged the Chinese Communist Party and Chinese citizenry to participate in rejuvenating the nation (Allison 2017). This dream includes China becoming one of the world's ascending powers where the Chinese citizenry is materially well off and China is "modernized."

Under the Xi administration, there has been a major cultural shift, with Chinese culture being promoted over other identities (Wang 2022). The China Dream has not been framed as inclusive of all, but instead reflects a cultural nationalist revival that is xenophobic, anti-Muslim, and anti-immigrant, mirroring in many ways how nationalism and ethnopopulism operate in the United States, the UK, and India. Difference is viewed as a threat to the China Dream. One study showed an increase in cyber-nationalism occurring online, with those who critiqued China being censored by the state or trolled by online nationalists (Zhang 2020). Furthermore, Chinese right-wing populists online argue that Muslims and people of color, aside from Chinese migrants, are a detriment to western and Chinese societies (Zhang 2020). A rise in Han nationalism, one where the Chinese state includes a Han population and excludes others, including Uyghurs, has been on the rise in China. A 2014 policy, "Incentive Measures Encouraging Uyghur–Chinese Intermarriage" is one of the many examples of the state's attempts to eradicate a Uyghur population. The policy claims that Uyghur women would be given financial incentives to marry Han men, but in reality it has resulted in forced marriages of Uyghur women (Kashgarian 2020). Uyghur women were threatened with punitive measures toward them

The Rise in Nationalism and Populism   135

and their families if they did not comply with this policy. The rationale behind it is to prevent Uyghur women from having Uyghur Muslim children. Thus, the racialization of Muslim women in this context is that they produce Muslim children, which threatens a national identity. Muslim intimate relationships are surveilled and policed by the Chinese state in an attempt to erase them from the polity to achieve a homogeneous national identity.

This nationalistic agenda by which Uyghur Muslims are targeted predates Xi Jinping's reign. After the creation of the People's Republic of China (PRC) language policies were implemented which made standard Chinese the national language. Uyghur Muslims who spoke Uyghur were allowed to speak this language even though it was not the national language. However, under President Xi and within the context of this hyper-nationalism and the GWOT, the state has put in place policies that require schools to teach in Mandarin rather than the native languages spoken in the various regions, including East Turkestan, where many Uyghurs reside. The justification given by the government is to promote and encourage a nationalist identity in China – but instead it is leading to cultural genocide in the name of nationalism (Lim 2021).

Painting Islamic culture as a threat to the nation justifies these policies. This relationship of the Chinese state to the Uyghur Muslims is a colonialist one, because the state is trying to eradicate the population and appropriate its resources (Roberts 2020; Byler 2022). In order to justify settler colonialism against Uyghur Muslims in the Xinjiang region of China, Muslims are ideologically presented as a threat to Chinese culture and security (Byler 2022). China is an example of how in today's global climate, the racialization of Muslim men and women is justified under a hyper-nationalist agenda.

Conclusion

In this chapter we show how Muslims' racialization plays a role in the rise of right-wing and authoritarian nationalism

136 A Global Racial Enemy

and populism in the United States, the UK, India, and China. Nationalism differs from right-wing populism in the United States and the United Kingdom, while the line between the two is blurry in authoritarian regimes like those under the current administrations in India and China. In this chapter we show that September 11th reified the idea that Muslims are a threat to national security and cultural values, which justified the Global War on Terror's policies in each of these countries. And although each country has a unique history and context and specific forms of nationalism and populism, they share situating Muslims as invaders of the nation-state. Muslims are treated as if they are bad for the nations, situating them outside of a national identity. They are viewed as cultural aberrations and threats to national security, which has justified protests against the building of mosques in the United States, surveilling children in schools in the UK, citizenship laws and preventing interreligious marriages in India, and forced marriages in China. Muslim men and women experience the consequences of a nationalism and populism that is inherently racist by being made to feel they are a problem and do not belong. In the next chapter we examine the counterterrorism policies that have been put into place in each of these countries, revealing how the racialization of Muslims is institutionalized globally.

–4–

Global Counterterrorism Policies: Racializing Muslims via Surveillance, Policing, and Detention

The attack took place on American soil, but it was an attack on the heart and soul of the civilized world. And the world has come together to fight a new and different war, the first, and we hope the only one, of the 21st century. A war against all those who seek to export terror, and a war against those governments that support or shelter them.

President George W. Bush, October 11, 2001

On October 11, 2001, one month after the terrorist attacks, President George W. Bush addressed the United States with a brief report on the military campaign that had just begun in Afghanistan. The two most visible acts by the United States in the Global War on Terror (GWOT) were the invasion of Afghanistan and then Iraq to weed out Al-Qaeda and protect the United States from another attack. In this short speech Bush's comments were revelatory in that it noted the attacks were not just against the United States, but it was an attack on the "civilized world," invoking the notion of a clash of civilizations between civilized and uncivilized societies.

138 A Global Racial Enemy

In his many speeches about the United States' campaign to rid the world of terrorism, Bush said that the GWOT would include traditional responses, like the military, along with other non-traditional strategies to fight this new enemy, requiring the cooperation of American allies globally. "Our staunch friends, Great Britain, our neighbors Canada and Mexico, our NATO allies, our allies in Asia, Russia and nations from every continent on the Earth have offered help of one kind or of another, from military assistance to intelligence information to crack down on terrorist financial networks" (Bush 2001). And while this statement at the time may have seemed innocuous, it hinted at how the rest of the world would eventually participate in the Global War on Terror. President Bush and his wife, Laura Bush, invoked women's rights as a test for civilized societies. Laura Bush gave a speech on the radio after the United States' invasion of Afghanistan, where she claimed that the women of Afghanistan would be liberated from abuse as a result of this war.

The GWOT has triggered mass surveillance and policing of Muslims around the world. The United Nations put into place one of the most important policies that institutionalized the racialization of Muslims internationally. Just weeks after the September 11th attacks, on September 28, 2001, the Counter-Terrorism Committee was established by the United Nation's Security Council's Resolution 1373. According to the meeting minutes, fifteen countries were a part of the committee to vote on the resolution. The entire meeting, including the vote, took a total of five minutes, starting at 9:55 pm and ending at 10:00 pm. According to the resolution, every country that is a member of the UN would be required to put into place domestic laws and policies that would aid in fighting the War on Terror. There are only two countries (Palestine and the Vatican City) in the world that are not recognized by the United Nations, reflecting the scope of this resolution. Some of the requests included preventing the financing of terrorism, denying safe haven to any individuals or groups marked as terrorists, cooperating with other governments in fighting terrorism

Global Counterterrorism Policies　　　139

within their borders, and cracking down on those seeking asylum to make sure they are not potential terrorists. Thus, a global concerted effort to fight terrorism emerged, which includes accountability of participation by each country to the UN.

Twenty-one years after the attacks, the efforts by the UN to combat terrorism are still going strong. On October 22–23, 2022 the Special Meeting of the Counter-Terrorism Committee took place in India. At this meeting, countries addressed how to use new technologies to combat terrorism.

> With the prevalence of technology and the rapid rise in digitization, the use of new and emerging technologies to counter terrorism is a topic of growing interest among Member States, policymakers and researchers, particularly in the context of the increasing role played by technology in terrorism and counterterrorism. This is addressed by the Security Council in a number of counter-terrorism related resolutions, most recently resolution 2617 (2021), which explicitly cited "emerging technologies." (UN 2022)

We should be critical of what constitutes these "emerging technologies." These technologies can include facial recognition, cameras at borders, body scanners in airports, and even tools to collect DNA. We should be deeply concerned when states invest in technologies that can be used to collect private information on its population. The GWOT has instigated this surveillance industry on a global scale that is driven by the racialization of Muslims. Khaled Beydoun (2020) argues that anti-Muslim animus is global, resulting in what he refers to as structural Islamophobia.

> Capitalizing on the global animus toward Muslims that proliferated after the 9/11 attacks, governments across the globe have enacted structural Islamophobic policies as a political expedient. The structural Islamophobia established and extended by three American presidential administrations embraced the fundamental assumption

140 A Global Racial Enemy

that Muslims were presumptive terrorists. Governments around the world interpreted American policy as a green light to adopt this presumption, and subsequently to implement their own policies and programs designed to police, punish, and prosecute their Muslim minority populations en masse. (pg. 92)

While the United States did push forth the narrative of the clash of civilizations, with Muslims being the uncivilized, it was with the help of the international community, like the United Nations, that we are witnessing how the racialization of Muslims is spread globally. Counterterrorism laws and policies and increased border security exemplify how racism toward Muslims is institutionalized across the world.

As we show in this chapter, counterterrorism policies in the United States, the UK, China, and India were implemented and justified as necessary to prevent terrorism in each of these countries. Many of these policies come from the same origins, like Preventing Terrorist Extremism (PVE), which originated in the Netherlands and later influenced counterterrorism policies across the globe, as we show below. And while counterterrorism policies may influence one another around the globe, they have a differential impact on Muslims based on where they are living. For example, citizenship may protect Muslims from some abuses in the UK and the United States, while in countries like India and China, citizenship is under attack for Muslims. While the crackdown on terrorism in each of these nations is unique to the sociopolitical context within which they exist, the idea that a Muslim is a threat to national security and the cultural values of the state has justified the monitoring, policing, and even detention of Muslims in the United States, the UK, India, and China. Counterterrorism policies rely on the racialized construction of a Muslim as a threat to both security and national identity, which have a differential impact on Muslim men and women in each of these nations. In this chapter we chronicle some of these policies to show how via counterterrorism laws, the racialization of Muslims is indeed a global racial project with gendered consequences.

Muslims and Surveillance in the United States

The terrorist attacks of 9/11 put into motion a hyper-surveillance society. Several laws and policies were passed immediately after the attacks, but the one that has had a tremendous impact on surveillance was the Uniting and Strengthening America by Providing Appropriate Tools Required to Intercept and Obstruct Terrorism Act of 2001 (USA PATRIOT Act). The PATRIOT Act was signed into law on October 26, 2001, just over a month after 9/11. In this moment of crisis, the majority of elected politicians in the United States voted to pass a bill that increased the state's surveillance capabilities. Title II of the Act, "Enhanced Surveillance Procedures," gave the government the power to monitor US citizens as well as non-citizens under the guise of gathering foreign intelligence. The targets under the Federal Information Surveillance Act (FISA) grew as a result of the PATRIOT Act (Cole 2003). Now the government could watch and monitor American citizens whereas under FISA the state had to prove the target was not a citizen of the United States and was a foreign agent. Edward Snowden, a whistleblower who worked for the National Security Agency (NSA), leaked classified information about the scope of the government's surveillance program. The documents showed that Muslims who were US citizens and had no history of criminal activity nor any proclivities toward committing acts of terrorism were targets of the government for surveillance (Greenwald and Hussain 2014). The Snowden leak showed that in this new era of hyper-surveillance, innocent people were being targeted by the government.

In addition to monitoring emails and phone calls, several other programs have been put into place in the name of national security that have targeted Muslims unfairly. Bush started the National Security Entry-Exit Registration System (NSEERS), which required non-citizen men over the age of sixteen from twenty-five countries to register with the state. Of these countries, twenty-four were Muslim majority, with North Korea being the only exception. Registration included

142   A Global Racial Enemy

being photographed, fingerprinted, and participating in an interview, revealing that the state collects biometric data of non-citizens (Cainkar 2009; Selod 2018). In 2011, the program was terminated under the Obama administration, however the damage NSEERS inflicted by instilling fear in the Muslim community had been done and data on Muslim non-citizens collected (Cainkar 2009).

These counterterrorism programs highlighted how Muslim men were specifically targeted as a threat to national security, revealing the gendered nature of this policy. Even though the majority of the countries on the list had no association with the 9/11 terrorists, the connection of Islam with terror via these policies institutionalized racism against Muslims. Targeting Muslim migrant men for surveillance exemplifies how a religious identity marks Muslim men as suspicious and thus racializes them as potential terrorists. Airport security practices and policies also accomplish this task of racializing Muslim men and women. The Transportation and Security Administration (TSA) utilizes a terrorist database housed by the FBI to determine who is a flight risk at airports. One study showed that Muslim men found themselves on these lists simply because of their Muslim name, while Muslim women who wear the hijab have been stopped and searched at the security line (Selod 2018).

Security policies and practices that are sold to the American public as keeping them safe from terrorist attacks target individuals based on their religious identity, resulting in racial bias and profiling. Documentary filmmaker Assia Boundaoui exposed FBI surveillance in her film *The Fear of Being Watched*, which chronicled her family's experiences with surveillance in Chicago. Her documentary highlights the insecurity Muslims feel when living under this threat of government surveillance.

One of the most outrageous examples of the inanity of these practices can be seen in the FBI's program entitled Operation Flex. The FBI recruited a fitness instructor, Craig Monteilh, to go undercover and spy on Muslims at a mosque in Irvine, California. Monteilh pretended to be a convert and went to the Islamic Center of Irvine where he offered to

Global Counterterrorism Policies 143

be a fitness trainer to members of the Muslim community. He got close to some members of the community, hoping to catch them plotting to commit acts of terror. Coming up empty handed after a year, Monteilh was encouraged by the FBI to entrap members of the community by expressing an interest in jihad and being a martyr. In an ironic twist, Muslims who interacted with Monteilh reported him to the FBI for his suspicious behavior, not realizing that they were the intended target of an FBI entrapment scheme. In 2011, Sheikh Yassir Fazaga, the imam of the community center, along with two other members brought a class action lawsuit against the FBI for spying on them because of their religious identity. The civil suit was initially blocked because a judge ruled that suing the FBI could compromise privileged information that would impact national security, but an appeals court overturned this and ruled in favor of Fazaga. The case, *FBI* v. *Fazaga*, eventually made its way to the Supreme Court where the justices unanimously voted to back the FBI arguing that it could compromise national security, leaving Muslims vulnerable with little recourse to discriminatory practices by the state. One of the major problems with counterterrorism policies is that they must operate under secrecy due to national security interests, enabling them to be carried out without any oversight and accountability. Thus, programs like Operation Flex are able to go on without any true oversight leaving Muslims susceptible to racialized surveillance.

CVE and TVTP

Another program that was put into place to curtail terrorism is Countering Violent Extremism (CVE). This program was created in 2009 under the Obama administration and viewed as a softer approach to preventing radicalization (Brennan Center 2019). CVE offered federal grants to various organizations for the purposes of identifying and weeding out radicalization. When the program was first rolled out, the Obama administration stated it would also target far-right extremist groups, like white nationalists. But according to

144 A Global Racial Enemy

the Brennan Center (2019), of the thirty-one organizations that received US$10 million only one group that focused on right-wing extremism received the funding.

CVE is an example of the global nature of counter-terrorism policies. For example, CVE was modeled after PREVENT that was rolled out in the UK, drawing on a similar initiative in the Netherlands (Kundnani and Hayes 2018). It is not just European and North American countries that are influencing one another with these policies, but Muslim majority ones also endure international pressure to participate in fighting the Global War on Terror. Countries like Pakistan, a Muslim majority nation, have also rolled out CVE (Mirahmadi et al. 2015). CVE has been introduced by the United States in Pakistan as a way to counter "Islamic radicals" that are viewed as a threat to the United States. According to a report by the Brookings Institution (Mirahmadi et al. 2015), Congress approved over a billion dollars in aid to Pakistan, some of which went to US organizations working with Pakistani civil organizations to combat radicalization and increase security. Instead of militarily occupying nations, programs like CVE are used in places like Pakistan by providing various civil organizations, including religious and nongovernmental agencies, financial assistance if they carry out surveillance and security for the United States, which can be seen as a form of one state exerting its control over another. CVE is the perfect example of how these racialized policies are global and even though they are used to serve different purposes in various nations, they are all justified in the name of securitizing spaces via the association of Muslims with terror.

CVE operates by providing federal funding to organizations (like mosques) where they are encouraged to surveil their own communities. Members who participate in the program often use the money to set up workshops and trainings for "community leaders" on how to identify radical behavior as well as putting in place a system to report suspicious individuals to law enforcement, like the FBI. Mosques and Islamic centers were some of the first organizations to receive CVE funding, but the funding was not limited to

Muslim organizations. The scope of CVE expanded over the years with social workers, hospitals, police departments, and teachers being brought into it. The state entertained rolling out programs like the "Shared Responsibility Committee," where the FBI would recruit social workers, counselors, teachers, and religious leaders to identify individuals they think may be susceptible to radicalization (Currier and Hussain 2016). Surveillance of Muslims extended beyond just the mosque and airports, but into every aspect of their lives.

The Obama administration was careful not to frame CVE as targeting Muslims exclusively, even if their programs did just that. The Trump administration, on the other hand, shifted the focus of the program to surveil Muslims specifically (Hussain 2017). The administration entertained renaming the program as "Countering Radical Islam" or "Countering Violent Jihad," revealing their true target of the state surveillance (Brennan Center 2019). The program was eventually rebranded as Targeting Violence and Terrorism Prevention (TVTP).

But what has come to surface in the twenty years after 9/11 and the implementation of many of these programs, is that they are based on inadequate research. Marc Sageman, a former CIA Operations Officer and counterterrorism consultant, testified as an expert witness in *Latif* v. *Lynch* (where the plaintiff was suing because he was put on a No-Fly List at airports). His testimony gives insight into the problems of counterterrorism research. "Despite decades of research, however, we still do not know what leads people to engage in political violence. Attempts to discern a terrorist 'profile' or to model terrorist behavior have failed to yield lasting insights, in part because of the lack of quality empirical data that could be used to test the validity of such a model" (*Latif* v. *Lynch* 2015). Additionally, in a letter to members of the House Committee on Homeland Security, community leaders and civil rights organizations wrote to persuade committee members against signing the Countering Violent Extremism Act of 2015, arguing that it unfairly targets Muslim civil liberties like free speech and religious

146 A Global Racial Enemy

freedoms. They also provided data on how right-wing attacks have been responsible for more violence as opposed to those committed by Muslims (Bergen and Sterman 2021). One scholar found that the FBI's hyper-focus on terrorism led to decreased recommendations to pursue white-collar crimes, showing how resources have been diverted toward counter-terrorism policies with virtually no terrorist plots uncovered while other crimes have been able to go on unchecked (Nguyen 2021). Diverting government resources to target a population that has been proven to have no connections to terrorism shows not only the inefficiency in security practices, but how some groups are racialized as a threat. Furthermore, programs like Operation Flex demonstrate how when there was no evidence collected, the FBI resorted to entrapping Muslims to justify the program.

The list of programs that have been rolled out since 9/11 that target Muslims is extensive. And while we are not able to chronicle each one of them, our purpose is to highlight how these policies in the United States reveal how the racialization of Muslims as threats to the state and society has become institutionalized. Programs like CVE can place Muslims under constant surveillance whether it is in school, hospitals, or mosques. Furthermore, these policies do not just stay within US borders, but have global implications.

Reach and impact of the War on Terror in the United States

It is important to note that the policies and programs put into place after 9/11 have had a far-reaching impact, beyond a Muslim population. The connection between the War on Terror and the War on Drugs, for example, is one that requires more scholarly attention. Federal law enforcement has been given more powers to conduct sneak and peek searches under the USA PATRIOT Act, whereby they would be able to search someone's property without informing the target of that search (Balko 2014). The number of requests for sneak and peek searches was forty-seven between 2001 and 2003 but jumped drastically to over 3,000 between 2009 and 2010. The Electronic Frontier Foundation's analysis revealed that of the thousands of sneak and peek warrants requested, fewer than 1 percent were for the purposes of surveilling terrorism. Instead, the majority were used in narcotics cases (Tien 2014). Thus, laws and policies, like the USA PATRIOT Act, that are passed and sold to the American public as protecting the nation from another terrorist attack, are in actuality being used in the War on Drugs. Law enforcement is thus able to expand its ability to surveil not just Muslims but other racialized groups as a result of September 11th. When policing powers are increased, so are the targets. One way this has been visible to the public in the United States is the increased militarization of the police. The military grade equipment that the police now wield has a direct connection to the fact that the United States was engaged militarily in Afghanistan for twenty years and still has a presence in Iraq. The resources put into the military can be seen in the types of tanks, tear gas, drones, rubber bullets, and sound cannons that the police have acquired and used on Black Lives Matter protesters, including the individuals who protested after the death of George Floyd (Katzenstein 2020).

In addition to targeting African Americans, the policies implemented have had a most detrimental impact on immigration policies in the United States. The creation of the Immigration and Customs Enforcement (ICE) as well as the Customs and Border Protection (CBP) agencies reflects the move from naturalization of immigrants to more punitive measures taken against them. The focus on national security after 9/11 resulted in a drastic increase in resources given to federal immigration enforcement. According to the Migration Policy Institute, the budget for the Immigration and Naturalization Services (INS) that preceded ICE was US$4.3 billion in 2000. In 2020 the budget was over $25 billion, six times more than twenty years earlier (Chishti and Bolter 2021). The attention paid to border security was enormous, with detentions and deportations seeing a massive increase. One of the most controversial clauses of the USA PATRIOT Act is that it allowed for the indefinite detention of non-citizens. According to the PATRIOT Act, if the government finds someone to be deportable and

148   A Global Racial Enemy

no country is willing to take that individual, they can be detained indefinitely (ACLU n.d.). Thus, it is important that scholars and policy makers pay attention to how the global racialization of Muslims triggers implementation of counter-terrorism policies that have a much larger reach and target other racialized populations.

The UK and PREVENT

In the UK it has been clearly established that Muslims, particularly since 2005, are fair game for critiques based on cultural determinism. Indeed, British Muslims find themselves discursively enmeshed in a religious and cultural net. The dominant discourse positions them as if they have only these dimensions and no economic, political, or other elements to their characters. The "Good" versus "Bad" Muslim binary revolves around whether or not they can break free of the presumed determining connection between Islamic culture and hostility to western values. Even the less hostile version of the Good/Bad Muslim narrative, which Kundnani (2014) calls "reformist," locates Muslims solely as reflections of religion and culture. British Muslims are never treated as potential political actors with views on every aspect of society (Rashid 2014), as other groups of actors are assumed to hold, "free" of religious framings. This restrictive understanding of Muslims leads to a tension in the principal state-driven scheme aimed at controlling terrorism.

The government's PREVENT policy, initially called Preventing Violent Extremism (PVE), was put in place to protect British citizens from the threat of a radicalized Muslim population. As we showed earlier, PREVENT in the UK was modeled after a Dutch security program that aimed to take a softer approach to counterterrorism. This program initiated the development of experts on radicalization, who created a program that included schools, youth clubs, and local organizations to participate in identifying early stages of radicalization (Kundnani and Hayes 2018). The purpose of PREVENT is to challenge the ideology that supports

Global Counterterrorism Policies   149

terrorism and those who promote it, to protect vulnerable people, and support sectors and institutions where there are risks of radicalization (Kundnani 2014). This counterterrorism law institutionalized an ideology, extremism, as a threat to the nation-state (Kundnani and Hayes 2018). Thus, one's worldviews can make one a target for policing.

PREVENT entails a statutory duty for educational institutions, the administrative bodies managing the health service, prisons, and municipal authorities to report people whom they consider at risk of turning to extremism. Critics argue, among other things, that the specifics of the parameters that define terrorism however overlap with the expression of completely legitimate opinions, such as being critical of UK foreign policy in relation to Muslim majority countries. At the same time, the parameters are vague enough to allow for dubious cases to be reported to police. Primary schoolchildren who have toy guns or discuss particular video games have been reported to the police, for example. Even if in some of these cases the police judge the accusation not worth investigating, the point is that Muslim children are surveilled and reported for doing things children from any background do because there is a state-imposed scheme that makes it the duty of people employed by the state to equate Islam with a heightened risk of radicalization. The fact that more than 300 children under six years old have been referred to Channel (the rehabilitation program for PREVENT) indicates that something is wrong with its parameters.

Ultimately, the scheme has been running for sixteen years and only around 11 percent of those referred are finally deemed "at risk," while more are referred to mental health services. Moreover, the proportion of far-right political activists referred under PREVENT has come to rival if not exceed the number of those linked to Islamic political groups. The numbers in 2016 reveal there were three Islamic for every one far-right. By 2019 for example 1,487 referrals fell into the latter category, with nearly 1,387 labeled as "right-wing extremists" (Grierson and Sabbagh 2020). Furthermore, the 2021 figures (Home Office 2022) show a drop to the lowest level (4,915) since figures were first recorded in 2016. Of the 697 referrals that actually ended up as cases discussed in Channel, twice as many were categorized as right-wing (317) than Islamic (154), with a further 205 labeled "mixed, unstable or unclear ideology."

O'Toole (2022) argues that despite its aim to understand and reduce radicalization, PREVENT actually developed into a system entailing both surveillance of Muslim communities (without their consent), but also "sousveillance" (from other Muslims) incentivized by the state to perform such functions. Indeed, the scheme is considered by critics to be primarily an intelligence-gathering exercise with low levels of success, which would consist according to the terms of the scheme of finding individuals being radicalized and preventing them from engaging in extremist political actions. Moreover, the existence of PREVENT helps sustain the racialization of Muslims by maintaining suspicion of them. The state's Universities Office for Students, for example, refers a minimal number of students to Channel every year while the compulsory training for staff seems to lead to self-censorship among Muslim students and continued suspicion of Muslims and Islam among non-Islamic students (Guest et al. 2020). It is not surprising that the official imposition of a frame of mistrust on a particular section of the population then fosters and may even reward suspicious attitudes. The state is the only body that can assert this level of power over so many institutions and this situates the state as the source of the definition of a Muslim problem. Massoumi et al. (2017), writing on the wider impact of counterterrorism policy, concluded that "We regard the state, and more specifically the sprawling official 'counter-terrorism' apparatus, to be absolutely central to production of contemporary Islamophobia – the backbone of anti-Muslim racism" (pg. 8).

The British state is dependent on the radicalization/cultural distinction and therefore cannot easily engage with the various critiques of PREVENT, particularly when they highlight social, economic, and political dimensions of radicalization not encompassed by PREVENT's narrow framing. The government effectively delayed the independent review of PREVENT, due in 2019, for three years. It finally nominated

William Shawcross to head the review. Shawcross is a high-profile former political journalist who was the director of the neoconservative Henry Jackson Society, which is prolific in producing the discourse of Islam as threatening to the West. While in this role in 2012, Shawcross was quoted as stating that "Europe and Islam is one of the greatest, most terrifying problems of our future. I think all European countries have vastly, very quickly growing Islamic populations" (Elgot and Dodd 2022). The appointment of Shawcross highlights the state's lack of sincerity in reviewing PREVENT.

On Shawcross' nomination, several civil society groups announced their intention to boycott the review as they felt Shawcross was biased against Islam. The alternative "People's Review" published its findings in 2022 (Holmwood and Aitlhadj 2022). This review concluded that PREVENT had undermined "multi-cultural equality grounded in rights of citizenship and protections against arbitrary state action. The latter is no less arbitrary if it is by an elected government claiming a popular mandate, [whose outcome] is an under-mining of people's rights, especially their rights to religious belief and expression, which is placed under suspicion by PREVENT" (pg. 134). The report goes on to urge the withdrawal of PREVENT, which it describes as "ideological," "for the sake of our children and young people and for the sake of our democracy" (pg. 155).

The state's dealings with terrorism suspects have also involved the establishment of a parallel system of legal practices, referred to as arbitrary in the report, with hearings in the absence of the suspect, extension of control orders with no evidence required, house arrests, and pre-emptive action resulting in rendition and ultimately deportation (Kapoor 2018). The burden of proving guilt is thus far lighter in suspected terrorism cases than in other areas of criminal law. Since the end of 2021, the government has codified its power to withdraw UK citizenship in the Nationality and Borders Bill (2021). Prabhat (2021) concludes that: "Citizenship stripping orders are not obtained from any court or tribunal and are based entirely on the discretion of the home secretary. UK law empowers the home secretary to deprive nationality of British citizens who have another nationality, if the secretary deems it 'conducive to the public good.'"

The threat of stripping citizenship is being used against people whom the government accuses of terrorist offenses. However, there are two things to note. First, the UK is not the only country in the world that seeks to do this. In the United States the US Citizenship and Immigration Services (USCIS) agency has put forth several criteria that justify revoking someone's citizenship. One of them is if someone has been associated with a terrorist organization within five years of their naturalization (American Immigrant Lawyers Association 2021). In contrast, in the UK this practice can only apply to people with dual nationality or whom the government thinks could obtain a second nationality. It therefore overwhelmingly targets immigrants.

In addition to PREVENT, there is the Terrorism Act of 2006. Preceded by the Terrorism Act of 2000, this legislation expands law enforcement's privileges in the name of preventing terrorism. For example, Schedule 7 as laid out in the 2000 Act allows for stops and searches of individuals at the border. Port officials were given the authority to stop and detain individuals at airports who they deem suspicious of terrorist activities. According to CAGE, a human rights organization in the UK, Muslims were stopped over 88 percent of the time and were detained for hours while officials interrogated them about their religious practices, went through their phones and computers, fingerprinted them, and even asked for DNA samples (Sabbagh 2019). According to the Counter Terrorism Policing website, a government site, individuals can be detained for up to six hours for questioning when traveling. This practice is reminiscent of NSEERS, mentioned above, where non-citizens from Muslim majority countries were required to register with the state where they were interrogated, fingerprinted, and photographed. The use of biometric surveillance is increasing in the Global War on Terror, as the case of China reveals below.

Another practice that is becoming more commonplace is "preventative" policing. For example, the Terrorism Act of 2006 expanded law enforcement's powers, including lengthening the time of detention for anyone suspected of terrorist activities, without proof they committed the act. According to CAGE, under the "pre-crime" offense are "offences relating to possession of banned material, or preparatory activity, but which place the burden of proof on the defendant who often faces a near-impossible environment, such as being faced with secret evidence and a judiciary that is in thrall to a discriminatory and compromised executive" (CAGE 2020). Before even committing an act, individuals are criminalized as potential terrorists due to their beliefs, making them susceptible to detention. This policy also justified the use of secret evidence, incriminating data the state has collected, but not shared with the person accused of committing a crime rendering them defenseless. These policies are similar to those in the United States. Section 215 of the USA PATRIOT Act allowed for secret evidence to be used and gathered in the name of national security until it expired in 2020. The similarities in counterterrorism policies and practices between the United States and the UK are important to highlight because they are evidence that security is a global industry that relies on similar constructions of the Muslim man as a threat, warranting these draconian surveillance and security policies.

An examination of PREVENT uncovers the ways in which problematic counterterrorism laws are not created in a vacuum, but instead are shared globally. The Terrorism Acts of 2000 and 2006 also highlight similarities between counterterrorism programs in Europe and the United States. While in the UK the majority of individuals who have been arrested under laws like the Terrorism Act of 2006 have been Muslim, in the United States these policies have also been used to indefinitely detain an undocumented population that is not Muslim. While Muslims experience hyper-surveillance in both the UK and the United States, their status as a citizen may afford some protection from punitive measures. Thus, we have to remain mindful of how systemic racism toward Muslims via these security and surveillance practices are expansive and their reach goes beyond the "intended" target and consider other factors like citizenship, race, ethnicity,

154 A Global Racial Enemy

class, gender, and sexual orientation in terms of who is vulnerable. In the next sections we turn our attention to China and India to show how counterterrorism laws racialize Muslims in non-western societies as well.

China and the Global War on Terror

A little over a month after the September 11th attacks, US President George Bush met with the former President of China, Jiang Zemin, in Shanghai to discuss China's support in the Global War on Terror. Bush stated that the President of China gave his support to the United States and was quoted as saying "civilized people like you and me can't understand how these people [terrorists] think" (McMillan and Garrett 2001). In this statement, Bush was delineating the civilized from the uncivilized (Muslims/terrorists) in an attempt to create a global coalition which would support US foreign policies. In this instance, the rhetoric of civilized and uncivilized that has been used to describe conflicts between Arab nations and western ones (Huntington 1993) was extended to include a Chinese population. The dichotomy of the civilized and uncivilized is a racialized concept, as described in detail in the introduction of this book. But this statement in particular exemplified how Muslim racialization is not limited to whiteness but incorporates other racialized groups. The racialization of Muslims extends into non-European and non-white spaces, operating in similar ways as in the majority of white countries. Bush's comments demonstrate how the racialization of Muslims is global because it transcends the notion of the West vs. the Rest. The narrative of who is part of the civilized world and who is outside of it justifies not only expanding military action but also acquisition of land and resources from within, as is the case in China.

After 9/11, China wanted to apply the same rhetoric around terrorism toward Uyghur Muslims, who had been referred to as separatists. Labeling Uyghur Muslims terrorists would allow the state to implement policies that would greatly control the Uyghur population, something the state had been wanting to do for a long time. The struggle for control of the region of East Turkestan by the Chinese state was one of the reasons they wanted to shift the narrative. Calling them terrorists would strip the Uyghurs of any humanity, justifying the horrific actions the state could take against them. While the United States sought to get China's support, it refused to acknowledge Uyghur separatists as terrorists, reflecting differences and tensions between the US and China (Chung 2002).

It was not long after Xi Jinping became President of China that he began seeking support for China to engage more critically in the Global War on Terror. At a UN General Assembly in 2015, Xi was quoted as saying, "No country can maintain absolute security with its own effort, and no country can achieve stability out of other countries' instability" (Xinhuanet 2021). The Chinese government had been trying to associate Uyghur Muslims with the Eastern Turkestan Islamic Movement (ETIM) and the Turkistan Islamic Party (TIP) to discredit their grievances with the Chinese government.

China's attempt to address terrorism predated the Xi administration and 9/11. For example, a coalition of five nations (China, Russia, Kazakhstan, Kyrgyzstan, and Tajikistan), dubbed the Shanghai Five, first met in 1996 to deal with border and diplomatic issues between China and the four Soviet states, which included the issue of terrorism. In 2001, the Shanghai Cooperation Organization (SCO) was founded to ensure security in the region (Roberts 2020). According to the UN, the SCO "was established as a multilateral association to ensure security and maintain stability across the vast Eurasian region, join forces to counteract emerging challenges and threats, and enhance trade, as well as cultural and humanitarian cooperation" (Alimov 2017: 34). One of their tasks was to address the threat of terrorism. There are two important takeaways from this UN quote. First, that global networks are created in counterterrorism efforts. The fact that fighting terrorism is seen as everyone's problem, in fact, eliminates the need to understand the specific geopolitical motivations behind the violence. Second, the labeling of terrorism as evil and irrational acts (Stampnitzky 2013) allows draconian policies to be put into place to curtail it. Moreover, because terrorism is reduced to irrational violence, everyone can get on board in the fight to eradicate it. Fighting terrorism can be everyone's problem since it is devoid of the context within which it exists. What we should not overlook is the economic and capitalistic motivation that drives counterterrorism policies in various spaces. The fact that security and trade are referenced in the UN quote is telling. The connection between securitizing spaces and acquisition of land reveals the capitalistic motivations behind global counterterrorist policies (Byler 2022). Control over land and territory is one of the main motivations behind the Chinese state's Global War on Terror policies, particularly those against the Uyghur Muslims.

Uyghur Muslims and camps

The People's War on Terror officially started in 2014, shortly after Xi Jinping became President of China. The campaign was in response to several violent protests perpetrated by Uyghur Muslims in cities, including Beijing (Byler 2021). The uptick in violence by Uyghur Muslims resembled other terrorist attacks seen in Europe and the United States (Byler 2021). But their grievances were tied to their displacement from their land, intensified discrimination in the workplace, and their increased surveillance. In 2014, the PRC began the "Strike Hard against Terrorism Campaign" that targeted Uyghur Muslims in the western part of Xinjiang (Van Schaack and Wang 2021). According to a Human Rights Watch report, part of this campaign included requiring Uyghur Muslims in the major city of Urumqi to return to their rural homelands to receive an identification card, known as the People's Convenience Card. Migrants who were denied the card were also prevented from returning to the city, essentially displacing them from Urumqi (Van Schaack and Wang 2021). Campaigns to target Uyghurs as terrorists continued via the "Regulation on De-Extremification Act" that passed in March of 2017. This law criminalized religious behaviors of Muslims, justifying the imprisonment of Uyghurs in the growing "re-education" camps where the state has argued it is de-extremifying this population. Article 4 of the law states, "De-extremification shall persist in the basic directives of the party's work on religion, persist in an orientation of making religion more Chinese and under law, and actively guide religions to become compatible with socialist society" (IUHRDF 2017). This provision of the Act set the stage for criminalizing any religion that appears to be incompatible with the state's definition of Chinese values. Article 9 of this law marks what actions, behaviors, and words are prohibited by the state. According to Article 9, wearing or forcing someone to wear the burqa, marrying or divorcing according to religious practices, and "spreading religious fanaticism through irregular beards or name selection" are illegal, and doing so results in individuals being imprisoned in detention facilities (Çaksu 2020). According to Roberts (2020), the law has "criminalized virtually all religious behavior and any consumption of religious information that was not explicitly promoted by the state" (pg. 210). Giving one's child a Muslim name was reason to be suspected of extremist behavior. This law funneled Uyghur Muslims into the de-extremification camps that were rapidly being built in 2017.

The camps in China that house Uyghur Muslims are an example of the extreme violence that is the result of the institutionalized racism against Muslims. Through the use of satellite imaging, the Australian Policy Institute estimates some 380 camps have been built that house over 1 million Uyghur Muslims (Ruser 2020). Reports show that men represent over 70 percent of the detainees in the camps, revealing again how Muslim men are racialized as terrorists (Cockerell n.d.). In his book *In the Camps: China's High-Tech Penal Colony* (2021) David Byler interviews Uyghur Muslims who had spent time in these camps. Byler (2021) shows how the "Regulation on De-Extremification Act" results in the detention of Uyghur Muslims for any adherence to Islam. In one case, a Uyghur man who is not religious and admitted to drinking alcohol was detained simply for having texted religious content to someone, highlighting the advanced surveillance tools of technology that are used against Uyghur Muslims (Byler 2021). Byler's interviews (2021) provide a horrific description of life in these camps, which included forcing dozens of men to sleep in one room with the lights on and a camera watching them at all times and rooms stinking from the one bucket used by prisoners as a toilet (Byler 2021). Byler's (2021) interviews also show how Uyghur Muslims are forced to work in these detention centers out of fear of being detained themselves. Muslims are required to completely disassociate from their religious identity, otherwise they face the threat of being placed into these camps. The camps have multiple purposes. They remove a Uyghur population from the Xinjiang region. Second, the camps are used for cheap labor: Uyghur Muslims are forced to work in these camps or are transported to nearby factories, producing clothing, textiles, and even technology (Buckley and Ramzy 2018). Human rights activists have stated that the entire fashion industry is implicated in this abuse because of the cotton and yarn that the Chinese state produces via this labor (Kelly 2020).

The media have also reported on the atrocities Uyghur Muslim women face in these camps, revealing how gendered the racialization of Muslims is in China. A BBC article uncovered some of the brutalities Uyghur women faced while in the camps. In the article, Tursunay Ziawudun describes how in her nine months in one of the camps she was blindfolded and taken to a room where she was repeatedly raped by men wearing a mask (Hill et al. 2021). The reporters also spoke with guards who worked at the facility, who corroborated the accounts of Uyghur women being sexually assaulted in these camps. There have furthermore been several reports about Uyghur women undergoing forced sterilization to control the Uyghur population (Hill et al. 2021). Uyghur women are targeted in different ways by the state than the men are. Forced sterilization is a tactic that has been used by colonizers to control the demographics of a particular population. Uyghur women have also been targeted in their own homes, showing how intimate spaces are also hyper-surveilled. One program, called "Pair Up and

Become Family," requires Uyghur households to "invite" Han officials to stay in their homes (Alexandra Ma 2019). Uyghur families have to share personal information as well as report their political views to these Han officials. There have also been several reports that many of the men have forced the women in these households to sleep in the same bed with them (Kang and Wang 2018). Thus, Uyghur women are policed in intimate spaces because they are racialized as producers of future terrorists.

The surveillance of Uyghur Muslims is extensive. They are not just physically detained, they also live in virtual camps via the intense surveillance they endure through what Byler (2022) calls "digital enclosure." The explosion of the use of smartphones and social media in China has played a significant role in the expansion of digital surveillance. Social media exposed Uyghur Muslims to more religious content, contributing to a rise in their religiosity and a strengthened identity (Byler 2022). At the same time, the PRC began to contract with tech companies to create sophisticated tracking and monitoring tools that would be used against Uyghur Muslims. While smartphones were used to educate Uyghurs about their religion, they were also used to track what they listened to, who they communicated with, and even their movements around the city. In addition to using Uyghur labor for monetary gains, their hyper-surveillance reflects a new form of capitalism that has been driven by policing populations. Shoshana Zuboff (2019) refers to this as surveillance capitalism, where big tech companies are profiting from the collection and selling of people's data.

But "terror capitalism" is the term Byler (2022) uses to describe the ways that capital is accumulated via the encampment of Uyghur Muslims both virtually and physically. Terror capitalism is the profit that is made from the labeling of Uyghur Muslims as potential terrorists (Byler 2022). For example, a program called "Physicals for All" was rolled out in 2016–17 where biometric data like DNA taken from blood samples and iris scans were collected from millions of Uyghur Muslims. The collection of these data aided in creating biometric surveillance tools and technologies

160 A Global Racial Enemy

(Wee 2019). There are many, including individuals and global corporations, that are benefiting from the marking of Uyghur Muslims as terrorists by creating advanced surveillance technologies. According to a *New York Times* article (Wee 2019), Thermo Fisher, a company that produces lab equipment in Massachusetts, financially benefited by selling equipment to China used to collect these blood samples. Some corporations and individuals are profiting through government contracts to create surveillance tools that track the movement of Uyghur Muslims. Corporations also benefit materially from Uyghur forced labor in the camps. Terror capitalism relies on the racialization of Muslims as an illness to society, which then justifies the security apparatus that has been created to detain and punish them as well as the cheap labor produced by their imprisonment.

While the treatment of Uyghur Muslims differs significantly from the treatment of Muslim citizens in the United States and the UK, there are important connections between them. The Chinese government is taking some of the policies put in place in the United States and the UK and greatly expanding them at the expense of human rights. The People's War on Terror "is premised on a rhetoric of a war on Muslim 'terrorism' that the Chinese state has imported from the US and its allies post-September 11, 2001. As recently as 2017, Xinjiang authorities hosted British counterterrorism experts as part of a diplomatic exchange called 'Countering the root causes of violent extremism undermining growth and stability in China's Xinjiang Region by sharing UK best practices'" (Byler 2021: 22–3). Thus, counterterrorism policies were not created in a vacuum, but instead are influenced by global policies created to combat terrorism. As shown above, American companies are invested in security practices abroad, thus the material benefits to China's draconian surveillance practices are not limited to Chinese companies because surveillance is often outsourced. The dehumanization of a terrorist gives authoritarian states like China the ability to create counterterrorism policies that strip individuals of all of their human rights in every aspect of their lives.

India and Counterterrorism Policies

Prior to the Global War on Terror, India had several laws and policies in place to address terrorism. The context for India's terrorism laws can be traced back to British colonialism, which was responsible for the partition of India and Pakistan, resulting in over a century of violence that has been perpetrated by both the state and individual actors. In 2008, for example, there were a series of terrorist attacks committed in Mumbai that resulted in the deaths of hundreds of individuals. But the Global War on Terror shifted the way the Indian government addressed terrorism through its laws. One of the major changes was in the way that terrorism was defined. Prior to 9/11, language such as "freedom fighters" was used to describe individuals who committed these acts of violence within the international community, something that the Indian government critiqued (Sasikumar 2010). By using the language of terrorism, motivations behind any attacks were not examined and the perpetrators of these attacks were reduced to "evil" individuals. Dehumanizing the terrorist along with making the definition of terrorism so ambiguous allowed for an expansive application of counterterrorism laws that had very few protections in place for people accused of committing acts of terror (Kalhan et al. 2006; Stampnitzky 2013). The Prevention of Terrorism Act of 2002 exemplifies how in a world hyper-obsessed with security, counterterrorism laws are used by the state to expand its powers, bypassing the rules and regulations set down to prevent human rights abuses within the criminal justice system.

The Prevention of Terrorism Act of 2002 (POTA) was passed after 9/11 and modeled after the USA PATRIOT Act (Jones 2009a). This law gave the Indian authorities more powers than they had under the criminal laws. The ambiguous definition of terrorism in this law enabled it to be used without oversight. It also gave the state the powers to detain individuals for a long period of time, 180 days, before they were charged with a crime, perpetuating preventative measures to combat terrorism. Furthermore, confessions

162   A Global Racial Enemy

obtained by the police were permitted in court, which were typically not allowed in other criminal cases, and government officials were given immunity from persecutions (Kalhan et al. 2006). The law was considered highly controversial and was eventually repealed, but many of the provisions were kept alive through an existing terrorism law known as the Unlawful Activities Prevention Act, or UAPA.

UAPA was originally passed in 1963, however it was later amended to be used as an anti-terrorism law. The law was originally enacted to protect the sovereignty of India from those whom the state viewed as a threat to it. It was used to curb political speech and demonstrations, however after POTA was repealed several of its provisions were placed under this existing law. This law gave the state the ability to determine who was a terrorist based on several vague guidelines. Furthermore, the law provided the National Investigation Agency (NIA) with the power to conduct raids and seize property under this amendment. As a result of this law, many groups that organized to protest against the Hindutva's discriminatory policies against Muslims and other groups are subjected to raids, arrests, and investigations by the NIA because they are labeled terrorists or terrorist sympathizers. For example, the Popular Front of India was accused of funding protests against India's citizenship laws and banning of the hijab that target Muslims (Al Jazeera 2022). Labeling groups that are organizing to resist the right-wing assault on religious freedom in India as terrorist groups ultimately strips them of rights of due process and legal protections from the criminal justice system. Yet, India is not alone in this practice, as we have shown in the other examples above. It is through these global efforts to combat terrorism that countries are enabled to use counterterrorism policies to silence dissent as well as justify increased border security.

India and border security in the Global War on Terror

In addition to justifying counterterrorism policies for the surveillance and detention of Muslims in India, the Global

War on Terror was also used to tighten border security. Similarly to the United States, India began building fences on the borders with Pakistan and Bangladesh (Jones 2009b). The Department of Border Management came into existence after 9/11, which oversaw the construction of the fence. In his book *Empire of Borders: The Expansion of the U.S. Border Around the World* (2019), journalist Todd Miller shows how the United States has been assisting in border security globally, what he and others refer to as "border imperialism." The BJP government pushed the narrative that India needed to secure the nation from neighboring Muslim countries. The relationship between Pakistan and India has always been fraught with tensions because of the history of colonialism and the partition of the countries into Muslim and Hindu majority states, but the relationship with Bangladesh was historically less contentious than that with Pakistan. Yet the BJP government continued to push the idea that terrorists were coming into India from Bangladesh. Barbed wire fences, CCTV cameras, floodlights, and checkpoints have been erected on the borders in the name of protecting India from terrorists and unwanted immigrants crossing the borders. It is also important to note that border security is a global project. Miller (2019) shows how the United States has assisted several countries, via training and resources, in forming and strengthening their borders, including India's Border Security Forces (BSF). Additionally, technologies for border security are shared across nations. In 2018, India erected smart fences on the border of Pakistan and Kashmir that utilize Israeli surveillance technology (Sen 2021). India and Israel are also part of a Joint Working Group on Counterterrorism where they share tactics and strategies to deal with the threat of terror (Sen 2021).

In an era of hyper-militarized borders in the name of protecting the nation, abuses at the border have become commonplace globally (Walia 2014). A report by Human Rights Watch (2010) has documented several abuses that have occurred on the border by the BSF. This includes torture, beatings, and shooting and killing individuals who were attempting to cross the border. According to the report, several people are trying to smuggle cattle into India. In one case, a seventeen-year-old Bengali boy named Shyamol Karmokar crossed into India to visit relatives. He traveled back to Bangladesh with cattle rustlers and was shot and killed by the BSF when they saw him. BSF did not attempt to arrest the group, but instead relied only on lethal force. There have been an estimated 1,000 individuals from Bangladesh killed by the BSF between 2000 and 2010 (Human Rights Watch 2010; Adams 2011). Since 2011, Bangladeshi organizations have claimed over 300 more deaths, with several of them being children (Human Rights Watch 2021). Furthermore, reporting indicates that those who have been tortured and killed were not carrying weapons on them, revealing how militarizing the borders brings with it human rights abuses that are committed in the name of national security.

Conclusion

It is beyond this single chapter to provide a comprehensive analysis of all of the counterterrorism laws and policies erected globally as a result of 9/11. There are many other countries, including those that are Muslim majority, that have instituted anti-terrorism laws and policies. The scope of counterterrorism policies is vast in the era of the Global War on Terror. These policies have become tools of the state for their political gain, whether it is acquiring territory, or silencing dissent, or for economic gain via the security industrial complex. We show in this chapter that the GWOT instigated a series of counterterrorism laws and policies, promoted by the international community, in the name of preventing the worldwide spread of terrorism. This war became everyone's war, making it one that differs from wars of the past. Rather than nation-states fighting one another, the GWOT targets people who are constructed as terrorists, mostly Muslim men. In the past, those that committed acts of violence were referred to as insurgents or freedom fighters, which warranted an understanding of the economic, political, and cultural motivations behind this violence (Stampnitzky 2013). By framing the terrorist as devoid of humanity, they are racialized as monsters, justifying the measures used against them (Kumar 2020). Preventative measures, like imprisonment before being charged with a crime, violence at borders, surveillance in every area of one's life including education and one's family life, become acceptable policies that governments enact without any accountability. The lack of accountability goes against democratic ideals of a just and fair society. India, the United States, and the UK claim to be democratic states, yet their counterterrorism policies grossly violate human rights. This calls into question whether or not they are practicing the values of equality and liberty they espouse. Nations, like China, that are characterized as authoritarian states are able to defend their abusive policies by justifying putting the nation first.

Whether a state is authoritarian or democratic, its abuses are equally permissible when the visible target is framed as a monster. Thus, counterterrorism policies thrive on the construction of the terrorist as an evil, blood thirsty murderer. As we show in this chapter, the Muslim as this violent inhumane terrorist is a global threat, revealing how anti-Muslim racism is a global phenomenon. It is important that we pay attention to how these policies are gendered. Some of these racialized policies impact Muslim men in unique ways compared to Muslim women. The forced marriages of Uyghur Muslims to Han men is one example of how Muslim women are surveilled in their intimate lives. Airport security since 9/11 has put Muslim men and women under hyper-surveillance, but the ways that they are watched and monitored is unique to their gender (Selod 2018). Thus, the global racialization of Muslims operates in gendered ways depending on the law and policy put in place. Furthermore, counterterrorism laws and policies cross borders, allowing each state to commit horrific human rights abuses against Muslims and other marginalized populations because of the global racialized construction of Muslim men and women as a threat to society.

Conclusion
Where Do We Go from Here? Possibilities for Resistance and Further Securitization

Anytime a mass shooting happens by a white perpetrator, we often hear a call to label that person a terrorist. When eighteen-year-old Peyton S. Gendron entered a grocery store in Buffalo, New York on May 14, 2022, and shot and killed ten Black shoppers, Democrats in the House of Representatives responded by pushing through a vote on the Domestic Terrorist Prevention Act. The vote narrowly passed in the House of Representatives, but was later stalled in the Senate. Grendon left a manifesto where he claimed to be an ethnonationalist and white supremacist who planned the massacre for political reasons. The Act would have required police departments to put more time and resources into identifying domestic terrorism in an attempt to thwart these horrific acts of violence. One major problem with surveilling and policing to prevent terrorist attacks is they are often done under secrecy, thus there is very little accountability over these policing tactics. However, often the intended targets of these laws and policies are not the only ones who are surveilled and policed, the scope extending to other racialized groups. Fusion centers are an example of this. After 9/11, fusion centers were created to coordinate intelligence gathering to prevent another terrorist attack. But a report by the Center for Security, Race, and Rights at Rutgers University revealed that these centers are being used to police Black neighborhoods under "broken windows policing" (Aziz 2023). This controversial theory justifies policing in neighborhoods that

Conclusion 167

have graffiti and abandoned buildings, neighborhoods that tend to be predominantly Black and Brown in the United States due to racial residential segregation. Thus, counterterrorism policies, like the creation of fusion centers, leads to more policing of Black communities. While labeling someone like G a terrorist may feel like the appropriate response to the general public, especially after he committed such a horrific act of racial violence, when counterterrorism laws are expanded to address violence it increases the state's ability to conduct racialized surveillance and police people of color, including Muslims.

Just like we should be critical of terrorist policies that are proposed when a white mass shooter commits an act of racial violence, we should also be skeptical of global counterterrorist policies. Although we only chronicled four countries in this book, there are many other examples that should be examined in order to understand the magnitude of how Muslims are racialized. The global racialization of Muslims allows for a wide range of surveillance and policing across borders. We do not argue that surveillance in China looks like surveillance in the United States, but the construct of Muslim men as terrorists and Muslim women as transgressors of cultural and national unity is present in each of these countries. Our goal has been to show that the GWOT was not limited to the United States or Europe, but in fact is being waged in non-western countries too. This allows us to think about how racialization can cross borders and racism is a global phenomenon. The global racialization of Muslims is one example of 21st-century racism. The call by the UN Security Council to demand that every country that is a member (which includes every country in the world except two) engage in the GWOT via their domestic laws ignited the racialization of Muslims globally. While Muslims have been racialized historically in many different countries, this allowed for the institutionalization of the racialization of Muslims via racialized surveillance and security practices.

The global racialization of Muslims allows us to think about race more broadly. In point of fact, a large proportion of the scholarship on racism centers whiteness. Edward Said

168 A Global Racial Enemy

showed this in his book as he argued that the construction of Arabs as uncivilized and barbaric was done in relation to the construction of Europeans as civilized and rational. Currently race scholarship focuses on how racism is a tool of white supremacy, however the global racialization of Muslims complicates this notion. In the United States and in Europe, we can see how the racialization of Muslims exists in relation to whiteness. But in India and China, even with phenotypical similarities, Muslims are racialized as threats to both the security of the nation and its cultural identity. Thus, in these spaces the racialization of Muslims does not serve whiteness. The global racialization of Muslims also allows us to think about how racisms are not only about differences in pigmentation and biology, but are also about culture, religion, language, nation of origin, and other factors. Sociology has long debunked the notion that race is a social construct, meaning it is something we created, yet we often only understand racism as tied to one's physical appearance or biology. We show in this book how Muslims who are phenotypically similar to the population in power can experience racisms because they are marked as suspect due to the racialization of their religious identity. Their racialization justifies the extraction of material resources, like land and labor, as the case of Uyghur Muslims exemplifies.

It is imperative to note that racialization is not a one-way street; there is always a response. Advocacy groups, activists, and politicians are working on bringing attention to the many ways the GWOT has stripped individuals of their human rights. We conclude the book on a hopeful note with some examples of resistance that we have identified in each of the countries we examined.

Advocacy and Protests: Resistance to Racialization

In each of the countries we have chronicled in this book, there are efforts being made to resist Muslim surveillance, racialization, and hyper-policing. These efforts are important to note because it shows how agency is an integral part of

Conclusion 169

the process of racialization. In other words, people do not passively accept their oppression, but in fact have always been resisting it. As we have shown throughout this book, one of the prominent social constructions about Muslim women is that they are abused by Muslim men and need saving. Yet, Muslim men and women have been resisting their racialization in each of these countries we examined.

The Muslim Justice League: United States

Some of the important work on resisting surveillance of Muslims in the United States is being done in Boston, Massachusetts by a small organization called the Muslim Justice League (MJL). MJL was started by four Muslim women in 2014. According to their website they organize the Muslim community to protect them from hyper-surveillance and policing.

> Muslim Justice League (MJL)'s mission is to organize and advocate for communities whose rights are threatened under the national security state in the United States. Led by Muslims, our organizing brings justice for ALL communities deemed "suspect." (MJL n.d.)

For example, they have campaigned against the Countering Violent Extremism (CVE) program that we chronicled in this book, and prevented the Boston police department from expanding their surveillance via fusion centers. The #STOPCVE campaign includes writing letters to policy makers, organizing protests, and sending advocates to schools to educate them on the dangers of participating in this program. As we mentioned earlier, schools, mosques, universities, social workers, police departments and unions, and hospitals are some of the recipients of CVE grants given out by the federal government to interrupt radicalization of a population. The reach of this program into the daily lives of Muslims, from schools to hospitals, is astounding. CVE specifically targets Muslims because of their association with radicalization and their perceived proclivities toward terrorist activities. MJL is one of the few organizations in the United States that is doing this work to educate the public on the dangers of this counterterrorism policy that puts Muslim civil rights in jeopardy.

MJL has also brought attention to fusion centers in Boston. Fusion centers were created after the terrorist attacks of September 11th with the goal of coordinating information gathering and sharing between local, state, and federal law enforcement agencies to prevent another terrorist attack. A Congressional report reveals that these centers have not uncovered any terrorist threats and are therefore wasting federal funding (Kopan 2012). Yet, fusion centers still exist and are being used instead to surveil racialized communities. MJL exposed Boston's fusion center, called the Boston Regional Information Center (BRIC), for collecting data on Black, Muslim, and immigrant populations. Because they operate as a counterterrorism program, they do so under secrecy and are therefore not held accountable (Aziz 2023). MJL in collaboration with the American Civil Liberties Union was successful in getting the city to deny funding for BRIC for surveillance analysts through their StoptheBRIC campaign. These may seem like small wins compared to the scope of surveillance in the United States, but through grassroots organizing and collaborating with other advocacy groups, like the ACLU, the Muslim Justice League has been successful in highlighting how problematic counterterrorism policies are for Muslims as well as other racialized groups, like African Americans and other immigrant populations.

The UK: Advocacy against PREVENT

CAGE started in 2003 and is an organization that works exclusively to dismantle racist policies in the UK that were put into place because of the War on Terror. The organization was founded by Moazzam Begg, a Pakistani British citizen, who had been held prisoner in Guantanamo Bay for three years. He was released without being charged and started CAGE to help those who are unfairly imprisoned in

Conclusion 171

Guantanamo. CAGE has done a lot of work to help those unjustly targeted as terrorists under counterterrorism policies and laws in the UK.

> CAGE is an independent advocacy organisation working to empower communities impacted by the "War on Terror". The organisation highlights and campaigns against repressive state policies, developed as part of increasing securitisation. In doing so, we strive for a world free from oppression and injustice.
>
> As such, we seek the application of principles like the presumption of innocence, the rule of law, due process, freedom from arbitrary imprisonment and torture; freedom from religious and racial discrimination; the right to privacy and freedom of movement and holding power to account. (CAGE n.d.)

Their website provides a lot of information for those who may be targeted by racialized surveillance. They write news articles and provide educational materials on the counterterrorism policies that impact Muslims in Britain. They have a "know your rights" section on the website that has one-page flyers with educational information on arrests, MI5 harassment, PREVENT, police doorstepping, and security practices at the border. Police doorstepping is when police make surprise visits to Muslims' houses to interrogate them. CAGE provides advice on dealing with this, like not letting police into one's home, recording the names of the officer and their badges, and questioning the reason for the visits. The CAGE hotline is printed on each flyer so that those who have been targeted can call and report the incident and get a referral for legal advice if needed. They also offer a program called Casework, where they help advocate for individuals unfairly targeted in the War on Terror. On the website they state they can connect people to legal counsel as well as journalists, so their stories can be made known. Like MJL, this is one of the few advocacy organizations that addresses counterterrorism policies that have impacted Muslims because of the War on Terror.

172   A Global Racial Enemy

Jamia Millia Islamia and Shaheen Bagh protests: India

In India, there was a mass protest organized by Muslim women in response to the Citizenship Amendment Act (CAA), which denied citizenship for Muslim migrants from Afghanistan, Pakistan, and Bangladesh. Muslim students at Jamia Millia Islamia, a university in Delhi, took to the streets on December 13, 2019, to protest the passage of this law. According to the protesters, they were beaten with batons and had tear gas deployed against them. Several Muslim students, both men and women, were arrested and detained. A few days later, a much larger protest was organized in response to the police brutality they encountered. Thousands of students joined the protests, which led to the Indian police raiding the Jamia Millia Islamia. CCTV cameras caught students who were not protesting, but studying in the library, brutally attacked by the Indian police. The videos show students scrambling over desks and trying to escape the attacks by jumping out of windows (Sunny and Sarfaraz 2019). During the raid, hundreds of Muslim students were tear gassed, beaten, and imprisoned. Students recalled how they were called "terrorists" and "jihadis" by the police as they were beating them (Ara 2021). The brutality that the students faced during their protests incited another protest led by Muslim women. In response to the passage of the CAA and the raid at Jamia Millia Islamia, Muslim women of all ages took to the street.

On December 15, 2019, several Muslim women blocked a highway that had access to the Muslim majority neighborhood of Shaheen Bagh, located in Delhi and close to Jamia Millia Islamia. The Muslim women who started the protest wore the hijab and consisted of mothers, students, and professors. Women brought their babies with them, sitting in the freezing cold on many days. The protest grew from a few dozen to thousands and lasted for months, until March 2020. The protesters installed a replica of the India Gate, which is a memorial to the soldiers of the British Indian Army who were killed between 1914 and 1921. On this makeshift India Gate were the names of the Muslim Indians

Conclusion 173

who had been killed by the police and government (Kuchay 2020). The protesters brought attention to the fact that Modi was changing the Indian Constitution, stripping Muslims of their rights. A piece chronicling the protest in *Frontline*, an Indian magazine, describes the communal feel of the protests. Women brought biryani and tea to share while they sat for hours in the streets. Men took over the household chores, while women were in the street. The crowd performed poetry and sang national songs together in unity. In the article, several women were interviewed about their experiences at Shaheen Bagh, such as Sarawari:

> We kept quiet when there was a ruling against the Babri Masjid. We kept quiet when they came with a ruling on triple talaq. We kept quiet when there was demonetisation. But when they entered Jamia and assaulted students in the library, in toilets, hostels, we decided enough is enough. Modi mistook our silence for weakness. We were quiet not out of fear but because we had faith in the Constitution. Now, when he wants to change the Constitution, enough is enough. We will speak up. *Hamari awaaz na dheemi hogi, hamare qadam na thhamenge, hum peechhe nahin hatenge* [Our voices shall not dim, our steps will not stop, we will not retreat]. It may take a year. It may take two. But we will not move away. (Salam 2020)

Shaheen Bagh highlights a few things. First, Muslim women are not passive recipients of the abuses they encounter because of the racialization of Muslims. The fact that Muslim women organized and led this protest should not be surprising, but it may seem unique given the narrative espoused in the GWOT of them needing to be saved. There has been a long history of women protesting globally, and India is no exception. Second, it shows that there is work being done to resist the racialization of Muslims in India. Muslim men and women are protesting these laws that are stripping them of their rights because their religious identity has racialized them as a threat to the nation-state.

174   A Global Racial Enemy

Uyghur women: Resistance from abroad

Resistance to Uyghur abuses has been difficult in a state where Uyghur Muslim men and women have their every move surveilled. Although there has been a long history of insurgency and separatist movements by Uyghur Muslims, the characterization of Uyghurs as terrorist by the Chinese state and the draconian laws put in place has made resistance difficult. As we have shown in earlier chapters, the crackdown on Uyghurs via their association as terrorists intensified through laws and policies meant to thwart terrorism. An Amnesty International report in 2004 reveals that Uyghur abuses by the Chinese state were intensified in the early 2000s because of its engagement in the Global War on Terror. The report also shows that getting information out about the abuses Uyghurs experience has been incredibly difficult in a state that has complete control of the media. One of the ways that Uyghurs are resisting their racialization is by speaking out about the abuses they have experienced in East Turkestan. Reports indicate that men make up the majority of people held in the camps (Cockerell n.d.). Thus, it is Uyghur Muslim women who constitute the majority of those who fled to other countries and have been speaking out about the human rights violations against Uyghur Muslims.

Campaign for Uyghurs is one example of an activist organization in the United States. It was founded by a Uyghur Muslim woman, Rushan Abbas, whose story we shared at the beginning of this book. Rushan had a history of participating in democratic protests when she a was a college student in Xinjiang University. She relocated to the United States, where she has continued to expose the abuses by the Chinese government on Uyghur Muslims. Her sister and aunt were both imprisoned because of her advocacy on Uyghur rights. Abbas organized the One Voice One Step campaign on March 15, 2018, where hundreds of Uyghur Muslim women demonstrated in cities around the world to bring attention to the mass detention of Uyghurs in East Turkestan (Abbas 2018). Additionally, in 2020 the Campaign for Uyghurs organized a protest during fashion week in New

Conclusion 175

York City. The purpose of the protest was to highlight how Uyghur forced labor in camps, farms, and factories is used by US-based companies like Gap, Adidas, and Calvin Klein, to produce clothes (Kelly 2020). There are also several other organizations that are doing the work to educate people about the abuses of Uyghurs. The Uyghur Human Rights Project (UHRP) produces educational materials and publishes reports in English and Chinese. They also submit policy recommendations to governmental agencies, like the EU and the UN (UHRP n.d.).

In addition to the work done by organizations, Uyghur women have been speaking out. Asiye Abdulaheb, a Uyghur Muslim woman who relocated to the Netherlands, shared internal documents she obtained while working in a government office in East Turkestan (Peltier et al. 2019). These secret documents, which were published in the *New York Times*, uncovered the details behind the government's surveillance and detention of Uyghur Muslims, revealing to the global community the atrocities that had been hidden by the Chinese state. Furthermore, Uyghur Muslim women who have escaped to other countries have been speaking out about forced sterilizations and rape that they endured while living in East Turkestan. Speaking out is a form of resistance, because these men and women know that their families who remain in the region could be imprisoned because of it, like Rushan Abbas. But many of them know that if they stay silent, the abuses will continue.

Final Thoughts

There is much more work that needs to be done to dismantle racism. But the first step is to recognize that it exists and identify where it has become part of the structure of society. We have shown that the global racialization of Muslims is an example of 21st-century racism. While we examine how it operates in only four countries, there are many other examples of how the racialization of Muslims has been institutionalized around the world. An analysis of

176   A Global Racial Enemy

counterterrorism policies is one way to find how states are beefing up security, surveillance, and policing under the guise of preventing terrorism. As we have shown, the policies put in place differ in each country. Muslims in the United States and the UK who are citizens still have some protections that Uyghur Muslims in China do not have. In the name of fighting terrorism, authoritarian regimes are able to commit horrific human rights violations, like forced sterilization, forced marriages, and disappearing people into camps. But each country relies on the same stereotypes of Muslims: that the men are potential terrorists and women are threats to a national identity via their cultural practices.

As we have shown in this book, rising nationalisms and ethnonationalist populism target Muslims as incapable of being a part of the nation in the United States, in the UK, in China, and in India. Although we are seeing some gains in political representation by Muslims in the United States and the UK, counterterrorism policies still remain and result in the hyper-surveillance of Muslims in these countries. As Edward Snowden revealed, even state actors of the US government who were Muslim were being surveilled (Currier and Hussain 2016). Thus, inclusion into the polity does not mean exclusion from surveillance practices. In China and India, the states are moving toward stripping Muslims of their status as citizens and policing intimate practices such as marriage, revealing the gendered nature of the racialization of Muslims.

We hope that others will research the global racialization of Muslims in other countries. What is happening in Palestine, France, and Yemen also requires scholarly attention. But to study the racialization of Muslims in a global context requires that we move away from only understanding racisms in relation to whiteness. The global racialization of Muslims reveals that Muslims have been raced to serve purposes other than white supremacy, European colonialism, or American empire. The racialization of Muslims is done in the service of power and material gain, whether it is in India or the United States. The global racialization of Muslims highlights that regardless of the boundaries created by nation-states, the world has always been connected. As we showed earlier in this book, trade and migration are not new, but have been ongoing with Muslims moving across borders for centuries. Racism is not a European invention but existed well before racial classifications were created by European colonists. We hope this book encourages readers, academics, and advocacy groups to think and theorize about racism globally, so that we can work toward dismantling it. First, we must put an end to the Global War on Terror, because the reach of these surveillance and security practices will go well beyond Muslim populations.

References

Abbas, Rushan. "My aunt and sister in China have vanished. Are they being punished for my activism?" *Washington Post*, October 19, 2018, https://www.washingtonpost.com /news/democracy-post/wp/2018/10/19/my-aunt-and-sister -in-china-have-vanished-are-they-being-punished-for-my -activism/.

Abbas, Rushan. "The rise of global Islamophobia and the Uyghur genocide." *Brown Journal of World Affairs* 28, no. 1 (2021).

Abbas, Tahir. "Media capital and the representation of South Asian Muslims in the British press: An ideological analysis." *Journal of Muslim Minority Affairs* 21, no. 2 (2001): 245–57.

Abu-Lughod, Lila. *Do Muslim Women Need Saving?* Cambridge, MA: Harvard University Press, 2013.

ACLU (American Civil Liberties Union). "Surveillance under the USA/Patriot Act." n.d., https://www.aclu.org/other /surveillance-under-usapatriot-act.

ACLU (American Civil Liberties Union). "Nationwide anti-mosque activity." December, 2022.

Adams, Brad. "India's shoot-to-kill policy on the Bangladesh border." *The Guardian*, January 23, 2011, https://www .theguardian.com/commentisfree/libertycentral/2011/jan /23/india-bangladesh-border-shoot-to-kill-policy.

Akram, Muhammad, Asim Nasar, and Muhammad Rizwan Safdar. "Holy cow in India: A political discourse and

References

179

social media analysis for restorative justice." *TRAMES: A Journal of the Humanities & Social Sciences* 25, no. 2 (2021): 219–37.

Al Jazeera. "What is India's Muslim group PFI?" *Al Jazeera*, September 29, 2022, https://www.aljazeera.com/news/2022/9/29/what-is-indian-muslim-group-pfi.

Al Jazeera Podcast Essential Middle East. "China's treatment of Uighur Muslims exposed." *Al Jazeera*, July 7, 2022, https://www.aljazeera.com/podcasts/2022/7/7/chinas-treatment-of-uighur-muslims-exposed.

Alimov, Rashid. "The role of the Shanghai Cooperation Organization in counteracting threats to peace and security." *UN Chronicle* 54, no. 3 (2017): 34–7.

Allen, Christopher. *Islamophobia*. Farnham: Ashgate Publishing, 2013.

Allison, Graham. "What Xi Jinping wants." *The Atlantic*, May 31, 2017, https://www.theatlantic.com/international/archive/2017/05/what-china-wants/528561/.

Alrababa'h, Ala', William Marble, Salma Mousa, and Alexandra A. Siegel. "Can exposure to celebrities reduce prejudice? The effect of Mohamed Salah on Islamophobic behaviors and attitudes." SocArXiv, May 31, 2019, https://immigrationlab.org/working-paper-series/can-exposure-celebrities-reduce-prejudice-effect-mohamed-salah-islamophobic-behaviors-attitudes-2/#:~:text=The%20survey%20experiment%20suggests%20that,role%20models%20can%20decrease%20prejudice.

Alsultany, Evelyn. *Arabs and Muslims in the Media*. New York: New York University Press, 2012.

Alsultany, Evelyn. "Arabs and Muslims in the media after 9/11: Representational strategies for a 'postrace' era." *American Quarterly* 65, no. 1 (2013): 161–9.

Alsultany, Evelyn. *Broken: The Failed Promise of Muslim Inclusion*. New York: New York University Press, 2022.

Ambedkar, Bhimrao Ramji. *Pakistan or Partition of India*. Mumbai: Thacker and Company, 1945.

Ameli, Saied Reza, Syed Mohammed Marandi, Sameera Ahmed, Seyfeddin Kara, and Arzu Merali. *The British Media and*

Muslim Representation: The Ideology of Demonisation. London: Islamic Human Rights Commission, 2007.

American Immigrant Lawyers Association. "Featured report: Denaturalization efforts by UNCIS." August 27, 2021, https://www.aila.org/infonet/featured-issue -denaturalization-efforts-by-uscis.

Amnesty International. *People's Republic of China: Uighurs Fleeing Persecution as China Wages its War on Terror.* London: International Secretariat, 2004.

Anderson, Edward. "'Neo-Hindutva': The Asia House MF Husain campaign and the mainstreaming of Hindu nationalist rhetoric in Britain." *Contemporary South Asia* 23, no. 1 (2015): 45–66.

Anderson, Edward, and Christophe Jaffrelot. "Hindu nationalism and the 'saffronisation of the public sphere': An interview with Christophe Jaffrelot." *Contemporary South Asia* 26, no. 4 (2018): 468–82.

Anderson, Edward, and Arkotong Longkumer. "'Neo-Hindutva': Evolving forms, spaces, and expressions of Hindu nationalism." *Contemporary South Asia* 26, no. 4 (2018): 371–7.

Ansari, Humayun. *"The Infidel Within": Muslims in Britain since 1800.* Oxford: Oxford University Press, 2018.

Ara, Ismat. "'Spirit of Anti-CAA protests lives on': Students, others recount police action at Jamia." *The Wire*, December 16, 2021, https://thewire.in/rights/jamia-university-police -action-two-years-caa.

Ashe, Stephen, Satnam Virdee, and Laurence Brown. "Striking back against racist violence in the East End of London, 1968–1970." *Race & Class* 58, no. 1 (2016): 34–54.

Awan, Imran. "'I am a Muslim not an extremist': How the Prevent Strategy has constructed a 'suspect' community." *Politics & Policy* 40, no. 6 (2012): 1158–85.

Awan, Imran. "Islamophobia and Twitter: A typology of online hate against Muslims on social media." *Policy & Internet* 6, no. 2 (2014): 133–50.

Awan, Imran. *Islamophobia in Cyberspace: Hate Crimes Go Viral.* Abingdon: Routledge, 2016.

Awan, Imran, and Irene Zempi. "We fear for our lives: Offline and online experiences of anti-Muslim hostility."

References 181

Tell MAMA, October 2015, https://tellmamauk.org/wp
-content/uploads/resources/We%20Fear%20For%20Our
%20Lives.pdf.

Aziz, Sahar F. *The Racial Muslim: When Racism Quashes
Religious Freedom*. Berkeley: University of California
Press, 2021.

Aziz, Sahar F. "Shining a light on New Jersey's secret intelligence system." *SSRN*, March 15, 2023, https://papers.ssrn
.com/sol3/papers.cfm?abstract_id=4400598.

Bachmann, Veit, and James D. Sidaway. "Brexit geopolitics."
Geoforum 77 (2016): 47–50.

Baharuddin, Andi Farid, and A. Zamakhsyari Baharuddin.
"Islamophobia, Indian media, and Covid-19 pandemic:
A critical discourse analysis." *Islam Realitas: Journal of
Islamic and Social Studies* 8, no. 1 (2022): 53–67.

Baker, Paul, Costas Gabrielatos, and Tony McEnery.
"Sketching Muslims: A corpus driven analysis of representations around the word 'Muslim' in the British press
1998–2009." *Applied Linguistics* 34, no. 3 (2013): 255–78.

Balch, Alex. "Tightening the grip: The coalition government
and migrant workers." In *Employment Relations under
Coalition Government*, edited by Steve Williams, pp.
144–64. Abingdon: Routledge, 2016.

Bald, Vivek. *Bengali Harlem and the Lost Histories of South
Asian America*. Cambridge, MA: Harvard University
Press, 2013.

Bale, Tim. "Who leads and who follows? The symbiotic
relationship between UKIP and the Conservatives – and
populism and Euroscepticism." *Politics* 38, no. 3 (2018):
263–77.

Balko, Radley. "Surprise! Controversial Patriot Act power now
overwhelmingly used in drug investigations." *Washington
Post*, October 29, 2014, https://www.washingtonpost.com
/news/the-watch/wp/2014/10/29/surprise-controversial
-patriot-act-power-now-overwhelmingly-used-in-drug
-investigations/.

Barker, Martin. *The New Racism: Conservatives and the
Ideology of the Tribe*. Seattle: Junction Books, 1981.

Bashri, Maha. "Elections, representations, and journalistic

schemas: Local news coverage of Ilhan Omar and Rashida Tlaib in the US mid-term elections." *ESSACHESS – Journal for Communication Studies* 12, no. 24 (2019): 129–46.

Basu, Soma. "Manufacturing Islamophobia on WhatsApp in India." *The Diplomat*, May 10, 2019, https://thediplomat.com/2019/05/manufacturing-islamophobia-on-whatsapp-in-india/.

Bayoumi, Moustafa. "Racing religion." *CR: The New Centennial Review* 6, no. 2 (2006): 267–93.

Bayoumi, Moustafa. *This Muslim American Life: Dispatches from the War on Terror*. New York: New York University Press, 2015.

Benjamin, Ruha. *People's Science: Bodies and Rights on the Stem Cell Frontier*. Stanford, CA: Stanford University Press, 2013.

Bergen, Peter, and David Sterman. "Terrorism in America after 9/11: A detailed look at jihadist terrorist activity in the United States and by Americans overseas since 9/11." *The New American*, September 10, 2021, https://www.newamerica.org/international-security/reports/terrorism-in-america/.

Beydoun, Khaled A. *American Islamophobia: Understanding the Roots and Rise of Fear*. Berkeley: University of California Press, 2018.

Beydoun, Khaled A. "Exporting Islamophobia in the global 'War on Terror'." *NYU Law Review Online* 95 (2020): article 81.

Bharucha, Rustom. "Muslims and others: Anecdotes, fragments and uncertainties of evidence." *Economic and Political Weekly* 38, no. 40 (2003): 4238–50.

Bhattacharya, Abanti. "Conceptualising Uyghur separatism in Chinese nationalism." *Strategic Analysis* 27, no. 3 (2003): 357–81.

Bier, David J. "Trump cut Muslim refugees 91%, immigrants 30%, visitors by 18%." CATO Institute, December 7, 2018, https://www.cato.org/blog/trump-cut-muslim-refugees-91-immigrants-30-visitors-18.

Biswas, Soutik. "Love jihad: The Indian law threatening

interfaith love." *BBC News*, December 8, 2020, https://www.bbc.com/news/world-asia-india-55158684.

Blake, A. "Let's have trial by combat: How Trump and allies egged on the violent scenes Wednesday." *Washington Post*, January 6, 2021, https://www.washingtonpost.com/politics/2021/01/06/lets-have-trial-by-combat-how-trump-allies-egged-violent-scenes-wednesday/.

Bolognani, Marta, Erum Haider, Humera Iqbal, and Zahra Sabri. "101 damnations: British Pakistanis, British cinema and sociological mimicry." *South Asian Popular Culture* 9, no. 2 (2011): 161–75.

Bolsover, Gillian. "Indian democracy under threat: The BJP's online authoritarian populism as a means to advance an ethnoreligious nationalist agenda in the 2019 general election." *International Journal of Communication* 16 (2022): 1940–68.

Bonikowski, Bart. "Ethno-nationalist populism and the mobilization of collective resentment." *The British Journal of Sociology* 68 (2017): S181–S213.

Bonilla-Silva, Eduardo. "From bi-racial to tri-racial: Towards a new system of racial stratification in the USA." *Ethnic and Racial Studies* 27, no. 6 (2004): 931–50.

Bonilla-Silva, Eduardo. *Racism without Racists: Color-blind Racism and the Persistence of Racial Inequality in the United States*. New York: Rowman & Littlefield, 2006.

Brass, Paul R. *The Production of Hindu–Muslim Violence in Contemporary India*. Seattle: University of Washington Press, 2005.

Brennan Center. "Why countering violent extremism programs are bad policy." Brennan Center for Justice, 2019, https://www.brennancenter.org/our-work/research-reports/why-countering-violent-extremism-programs-are-bad-policy.

Brown, Anna. "The changing categories the US census has used to measure race." Pew Research Center, February 20, 2020, https://www.pewresearch.org/short-reads/2020/02/25/the-changing-categories-the-u-s-has-used-to-measure-race/.

Brown, James D. "The history of Islam in India." *The Muslim World* 39, no. 1 (1949): 11–25.

Brown, Lorraine, Joanne Brown, and Barry Richards. "Media representations of Islam and international Muslim student well-being." *International Journal of Educational Research* 69 (2015): 50–8.

Browne, Simone. *Dark Matters: On the Surveillance of Blackness.* Durham, NC: Duke University Press, 2015.

Bruce-Lockhart, Anna. "China's $900 billion New Silk Road. What you need to know." The World Economic Forum, June 26, 2017, https://www.weforum.org/agenda/2017/06/china-new-silk-road-explainer/.

Buckley, Chris and Austin Ramzy. "China's detention camps for Muslims turn into forced labor." *New York Times*, December 16, 2018, https://www.nytimes.com/2018/12/16/world/asia/xinjiang-china-forced-labor-camps-uighurs.html.

Burghart, Devin, and Leonard Zeskind. *Tea Party Nationalism: A Critical Examination of the Tea Party Movement and the Size, Scope, and Focus of its National Factions.* Kansas City, MO: Institute for Research and Education on Human Rights, 2010.

Bush, George. "Address to a Joint Session of Congress and the American People." September 20, 2001, https://georgewbush-whitehouse.archives.gov/news/releases/2001/09/20010920-8.html.

Bush, George. "President delivers State of the Union Address." January 29, 2002, https://georgewbush-whitehouse.archives.gov/news/releases/2002/01/20020129-11.html.

Byler, Darren. *In the Camps: China's High-Tech Penal Colony.* New York: Columbia University Press, 2021.

Byler, Darren. *Terror Capitalism: Uyghur Dispossession and Masculinity in a Chinese City.* Durham, NC: Duke University Press, 2022.

Byrd, Jodi A. *The Transit of Empire: Indigenous Critiques of Colonialism.* Minneapolis: University of Minnesota Press, 2011.

Cadell, Cate. "Overseas Uyghurs struggle to locate relatives in Xinjiang prisons." *Reuters*, September 21, 2021, https://

References

www.reuters.com/world/asia-pacific/overseas-uyghurs-struggle-locate-relatives-xinjiang-prisons-2021-09-21/.

CAGE. "About us." n.d., https://www.cage.ngo/cage-about-us.

CAGE. "20 years of TACT: Justice under threat executive summary." October 19, 2020, https://www.cage.ngo/20-years-of-tact-justice-under-threat-executive-summary.

Cainkar, Louis A. *Homeland Insecurity: The Arab American and Muslim American Experience after 9/11*. New York: Russell Sage Foundation, 2009.

Çaksu, Ali. "Islamophobia, Chinese style: Total internment of Uyghur Muslims by the People's Republic of China." *Islamophobia Studies Journal* 5, no. 2 (2020): 175–98.

Caldwell, Christopher. *Reflections on the Revolution in Europe: Immigration, Islam, and the West*. New York: Doubleday, 2009.

CBS/AP News. "More ads with inflammatory messages about Islam appear in NYC subway." January 8, 2013, https://www.cbsnews.com/newyork/news/more-ads-with-inflammatory-messages-about-islam-appear-in-nyc-subway/.

CfMM (Centre for Media Monitoring). *British Media's Coverage of Muslims and Islam (2018–2020)*. Report for the Centre for Media Monitoring, Muslim Council of Britain, 2021, https://cfmm.org.uk/wp-content/uploads/2021/11/CfMM-Annual-Report-2018-2020-digital.pdf.

Chadha, Kalyani, and Anandam P. Kavoori. "Exoticized, marginalized, demonized." In *Global Bollywood,* edited by Anandam P. Kavoori and Aswin Punathambekar, pp. 131–45. New York: New York University Press, 2008.

Cháirez-Garza, Jesús F., Mabel Denzin Gergan, Malini Ranganathan, and Pavithra Vasudevan. "Introduction to the special issue: Rethinking difference in India through racialization." *Ethnic and Racial Studies* 45, no. 2 (2022): 193–215.

Chishti, Muzaffar, and Jessica Bolter. "Two decades after 9/11, national security focus still dominates US immigration system." Migration Policy Institute,

2021, https://www. migrationpolicy. org/article/ two-decades-after-sept-11-immigration-national-security.

Choudhary, Vikas K. "The idea of religious minorities and social cohesion in India's Constitution: Reflections on the Indian experience." *Religions* 12, no. 11 (2021): article 910.

Chung, Chien-peng. "China's 'war on terror': September 11 and Uighur separatism." *Foreign Affairs* 81, no. 4 (2002): 8–12.

Civila, Sabina, Luis M. Romero-Rodríguez, and Amparo Civila. "The demonization of Islam through social media: A case study of #StopIslam in Instagram." *Publications* 8, no. 4 (2020): article 52.

Cockerell, Isobel. "The Uyghur women fighting China's surveillance state." *Coda Story*, n.d., https://www .codastory.com/authoritarian-tech/uyghur-women -fighting-china-surveillance/.

Cole, David. *Enemy Aliens: Double Standards and Constitutional Freedoms in the War on Terrorism*. New York: New Press, 2003.

Copsey, Nigel, Janet Dack, Mark Littler, and Matthew Feldman. "Anti-Muslim hate crime and the far right." Centre for Fascist, Anti-Fascist, and Post-Fascist Studies, 2013, https://research.tees.ac.uk/ws/files/8963116/Anti _Muslim_Hate_Crime_and_the_Far_Right.pdf.

Counihan, Christopher R. "American immigration policy since 9/11: Impact on Muslim migrants." Institute for Social Policy and Understanding, Policy Brief 19, 2007.

Counter Terrorism Policing. "Schedule 7." https://www .counterterrorism.police.uk/what-we-do/protect/schedule -7/.

Crawley, Heaven. "Evidence on attitudes to asylum and immigration: What we know, don't know and need to know." *COMPAS*, 2005, https:// www.compas.ox.ac.uk/wp-content/uploads/WP-2005- 023-Crawley_Attitudes_Asylum_Immigration.pdf.

Currier, Cora, and Murtaza Hussain. "Letter details FBI plan for secretive anti-radicalization committees." *The Intercept,* April 28, 2016, https://theintercept.com/2016/04

References

/28/letter-details-fbi-plan-for-secretive-anti-radicalization -committees/.

Daniel, Joseph. "Indian secularism: Affirming religious and cultural diversities." *Studies in Interreligious Dialogue* 26, no. 2 (2016): 176–89.

Daniyal, Shoaib. "Explained: Sampling bias drove sensationalist reporting around Tablighi coronavirus cases." *Scroll.in*, April 7, 2020, https://scroll. in/article/958392/ explained-sampling-bias-drove-sensationalist-reporting-around-tablighi-coronavirus-cases.

Dhulipala, Venkat. "Parties and politics in the 'parting of ways' narrative: Reevaluating Congress-Muslim League negotiations in late colonial India." *Asiatische Studien-Études Asiatiques* 74, no. 2 (2021): 269–323.

Diouf, Sylviane A. *Servants of Allah: African Muslims Enslaved in the Americas*. New York: New York University Press, 2013.

Doyle, Mark. *Communal Violence in the British Empire: Disturbing the Pax*. London: Bloomsbury Academic Publishing, 2016.

Drabu, Onaiza. "Who is the Muslim? Discursive representations of the Muslims and Islam in Indian prime-time news." *Religions* 9, no. 9 (2018): 1–23.

Dreyer, June. "China's minority nationalities in the Cultural Revolution." *The China Quarterly* 35 (1968): 96–109.

Ejiofor, Promise Frank. "Decolonising Islamophobia." *Ethnic and Racial Studies* (2023): 1–30.

Elgenius, Gabriella, and Steve Garner. "Gate-keeping the nation: Discursive claims, counter-claims and racialized logics of whiteness." *Ethnic and Racial Studies* 44, no. 16 (2021): 215–35.

Elgot, Jessica, and Vikram Dodd. "Leaked PREVENT review attacks 'double standards' on far right and Islamists." *The Guardian*, May 16, 2022, https://www.the guardian.com/uk-news/2022/may/16/leaked-prevent-review-attacks-double-standards-on-rightwingers-and-islamists.

Elliott, Andrea. "The man behind the anti-sharia movement." *New York Times*, July 30, 2011, https://www.nytimes.com /2011/07/31/us/31shariah.html?_r=0.

188   A Global Racial Enemy

Elshayyal, Khadijah. *Muslim Identity Politics: Islam, Activism and Equality in Britain.* London: Bloomsbury Publishing, 2019.

Evolvi, Giulia. "Hate in a tweet: Exploring internet-based Islamophobic discourses." *Religions* 9, no. 10 (2018): article 307.

Falah, Ghazi-Walid. "The visual representation of Muslim/Arab women in daily newspapers." In *Geographies of Muslim Women: Gender, Religion, and Space,* edited by Falah Ghazi-Walid and Caroline Rose Angel, pp. 300–19. New York: Guilford Press, 2005.

Fallert, Nicole. "Gynecologist exiled from China says 80 sterilizations per day forced on Uyghurs." *Newsweek,* April 14, 2021, https://www.newsweek.com/gynecologist-exiled-china-says-80-sterilizations-per-day-forced-uyghurs-1583678.

Fisher, Max. "54% of Republicans say that, 'deep down,' Obama is a Muslim." *Vox,* February 25, 2015, https://www.vox.com/2015/2/25/8108005/obama-muslim-poll.

Fisher, Michael. *A Short History of the Mughal Empire.* London: Bloomsbury Publishing, 2015.

Frangville, Vanessa. "Chinese cinema's push to produce the ideal Uyghur citizen." *.coda,* February 5, 2020, https://www.codastory.com/disinformation/uyghurs-movies-propaganda/.

Fryer, Peter. *Staying Power: The History of Black People in Britain.* London: Pluto Press, 1986.

Gardiner, Dustin, and Mark Olalde. "These copycat bills on sharia law and terrorism have no effect. Why do states keep passing them?" *USA Today,* July 17, 2019, https://www.usatoday.com/in-depth/news/investigations/2019/07/17/islam-sharia-law-how-far-right-group-gets-model-bills-passed/1636199001/.

Garner, Steve. *The Moral Economy of Whiteness: Four Frames of Racializing Discourse.* Abingdon: Routledge, 2015.

Garner, Steve, and Saher Selod. "The racialization of Muslims: Empirical studies of Islamophobia." *Critical Sociology* 41, no. 1 (2015): 9–19.

GhaneaBassiri, Kambiz. *A History of Islam in America: From*

References

189

the New World to the New World Order. Cambridge: Cambridge University Press, 2010.

Ghurye, Govind Sadashiv. *Social Tensions in India.* Mumbai: Popular Prakash, 1968.

Gilliat-Ray, Sophie. *Muslims in Britain: An Introduction.* Cambridge: Cambridge University Press, 2010.

Gilroy, Paul. *Ain't No Black in the Union Jack.* London: Hutchinson, 1987.

Glenza, Jessica and Nicky Woolf. "Texas schoolboy arrested over clock to visit Obama as authorities defend action." *The Guardian,* September 17, 2015, https://www .theguardian.com/us-news/2015/sep/16/homemade-clock -ahmed-mohamed-texas-officials-we-were-right.

Goodhart, David. "Too diverse?" *Prospect Magazine 95,* no. 30 (2004): 30–7.

Gottschalk, Peter, and Gabriel Greenberg. *Islamophobia: Making Muslims the Enemy.* Lanham, MD: Rowman & Littlefield, 2008.

Greenwald, Glenn, and Murtaza Hussain. "Meet the Muslim-American leaders the FBI and NSA have been spying on." *The Intercept,* February 18, 2014, https://theintercept.com /2014/07/09/under-surveillance/.

Grewal, Zareena. *Islam is a Foreign Country: American Muslims and the Global Crisis of Authority,* Vol. 22. New York: New York University Press, 2014.

Grierson, Jamie, and Dan Sabbagh. "Largest number of PREVENT referrals related to far-right extremism." *The Guardian,* November 26, 2020, https://www.theguardian .com/uk-news/2020/nov/26/just-one-in-10-prevent -referrals-found-at-risk-of-radicalisation.

Grieshaber, Kirsten. "US museum condemns use of its art by German far-right party." *The Seattle Times,* April 30, 2019, https://www.seattletimes.com/entertainment /us-museum-condemns-use-of-its-art-by-german-far-right -party/.

Groves, Matthew. "Law, religion and public order in colonial India: Contextualising the 1887 Allahabad high court case on 'sacred' cows." *South Asia: Journal of South Asian Studies 33* (2010): 87–121.

Gualtieri, Sarah. *Between Arab and White: Race and Ethnicity in the Early Syrian American Diaspora*. Berkeley: University of California Press, 2009.

Guest, Mathew, Alison Scott-Baumann, Sariya Cheruvallil-Contractor, Shuruq Naguib, Aisha Phoenix, Yenn Lee, and Tarek Al Baghal. *Islam and Muslims on UK University Campuses: Perceptions and Challenges*. Technical Report. Durham: Durham University, London: SOAS, Coventry: Coventry University and Lancaster: Lancaster University, 2020, https://blogs.soas.ac.uk/cop/wp-content/uploads/2020/07/Islam-on-Campus.pdf.

Guha, Ramachandra. *India after Gandhi*. Basingstoke: Macmillan, 2007.

Gupta, Charu. "Love taboos: Controlling Hindu–Muslim romances." *India Forum*, January 7, 2021, https://www.theindiaforum.in/article/love-laws-making-hindu-muslim-romances-illegitimate.

Haji, Reeshma, Shelley McKeown, Alex Matthews, and Samantha Platten. "(De) humanization and (dis) trust: Representations of Muslims in the UK newspapers following the 7/7 London bombings." *Peace and Conflict: Journal of Peace Psychology* 27, no. 2 (2021): 256–57.

Halliday, Fred. "Islamophobia reconsidered." *Ethnic and Racial Studies* 22, no. 5 (1999): 892–902.

Hajjat, Abdellali and Marwan Mohammed. *Islamophobie: comment les élites françaises fabriquent le 'problème musulman'*. Paris: La Découverte, 2013.

Hartig, Hannah, and Carroll Doherty. "Two decades later, the enduring legacy of 9/11." Pew Research Center, September 2, 2021, https://www.pewresearch.org/politics/2021/09/02/two-decades-later-the-enduring-legacy-of-9-11/.

Harwell, Drew, and Eva Dou. "Huawei tested AI software that could recognize Uighur minorities and alert police, report says." *Washington Post*, December 8, 2020, https://link.gale.com/apps/doc/A644186899/ITOF?u=mlin_b_simmcol&sid=bookmark-ITOF&xid=b7295968.

Hilal, Maha. *Innocent Until Proven Muslim: Islamophobia, the War on Terror, and the Muslim Experience Since 9/11*. Minneapolis: Broadleaf Books, 2022.

References 191

Hill, Matthew, David Campanale, and Joel Gunter. "'Their goal is to destroy everyone': Uighur camp detainees allege systematic rape." *BBC News*, February 2, 2021, https://www.bbc.com/news/world-asia-china-55794071

Hillman, Ben. "Unrest in Tibet and the limits of regional autonomy." In *Ethnic Conflict and Protest in Tibet and Xinjiang*, edited by Ben Hillman and Gray Tuttle, pp. 18–39. New York: Columbia University Press, 2016.

Hirji, Faiza. "Change of pace? Islam and tradition in popular Indian cinema." *South Asian Popular Culture* 6, no. 1 (2008): 57–69.

Holmwood, John, and L. Aitlhadj. "The people's review of Prevent." *Prevent Watch* (2022).

Holmwood, John, and Therese O'Toole. *Countering Extremism in British Schools? The Truth about the Birmingham Trojan Horse Affair*. Bristol: Policy Press, 2018.

Home Office. *Hate Crime: England and Wales, 2018–19*. London: HM Government, 2019, https://assets.publishing.service.gov.uk/government/uploads/system/uploads/attachment_data/file/839172/hate-crime-1819-hosb2419.pdf.

Home Office. *Official Statistics. Hate Crime, England and Wales, 2021 to 2022*. London: HM Government, 2022, https://www.gov.uk/government/statistics/hate-crime-england-and-wales-2021-to-2022/hate-crime-england-and-wales-2021-to-2022#police-recorded-hate-crime.

Huffington Post. "Minister in Modi's cabinet garlands cow vigilantes convicted for lynching a Muslim trader in Jharkhand." July 6, 2018, https://www.huffpost.com/archive/in/entry/union-minister-jayant-singh-garlands-cow-vigilantes-convicted-for-lynching-a-muslim-trader-in-jharkhand_a_23476652.

Human Rights Watch. "'We have no orders to save you': State participation and complicity in communal violence in Gujarat." April 30, 2002, https://www.hrw.org/report/2002/04/30/we-have-no-orders-save-you/state-participation-and-complicity-communal-violence.

Human Rights Watch. "Trigger happy excessive use of force

by Indian troops." December 9, 2010, https://www.hrw.org/report/2010/12/09/trigger-happy/excessive-use-force-indian-troops-bangladesh-border.

Human Rights Watch. "India: Investigate alleged border force killings." February 9, 2021, https://www.hrw.org/news/2021/02/09/india-investigate-alleged-border-force-killings.

Huntington, Samuel. "The clash of civilizations." *Foreign Affairs* 72 (1993): 22–49.

Husain, Atiya. "Deracialization, dissent, and terrorism in the FBI's most wanted program." *Sociology of Race and Ethnicity* 7, no. 2 (2021a): 208–25.

Husain, Atiya. "Official antiracism and the limits of 'Islamophobia'." *Social Identities* 27, no. 6 (2021b): 611–25.

Hussain, Murtaza. "Trump signals cuts to unpopular 'countering extremism' programs, but worse could be coming." *The Intercept*, August 4, 2017, https://theintercept.com/2017/08/04/cve-trump-cuts-worse-coming-radicalization-islamic-extremism/.

Islam, Inaash. "Muslim American double consciousness." *Du Bois Review: Social Science Research on Race* 17, no. 2 (2020): 429–48.

Islamic Human Rights Commission. "Islamophobia by any other name smells just as rank." September 5, 2018, https://www.ihrc.org.uk/bodyguard-islamophobia-by-any-other-name-smells-just-as-rank/.

IUHRDF (International Uyghur Human Rights and Democracy Foundation). "Xinjiang Uyghur autonomous region regulation on de-extremification." 2017.

Jackson, Leonie. "Images of Islam in US media and their educational implications." *Educational Studies*, 46 (2010): 3–24.

Jackson, Leonie. *The Monstrous and the Vulnerable: Framing British Jihadi Brides*. London: C. Hurst & Co., 2021.

Jackson, Sherman A. *Islam and the Black American: Looking toward the Third Resurrection*. Oxford: Oxford University Press, 2005.

Jaffrelot, Christophe. "Communal riots in Gujarat: The state at risk?" Heidelberg Papers in South Asian and Comparative

References

Politics, Working Paper 17, 2003, http://archiv.ub.uni -heidelberg.de/volltextserver/4127/1/hpsacp17.pdf.

Jaffrelot, Christophe. "The Modi-centric BJP 2014 election campaign: New techniques and old tactics." *Contemporary South Asia* 23, no. 2 (2015): 151–66.

Jain, Pankaj. "From Padosi to My Name is Khan: The portrayal of Hindu–Muslim relations in South Asian films." *Visual Anthropology* 24, no. 4 (2011): 345–63.

Jain, Ritika. "Covid-19: How fake news and Modi government messaging fuelled India's latest spiral of Islamophobia." *Scroll.in*, April 21, 2020, https://scroll.in/article/959806 /covid-19-how-fake-news-and-modi-government -messaging-fuelled-indias-latest-spiral-of-islamophobia.

Jaspal, Rusi, and Marco Cinnirella. "Media representations of British Muslims and hybridised threats to identity." *Contemporary Islam* 4 (2010): 289–310.

Jiwani, Yasmin. "Orientalizing 'war talk': Representations of the gendered Muslim body post-9/11 in the Montreal Gazette." In *Situating "Race" and Racisms in Time, Space, and Theory: Critical Essays for Activists and Scholars*, edited by Jo Ann Lee and John S. Lutz, pp. 178–203. Montreal: McGill Queen's University Press, 2005.

Jones, Reece. "Agents of exception: Border security and the marginalization of Muslims in India." *Environment and Planning D: Society and Space* 27, no. 5 (2009a): 879–97.

Jones, Reece. "Geopolitical boundary narratives, the global war on terror and border fencing in India." *Transactions of the Institute of British Geographers* 34, no. 3 (2009b): 290–304.

Jones, Stephen, and Amy Unsworth. *The Dinner Table Prejudice: Islamophobia in Contemporary Britain.* University of Birmingham / YouGov, 2022, https://www .birmingham.ac.uk/documents/college-artslaw/ptr/90172 -univ73-islamophobia-in-the-uk-report-final.pdf.

Kalhan, Anil, Gerald P. Conroy, Mamta Kaushal, and Sam Scott Miller. "Colonial continuities: Human rights, terrorism, and security laws in India." *Columbia Journal of Asian Law* 20 (2006): 93–234.

Kang, Dake, and Yanan Wang. "China's Uighurs told

to share beds, meals with party members." *AP News*, November 30, 2018, https://apnews.com/article/ap-top-news-international-news-prayer-weddings-occasions-9ca1c29fc9554c1697a8729bba4dd93b.

Kapoor, Nisha. *Deport, Deprive, Extradite: 21st Century State Extremism*. London: Verso Books, 2018.

Kashgarian, Asim. "China video ad calls for 100 Uighur women to 'urgently' marry Han men." *Voice of America*, August 21, 2020, https://www.voanews.com/a/east-asia-pacific_voa-news-china_china-video-ad-calls-100-uighur-women-urgently-marry-han-men/6194806.html.

Katzenstein, Jessica. "The wars are here: How the United States' post-9/11 wars helped militarize US police." Watson Institute Costs of War Project, 2020.

Kausar, Zeenath. "Communal riots in India: Hindu–Muslim conflict and resolution." *Journal of Muslim Minority Affairs* 26, no. 3 (2006): 353–70.

Kazi, Nazia. *Islamophobia, Race, and Global Politics*. New York: Rowman & Littlefield, 2021.

Kelly, Annie. "Virtually entire fashion industry complicit in Uighur forced labour, say rights groups." *The Guardian*, July 23, 2020, https://www.theguardian.com/global-development/2020/jul/23/virtually-entire-fashion-industry-complicit-in-uighur-forced-labour-say-rights-groups-china.

Kerboua, Salim. "From Orientalism to neo-Orientalism: Early and contemporary constructions of Islam and the Muslim world." *Intellectual Discourse* 24, no. 1 (2016): 7–34.

Khan, Sabah. "Social exclusion of Muslims in India and Britain." *Journal of Social Inclusion Studies* 6, no. 1 (2020): 56–77.

Khatun, Nadira. "Imagining Muslims as the 'Other' in Muslim political films." *Journal of Arab & Muslim Media Research* 9, no. 1 (2016): 41–60.

Khurshid, Ahmad. "Pakistan: Vision and reality, past and future." *The Muslim World* 96, no. 2 (2006): 363–79.

Kim, Heewon. "Understanding Modi and minorities: The BJP-led NDA government in India and religious minorities." *India Review* 16, no. 4 (2017): 357–76.

References

Kirkup, James. "Muslims must embrace our British values, David Cameron says." *Daily Telegraph*, February 7, 2011.

Knott, Kim. "British Muslims: A history." Centre for Research and Evidence on Security Threats, March 26, 2018, https://crestresearch.ac.uk/resources/british-muslims-history/.

Kopan, Tal. "Lawmakers split over fusion center report." *Politico*, October 3, 2012, https://www.politico.com/blogs/under-the-radar/2012/10/lawmakers-split-over-fusion-center-report-137411.

Kuchay, Bilal. "Shaheen Bagh protesters pledge to fight, seek rollback of CAA law." *Al Jazeera*, January 15, 2020, https://www.aljazeera.com/news/2020/1/15/shaheen-bagh-protesters-pledge-to-fight-seek-rollback-of-caa-law.

Kumar, Deepa. "Terrorcraft: Empire and the making of the racialised terrorist threat." *Race & Class* 62, no. 2 (2020): 34–60.

Kumar, Deepa. *Islamophobia and the Politics of Empire: Twenty Years after 9/11*. London: Verso Books, 2021.

Kundnani, Arun. *Spooked! How not to Prevent Violent Extremism*. London: Institute for Race Relations, 2009, https://www.kundnani.org/wp-content/uploads/spooked.pdf.

Kundnani, Arun. *The Muslims Are Coming! Islamophobia, Extremism, and the Domestic War on Terror*. London: Verso Books, 2014.

Kundnani, Arun, and Ben Hayes. "The globalisation of countering violent extremism policies." In *Undermining Human Rights, Instrumentalising Civil Society*. Amsterdam: Transnational Institute, 2018, https://www.preventwatch.org/wp-content/uploads/2021/08/014092_26ca35cecec34464a5419fb6e72bf7e9.pdf.

La Barbera, Maria Caterina, ed. *Identity and Migration in Europe: Multidisciplinary Perspectives*, Vol. 13. Cham: Springer, 2014.

Labidi, Imed Ben. "Hollywood's bad Muslims: Misrepresentations and the channeling of racial violence." *The Journal of Religion and Popular Culture* 33, no. 3 (2021): 126–37.

Latif v. *Lynch*, 3:10-cv-00750-BR (D. Or. Mar. 28, 2016), https://casetext.com/case/latif-v-lynch.

Leidig, Eviane Cheng. "Immigrant, nationalist and proud: A Twitter analysis of Indian diaspora supporters for Brexit and Trump." *Media and Communication* 7, no. 1 (2019): 77–89.

Lewis, Bernard. "The roots of Muslim rage." *The Atlantic Monthly* 266, no. 3 (1990): 47–60.

Li, Qiong, and Marilynn B. Brewer. "What does it mean to be an American? Patriotism, nationalism, and American identity after 9/11." *Political Psychology* 25, no. 5 (2004): 727–39.

Liberhan Ayodhya Commission of Inquiry. *Report of the Commission of Enquiry*, 2009.

Lim, Peh Hong. "China steps up assimilation of ethnic minorities by banning languages in schools." *Voice of America*, October 24, 2021, https://www.voanews.com /a/china-steps-up-assimilation-of-ethnic-minorities-by-banning-languages-in-schools-/6281558.html#:~:text=The%20 Chinese%20Constitution%20states%20that,own%20 spoken%20and%20written%20languages.%22.

Liu, Jiehan and Shen, Xiaoxiao. "Measuring populism: Evidence from China." *SSRN*, July 8, 2022, http://dx.doi .org/10.2139/ssrn.4177268.

Loomba, Ania. "Race and the possibilities of comparative critique." *New Literary History* 40, no. 3 (2009): 501–22.

Lopez, Ian Haney. *White by Law 10th Anniversary Edition*. New York: New York University Press, 2006.

Lord Ashcroft. "How the United Kingdom voted on Thursday... and why." *Lord Ashcroft Polls*, June 24, 2016, https://lordashcroftpolls.com/2016/06/how-the -united-kingdom-voted-and-why/.

Love, Erik. *Islamophobia and Racism in America*. New York: New York University Press, 2017.

Lowe, Lisa. *Critical Terrains: French and British Orientalisms*. Ithaca, NY: Cornell University Press, 1991.

Ludden, David. *India and South Asia: A Short History*. New York: Simon and Schuster, 2002.

Luqiu, Luwei Rose, and Fan Yang. "Islamophobia in China: News coverage, stereotypes, and Chinese Muslims'

References

perceptions of themselves and Islam." *Asian Journal of Communication* 28, no. 6 (2018): 598–619.

Ma, Alexandra. "China is reportedly sending men to sleep in the same beds as Uighur Muslim women while their husbands are in prison camps." *Business Insider*, November 4, 2019, https://www.businessinsider.com/china-uighur-monitor-home-shared-bed-report-2019-11.

Ma, Haiyun. "The anti-Islamic movement in China." *Current Trends in Islamist Ideology*, July 13, 2019, https://www.hudson.org/research/15095-the-anti-islamic-movement-in-china.

Maghbouleh, Neda. "From white to what? MENA and Iranian American non-white reflected race." *Ethnic and Racial Studies* 43, no. 4 (2020): 613–31.

Mamdani, M. *Good Muslim, Bad Muslim: America, the Cold War, and the Roots of Terror*. New York: Three Leaves Press, 2004.

Mamonova, Natalia. "Understanding the silent majority in authoritarian populism: What can we learn from popular support for Putin in rural Russia?" *Critical Agrarian Studies* 46, no. 3 (2019): 201–26.

Mandal, Rakesh. "Rights of minorities in India and Pakistan: A comparative study." *Indian Journal of Law and Justice* 13, no. 1 (2022): 192–206.

Massoumi, Narzanin, Tom Mills, and David Miller. *What is Islamophobia? Racism, Social Movements and the State.* New York: Pluto Press, 2017.

Maurer-Fazio, Margaret, and Reza Hasmath. "The contemporary ethnic minority in China: An introduction." *Eurasian Geography and Economics* 56, no. 1 (2015): 1–7.

McCloud, Aminah Beverly. *African American Islam*. New York: Routledge, 2014.

McMillan, Alex Frew, and Major Garrett. "U.S. wins support from China." *CNN*, October 19, 2001, https://www.cnn.com/2001/WORLD/asiapcf/east/10/19/bush.jiang.apec/index.html.

MEND (Muslim Engagement and Development) and Muslim Census. *Mosque Security Report*. 2022. https://www.mend.org.uk/mosque-security-report/.

Menon, Kalyani Devaki. *Making Place for Muslims in Contemporary India*. Ithaca, NY: Cornell University Press, 2022.

Miao, Ying. "Sinicisation vs. Arabisation: Online narratives of Islamophobia in China." *Journal of Contemporary China* 29, no. 125 (2020): 748–62.

Michelutti, Lucia. *The Vernacularisation of Democracy: Politics, Caste and Religion in India*. New Delhi and Abingdon: Routledge, 2020.

Miles, Robert, and Annie Phizacklea. *White Man's Country: Racism in British Politics*. London: Pluto Press, 1984.

Miller, Todd. *Empire of Borders: The Expansion of the U.S. Border around the World*. London: Verso Books, 2019.

Mills, Charles W. *The Racial Contract*. Ithaca, NY: Cornell University Press, 1997.

Mirahmadi, Hedieh, Waleed Ziad, Mehreen Farooq, and Robert D. Lamb. *Empowering Pakistan's Civil Society to Counter Global Violent Extremism*. Washington DC: Center for Middle East Policy at Brookings, 2015.

Mishra, Smeeta. "Saving Muslim women and fighting Muslim men: Analysis of representations in the New York Times." *Global Media Journal* 6, no. 11 (2007): 1–20.

MJL (Muslim Justice League). "Our work." n.d., https://muslimjusticeleague.org/our-work/.

Modood, Tariq. "Political blackness and British Asians." *Sociology* 28, no. 4 (1994): 859–76.

Mohammad, Niala. "I didn't realize how often Muslims get kicked off planes, until it happened to me." *The Guardian*, September 8, 2016, https://www.theguardian.com/world/2016/sep/08/muslim-woman-kicked-off-american-airlines-flight-islamophobia.

Moore, D.W. "War makes Americans confident, sad: Personal lives less affected than during the first Gulf War and 9/11." *Gallup News Service*, Washington DC, 2003, http://www.gallup.com/poll/8077/War-Makes-Americans-Confident-Sad.aspx.

Moore, Kerry, Paul Mason, and Justin Matthew Wren Lewis. *Images of Islam in the UK: The Representation of British*

Muslims in the National Print News Media 2000–2008. Cardiff School of Journalism, Media and Cultural Studies, July 7, 2008, https://orca.cardiff.ac.uk/id/eprint/53005/1/08channel4-dispatches.pdf.

Moussawi, Ghassan. *Disruptive Situations: Fractal Orientalism and Queer Strategies in Beirut.* Philadelphia: Temple University Press, 2020.

Muslim Advocates. *Complicit: The Human Cost of Facebook's Disregard for Muslim Life.* 2020, https://muslimadvocates.org/wp-content/uploads/2020/10/Complicit-Report.pdf.

Naber, Nadine. "Introduction: Arab Americans and U.S. racial formations." In *Race and Arab Americans Before and After 9/11: From Invisible Citizens to Visible Subjects,* edited by Amaney Jamal and Nadine Naber. Syracuse, NY: Syracuse University Press, 2007.

Naber, Nadine and Junaid Rana. "The 21st century problem with anti-Muslim racism." *Jadaliyyah,* July 25, 2019, https://www.jadaliyya.com/Details/39830.

Nandi, Alita, and Lucinda Platt. Patterns of minority and majority identification in a multicultural society. *Ethnic and Racial Studies* 38, no. 15 (2015): 2615–34.

Natrajan, Balmurli. "Racialization and ethnicization: Hindutva hegemony and caste." *Ethnic and Racial Studies* 45, no. 2 (2022): 298–318.

Nazeer, Tasnim. "Memo to Bodyguard writers: Muslim women are more than victims or terrorists." *The Guardian,* September 24, 2018, https://www.theguardian.com/commentisfree/2018/sep/24/bodyguard-muslim-islamophobic-attacks-muslim-terrorist-stereotype.

Nguyen, Trung. "The effectiveness of white-collar crime enforcement: Evidence from the War on Terror." *Journal of Accounting Research* 59, no. 1 (2021): 5–58.

Oboler, Andre. "The normalisation of Islamophobia through social media: Facebook." In *Islamophobia in Cyberspace,* edited by Imran Awan, pp. 55–76. Abingdon: Routledge, 2016.

Omar, Ilhan. "Rep. Omar remarks on Islamophobia." Press Release, December 21, 2021, https://omar.house.gov/media/press-releases/rep-omar-remarks-islamophobia.

Omi, Michael, and Howard Winant. *Racial Formation in the United States*. New York: Routledge, 2015.

ONS (Office for National Statistics). "How life has changed in Bradford." 2021a, https://www.ons.gov.uk/visualisations/censusareachanges/E08000032/.

ONS (Office for National Statistics). "How life has changed in Birmingham." 2021b, https://www.ons.gov.uk/visualisations/censusareachanges/E08000025/.

ONS (Office for National Statistics). "Religion: England and Wales, 2021." 2022, https://www.ons.gov.uk/peoplepopulationandcommunity/culturalidentity/religion/bulletins/religionenglandandwales/census2021.

O'Toole, Therese. "The political inclusion of British Muslims: From multiculturalism to muscular liberalism." *Ethnicities* 22, no. 4 (2022): 589–602.

O'Toole, Therese, Daniel DeHanas, and Tariq Modood. "Balancing tolerance, security and Muslim engagement in the United Kingdom: The impact of the 'Prevent' agenda." *Critical Studies on Terrorism* 5, no. 3 (2012): 373–89.

Paul, Kathleen. *Whitewashing Britain: Race and Citizenship in the Postwar Era*. Ithaca, NY: Cornell University Press, 1997.

Peek, Lori. *Behind the Backlash: Muslim Americans after 9/11*. Philadelphia: Temple University Press, 2011.

Pelinka, Anton. "The European Union as an alternative to the nation-state." *International Journal of Politics, Culture, and Society* 24 (2011): 21–30.

Peltier, Elian, Claire Moses, and Edward Wong. "'I have told everything,' Says whistle-blower in China crackdown." *New York Times*, December 7, 2019, https://www.nytimes.com/2019/12/07/world/europe/uighur-whistleblower.html.

Pengelly, Martin. "Trump defended rioters who threatened to hang 'Mike Pence', audio reveals." *The Guardian*, November 12, 2021, https://www.theguardian.com/us-news/2021/nov/12/trump-capitol-attack-rioters-mike-pence.

Pew Research Center. "How 9-11 changed the evening news." September 11, 2006, https://www.pewresearch.org

/journalism/2006/09/11/how-9-11-changed-the-evening-news/.

Pew Center for Research. "What census calls us." February 6, 2020, https://www.pewresearch.org/interactives/what-census-calls-us/.

Philips, C.H., ed. *Politics and Society in India*. New York: Routledge, 2021.

Phillips, Melanie. *Londonistan: How Britain Created a Terror State Within*. London: Encounter Books, 2007.

Poole, Elizabeth. *Reporting Islam: Media Representations of British Muslims*. London: I.B. Tauris, 2002.

Poole, Elizabeth. "The effects of September 11 and the war in Iraq on British newspaper coverage." In *Muslims and the News Media*, edited by Elizabeth Poole and John Richardson, pp. 89–102. London: I.B. Tauris, 2006.

Poole, Elizabeth, and Milly Williamson. "Disrupting or reconfiguring racist narratives about Muslims? The representation of British Muslims during the Covid crisis." *Journalism* 24, no. 2 (2023): 262–79.

Prabhat, D. "Stripping British citizenship: The government's new bill explained." *The Conversation*, December 14, 2021, https://theconversation.com/stripping-british-citizenship-the-governments-new-bill-explained-173547#:~:text=Citizenship%20stripping%20orders%20are%20not%20obtained%20from%20any,secretary%20deems%20it%20%E2%80%9Cconducive%20to%20the%20public%20good%E2%80%9D.

Prakash, Gyan. *Emergency Chronicles: Indira Gandhi and Democracy's Turning Point*. Princeton, NJ: Princeton University Press, 2019.

Prince, Stephen. *Firestorm: American Film in the Age of Terrorism*. New York: Columbia University Press, 2009.

Puar, Jasbir K. *Terrorist Assemblages: Homonationalism in Queer Times*. Durham, NC: Duke University Press, 2009.

Pugh, Martin. *Britain and Islam: A History from 622 to the Present Day*. New Haven, CT: Yale University Press, 2019.

Puri, Jyoti. *Encountering Nationalism*. Chichester: John Wiley & Sons, 2008.

Puri, Jyoti. *Sexual States*. Durham, NC: Duke University Press, 2016.

Rahman, Khalid. "Indian secularism and religious minorities: The case of Muslims." *Policy Perspectives: The Journal of the Institute of Policy Studies* 14, no. 2 (2017): 35–53.

Rai, Amit. "Patriotism and the Muslim citizen in Hindi films." *Harvard Asia Quarterly* 7 (2003): 4–15.

Rajgopal, Shoba Sharad. "Bollywood and neonationalism: The emergence of nativism as the norm in Indian conventional cinema." *South Asian Popular Culture* 9, no. 3 (2011): 237–46.

Ramamurthy, Anandi. *Black Star: Britain's Asian Youth Movements*. London: Pluto Press, 2013.

Ramzy, Austin and Chris Buckley. "'Absolutely no mercy': Leaked files expose how China organized mass detentions of Muslims." *New York Times*, November 16, 2019, https://www.nytimes.com/interactive/2019/11/16/world/asia/china-xinjiang-documents.html.

Rana, Junaid. *Terrifying Muslims: Race and Labor in the South Asian Diaspora*. Durham, NC: Duke University Press, 2011.

Rana, Junaid. "The racial infrastructure of the terror-industrial complex." *Social Text* 34, no. 4 (2016): 111–38.

Rashid, Naaz. "Giving the silent majority a stronger voice? Initiatives to empower Muslim women as part of the UK's 'War on Terror'." *Ethnic and Racial Studies* 37, no. 4 (2014): 589–604.

Rathborn, Jack. "Chelsea fans filmed singing 'Mohamed Salah is a bomber' ahead of Slavia Prague match." *The Independent*, April 11, 2019, https://www.independent.co.uk/sport/football/european/chelsea-fans-mohamed-salah-islamophobic-racist-song-slavia-prague-europa-league-a8865491.html.

Razack, Sherene H. *Nothing Has to Make Sense: Upholding White Supremacy through Anti-Muslim Racism*. Minneapolis: University of Minnesota Press, 2022.

Regan, Helen. "China passes sweeping Hong Kong national security law." *CNN*, June 30, 2020, https://www.cnn.com/2020/06/29/china/hong-kong-national-security-law-passed-intl-hnk/index.html.

References 203

Rex, John and Robert Moore. *Race, Community and Conflict: A Study of Sparkbrook.* Oxford: Oxford University Press/ Institute for Race Relations, 1967.

Roberts, Dorothy. *Fatal Invention: How Science, Politics, and Big Business Re-create Race in the Twenty-First Century.* New York: New Press, 2011.

Roberts, Sean R. *The War on the Uyghurs: China's Campaign against Xinjiang's Muslims.* Princeton, NJ: Princeton University Press, 2020.

Rudolph, Lloyd I., and Susanne Hoeber Rudolph. *In Pursuit of Lakshmi: The Political Economy of the Indian State.* Chicago: Chicago University Press, 1987.

Ruser, Nathan. *Documenting Xinjiang's Detention System.* Barton, Australian Capital Territory: Australian Strategic Policy Institute, 2020.

Sabbagh, Dan. "Detention of Muslims at UK ports and airports 'structural Islamophobia'." *The Guardian*, August 20, 2019, https://www.theguardian.com/news/2019/aug/20/detention-of-muslims-at-uk-ports-and-airports-structural-islamophobia.

Sacirbey, Omar. "Shariah or not, Muslim divorces can get tricky." *Washington Post*, October 1, 2012, https://www.washingtonpost.com/national/on-faith/shariah-or-not-muslim-divorces-can-get-tricky/2012/10/01/13d014da-0c15-11e2-97a7-45c05ef136b2_story.html.

Said, Edward. *Orientalism: Western Conceptions of the East.* New York: Pantheon, 1978.

Salam, Ziya Us. "CAA protests: Making it count in Delhi." *Frontline*, January 18, 2020, https://frontline.thehindu.com/the-nation/article30544019.ece.

Saldanha, A. "Cow-related hate crimes peaked in 2017, 86% of those killed Muslim." *The Wire*, December 8, 2017, https://thewire.in/communalism/cow-vigilantism-violence-2017-muslims-hate-crime.

Saleem, Shahed. *The British Mosque: An Architectural and Social History.* Liverpool: Liverpool University Press, 2018.

Samaie, Mahmoud, and Bahareh Malmir. "US news media portrayal of Islam and Muslims: A corpus-assisted Critical

Discourse Analysis." *Educational Philosophy and Theory* 49, no. 14 (2017): 1351–66.

Sarkar, Tanika. "Special guest contribution: Is love without borders possible?" *Feminist Review* 119, no. 1 (2018): 7–19.

Sarkar, Tanika. *Hindu Nationalism in India*. Oxford: Oxford University Press, 2022.

Sasikumar, Karthika. "State agency in the time of the global war on terror: India and the counter-terrorism regime." *Review of International Studies* 36, no. 3 (2010): 615–38.

Sayyid, Salman, and AbdoolKarim Vakil. *Thinking through Islamophobia: Global Perspectives*. New York: Columbia University Press, 2010.

Selod, Saher. *Forever Suspect: Racialized Surveillance of Muslim Americans in the War on Terror*. New Brunswick, NJ: Rutgers University Press, 2018.

Selod, Saher. "Gendered racialization: Muslim American men and women's encounters with racialized surveillance." *Ethnic and Racial Studies* 42, no. 4 (2019): 552–69.

Selod, Saher, and David G. Embrick. "Racialization and Muslims: Situating the Muslim experience in race scholarship." *Sociology Compass* 7, no. 8 (2013): 644–55.

Sen, Somdeep. "India's deepening love affair with Israel: Under Modi's Hindu nationalist government, the strategic, military, and ideological ties between Israel and India are growing stronger." *Al Jazeera*, September 9, 2021, https://www.aljazeera.com/opinions/2021/9/9/indias-deepening-love-affair-with-israel.

Sengupta, Nitish. *Land of Two Rivers: A History of Bengal from the Mahabharata to Mujib*. London: Penguin, 2011.

Serwer, Adam. "Birtherism of a nation: The conspiracy theories surrounding Obama's birthplace and religion were much more than mere lies. They were ideology." *The Atlantic*, May 13, 2020, https://www.theatlantic.com/ideas/archive/2020/05/birtherism-and-trump/610978/.

Seshia, Shaila. "Divide and rule in Indian party politics: The rise of the Bharatiya Janata Party." *Asian Survey* 38, no. 11 (1998): 1036–50.

References

Shaheen, Jack G. *Reel Bad Arabs: How Hollywood Vilifies a People*. Northampton: Olive Branch Press, 2001.

Shaheen, Jack G. "Reel bad Arabs: How Hollywood vilifies a people." *The ANNALS of the American Academy of Political and Social Science* 588, no. 1 (2003): 171–93.

Shanmugasundaram, Swathi. "Anti-Sharia law bills in the United States." Southern Poverty Law Center, February 5, 2018.

Sharma, Betwa, and Ahmer Khan. "Hindu vigilantes work with police to enforce 'Love Jihad' law in North India." *The Intercept*, July 3, 2021, https://theintercept.com/2021/07/03/love-jihad-law-india/.

Sharma, Parth, and Abhijit Anand. "Indian media coverage of Nizamuddin Markaz event during COVID-19 pandemic." *Asian Politics & Policy* 12, no. 4 (2020): 650–4.

Sherwood, Marika. "Race, nationality and employment among Lascar seamen, 1660 to 1945." *Journal of Ethnic and Migration Studies* 17, no. 2 (1991): 229–44.

Shryock, Andrew, ed. *Islamophobia/Islamophilia: Beyond the Politics of Enemy and Friend*. Bloomington: Indiana University Press, 2010.

Siddiqui, Kalim. *The Muslim Manifesto: A Strategy for Survival*. London: The Muslim Institute, 1990, http://kalimsiddiqui.com/wp-content/uploads/2016/01/Muslim-Manifesto-1990.pdf.

Singh, Gurharpal. "Hindu nationalism in power: Making sense of Modi and the BJP-led National Democratic Alliance government, 2014–19." *Sikh Formations* 15, no. 3–4 (2019): 314–31.

Skitka, Linda J. "Patriotism or nationalism? Understanding post-September 11, 2001, flag-display behavior." *Journal of Applied Social Psychology* 35, no. 10 (2005): 1995–2011.

Speakman, Burton, and Anisah Bagasra. "Reinforcing Islamophobic rhetoric through the use of Facebook comments: A study of imagined community." *Journal of Communication & Religion* 45, no. 1 (2022): 43–60.

Squire, Megan. "Network analysis of anti-Muslim groups on Facebook." In *Social Informatics: 10th International Conference, SocInfo 2018, St. Petersburg, Russia,*

September 25–28, 2018, Proceedings, Part I 10, pp. 403–19. Cham: Springer International Publishing, 2018.

Stableford, Dylan. "'Born in Kenya': Obama's literary agent misidentified his birthplace in 1991." *ABC News*, May 17, 2012, https://abcnews.go.com/Politics/OTUS/born-kenya -obamas-literary-agent-misidentified-birthplace-1991 /story?id=16372566#.T7WvDXlYtR8.

Stampnitzky, Lisa. *Disciplining Terror: How Experts Invented "Terrorism"*. Cambridge: Cambridge University Press, 2013.

Steinback, Robert. "Jihad against Islam." *Southern Poverty Law Center*, June 17, 2011.

Steiner, Kristian. "Images of Muslims and Islam in Swedish Christian and secular news discourse." *Media, War & Conflict* 8, no. 1 (2015): 20–45.

Su, Ping. "The floating community of Muslims in the island city of Guangzhou." *Island Studies Journal* 12, no. 2 (2017): 83–96.

Sunny, Shiv, and Kainat Sarfaraz. "Bloodstains, used tear gas shell in Jamia library capture Sunday's violence." *Hindustan Times*, December 17, 2019, https://www .hindustantimes.com/delhi-news/bloodstains-used-tear -gas-shell-in-library-capture-sunday-s-violence/story -FRVJH7Im0JGQU8kf5nqFAL.html.

Swales. Kirby. "Understanding the leave vote." *UK in a Changing Europe*, December 8, 2016, https://ukandeu.ac .uk/partner-reports/understanding-the-leave-vote/.

Tam, Wai-Chu Maria. "The basic law and Hong Kong – The 15th anniversary of reunification with the Motherland." Hong Kong: Working Group on Overseas Community of the Basic Law Promotion Steering Committee, 2012.

Taylor, Max, and Audrey Gillan. "Racist slur or army banter? What the soldiers say." *The Guardian*, January 12, 2009, https://www.theguardian.com/uk/2009/jan/13 /military-prince-harry-race-issues.

Tell MAMA. "CST blog: Tell Mama first annual report." March 11, 2013, https://cst.org.uk/news/blog/2013/03/11 /tell-mama-first-annual-report.

Tell MAMA. "Tell MAMA annual report for 2017 shows

highest number of anti-Muslim incidents." July 22, 2018a, https://tellmamauk.org/tell-mamas-annual-report-for-2017-shows-highest-number-of-anti-muslim-incidents/.

Tell MAMA. "Understanding hate incident patterns after the Westminster terrorist attack of the 22nd of March 2017. Building a pattern of community resilience against hate – what worked?" December 4, 2018b, https://tellmamauk.org/understanding-hate-incident-patterns-after-the-westminster-terrorist-attack-of-the-22nd-of-march-2017-building-a-pattern-of-community-resilience-against-hate-what-worked/.

Tell MAMA. "Tell MAMA annual report 2018: Normalizing hatred." September 2, 2019, https://tellmamauk.org/tell-mama-annual-report-2018-_-normalising-hate/.

Terman, Rochelle. "Islamophobia and media portrayals of Muslim women: A computational text analysis of US news coverage." *International Studies Quarterly* 61, no. 3 (2017): 489–502.

Tien, Lee. "Peekaboo, I see you: Government authority intended for terrorism is used for other purposes." Electronic Frontier Foundation, October 26, 2014, https://www.eff.org/deeplinks/2014/10/peekaboo-i-see-you-government-uses-authority-meant-terrorism-other-uses.

Tope, Daniel, Justin T. Pickett, and Ted Chiricos. "Anti-minority attitudes and Tea Party Movement membership." *Social Science Research* 51 (2014): 322–37.

Tozawa, Kenji. "Narendra Modi's government and the RSS." 愛媛大学法文学部論集. 総合政策学科編 38 (2015): 1–11, https://opac1.lib.ehime-u.ac.jp/iyokan/bdyview.do?bodyid=TD00003276&elmid=Body&fname=AN10593675_2015_38-1.pdf

Treitler, Vilna Bashi. *The Ethnic Project: Transforming Racial Fiction into Ethnic Factions.* Stanford, CA: Stanford University Press, 2013.

TUC. *Challenging Racism after the EU Referendum: An Action Plan for Challenging Racism and Xenophobia.* Report compiled by Trades Union Congress, 2016, https://www.tuc.org.uk/sites/default/files/ChallengingracismaftertheEUreferendum2.pdf.

Tyrer, David. *The Politics of Islamophobia: Race, Power and Fantasy*. London: Pluto Press, 2013.

UHRP (Uyghur Human Rights Project). "About." n.d., https://uhrp.org/about/.

United Nations. "Security Council Counter-Terrorism Committee will hold special meeting in India focused on new and emerging technologies." The United Nations, 2022, https://www.un.org/securitycouncil/ctc/news /security-council-counter-terrorism-committee-will-hold -special-meeting-india-focused-new-and.

Van Schaack, Beth, and Maya Wang. *"Break Their Lineage, Break Their Roots:" China's Crimes against Humanity Targeting Uyghurs and Other Turkic Muslims*. Human Rights Watch report, 2021, https://www.hrw.org/sites /default/files/media_2021/04/china0421_web_2.pdf.

Vasudeva, Feeza, and Nicholas Barkdull. "WhatsApp in India? A case study of social media related lynchings." *Social Identities* 26, no. 5 (2020): 574–89.

Visram, Rozina. *Lascars, Ayahs and Princes: The Story of Indians in Britain 1700–1947*. London: Pluto Press, 1986.

Walia, Harsha. *Undoing Border Imperialism*, Vol. 6. Chico, CA: AK Press, 2014.

Wang, Vivian. "How China under Xi Jinping is turning away from the world." *New York Times*, February 23, 2022, https://www.nytimes.com/2022/02/23/world/asia/china-xi -jinping-world.html.

Wee, Su-Lee. "How China uses DNA to track its people, with the help of American expertise: The Chinese authorities turned to a Massachusetts company and a prominent Yale researcher as they built an enormous system of surveillance and control." *New York Times*, February 21, 2019, https://www.nytimes.com/2019/02/21/business /china-xinjiang-uighur-dna-thermo-fisher.html#:~:text= In%20Xinjiang%2C%20in%20northwestern%20China ,Uighurs%20and%20human%20rights%20groups.

Weiner, Melissa F. "Towards a critical global race theory." *Sociology Compass* 6, no. 4 (2012): 332–50.

Werbner, Pnina. "Islamophobia: Incitement to religious

References

hatred – legislating for a new fear?" *Anthropology Today* 21, no. 1 (2005): 5–9.

Williams, Johnny E. "Biological pre-emption: 'Race', class, and genomics." *Sociology Compass* 7, no. 9 (2013): 711–25.

Williamson, Vanessa, Theda Skocpol, and John Coggin. "The Tea Party and the remaking of Republican conservatism." *Perspectives on Politics* 9, no. 1 (2011): 25–43.

Xinhuanet. "Xi Jinping – On war against 'common enemy of mankind.'" September 11, 2021, http://www.news.cn/english/2021-09/11/c_1310181993.htm.

Yang, Anand A. "Sacred symbol and sacred space in rural India: Community mobilization in the 'anti-cow killing' riot of 1893." *Comparative Studies in Society and History* 22 no. 4 (1980): 576–96.

Yasir, Sameer. "India is scapegoating Muslims for the spread of the Coronavirus." *Foreign Policy*, April 22, 2020, https://foreignpolicy.com/2020/04/22/india-muslims-coronavirus-scapegoat-modi-hindu-nationalism/.

Ye, Meng. "Ideological representations of Chinese Muslim groups in Chinese and US media (2001–2015): A comparative approach." Dissertation, The Hong Kong Polytechnic University, 2019, https://theses.lib.polyu.edu.hk/bitstream/200/10073/1/991022255759203411.pdf90.

Zajączkowska, Natalia. "On the politics of fear: The role of politicians in stoking Islamophobia during the COVID-19 pandemic in India." *Sprawy Miedzynarodowe/International Affairs* 74, no. 3 (2021): 237–66.

Zhang, Chenchen. "Right-wing populism with Chinese characteristics? Identity, otherness and global imaginaries in debating world politics online." *European Journal of International Relations* 26, no. 1 (2020): 88–115.

Zhao, Suisheng. "From affirmative to assertive patriots: Nationalism in Xi Jinping's China." *The Washington Quarterly* 44, no. 4 (2021): 141–61.

Ziegfeld, Adam. "The authoritarian origins of dominant parties in democracies: Opposition fragmentation and asymmetric competition in India." *Studies in Comparative International Development* 56, no. 4 (2021): 435–62.

Zopf, Bradley J. "A different kind of brown: Arabs and

Middle Easterners as anti-American Muslims." *Sociology of Race and Ethnicity* 4, no. 2 (2018): 178–91.

Zuboff, Shoshana. *The Age of Surveillance Capitalism: The Fight for a Human Future at the New Frontier of Power.* London: Profile Books, 2019.

Index

Abbas, Dr. Gulshan 1, 2
Abbas, Rushan 1, 174, 175
Abdulaheb, Asiye 175
Abliz, Abdukerim 85
Abu-Lughod, Lila 64, 77
  *Do Muslim Women Need
    Saving?* 79
ACT for America 115
Action Committee on Islamic
  Affairs 36
Afghanistan
  resistance to British army by
    Muslims 33
  US invasion of 9, 11, 12, 72,
    111, 137, 138, 147
  women in 11
African Americans 13, 21, 41,
  147, 170
African Muslims 6, 39–40, 46
airports/airport security 165
  racializing/racial profiling of
    Muslim passengers 15–16,
    142
  stopping and detaining
    people at British 152
  surveillance technologies 21
Akbar 47
Al-Qaeda 137
Ali, Noble Drew 41
Ali, Tosir and Altab 36

Ali, Wajahat 103
All-Indian Muslim League 33,
  49
Alsultany, Evelyn 5, 63, 66,
  67, 68, 70, 71, 78, 80
  104
Alternative for Germany (AfD)
  campaign ad (2019) 107–8
Ameli, Saied Reza et al. 80
America First campaign 75–6
American Civil Liberties Union
  (ACLU) 113, 148, 170
American Freedom Defense
  Institute 113
American Freedom Law Center
  114
American Sniper (film) 69–70
Amritsar massacre (1919)
  49–50
Anand, Abhijit 98, 99
anti-immigration sentiments
  26–7, 28, 107
  Brexit 81, 83
  Britain 35–6, 38, 81, 83,
    118
  China 26, 91, 134
  right-wing populist
    movements 106
  United States 26, 42, 46,
    111, 113, 115

212   A Global Racial Enemy

anti-Muslim hate crimes 84
  influenced by trigger events
    84
  online 82–4
anti-sharia movement
  in United States 114–15, 117
Arabs 5
  migration to the United
    States 42–7
  and US Census 16–17
Arya Samaj 48
Asian Youth Movements 36
Atlas Shrugs, The 75
Aurangzeb, Emperor 47
Awan, Imran 84
Aziz, Sahar F. 13

Babar 47
Babri Masjid mosque (India)
  destruction of (1992) 94,
    126, 127
Baharuddin, A. Zamakhsyari
  98
Baharuddin, Andi Farid 98
Bald, Vivek 44
Bangladesh 51, 127, 131, 163,
  164
Begg, Moazzam 170–1
Begum, Shamima 65
Bellingham riots (1907) 43
Bengal
  partition of (1905) 33, 48–9
  rescinding of partition (1911)
    49
Bengali Muslims 34, 43, 44
Beydoun, Khaled 139–40
Bharatiya Janata Party see BJP
Biden, President Joe 106
bio-terrorism/terrorists 98, 99
biological racism 12–13
biometric surveillance 22, 152,
  159–60
Birmingham City Council
  120–1

birther movement, in United
  States 115–17
BJP (Bharatiya Janata Party)
  53, 64, 97, 123, 124, 125,
  130, 163
  and cow vigilantes 128–9
  use of social media 99, 100
Black Americans
  negative depiction of in
    minstrel shows 62
blackness
  surveillance of in United
    States 20–1
Blair, Tony 2
BNP (British National Party)
  36, 82, 118, 119
Body of Lies (film) 70
Bodyguard (tv series) 78–9
Bollywood 95
Bonikowski, Bart 108
border imperialism 163
border security 140
  India 162–4
  United States 147–8, 163
Border Security Forces (BSF)
  (India) 163, 164
Borough Market attack (2017)
  38
Bosnian Muslims
  migration to the United
    States 43
Boston Regional Information
  Center (BRIC) 170
Boundaoui, Assia 142
Bouyeri, Mohammed 3
Brexit 38, 75, 80, 103, 108
  anti-immigration sentiment
    and 81, 83
  impact on online
    anti-Muslim racism 83
  mobilization of Hindutva
    ideologies by diasporic
    Indians 101, 102
  and negative attitude towards

Index

immigrants and minorities
118
news media frames of
Muslims during 81
Britain 22–3, 32–9
anti-immigration sentiments
and restrictions 35–6, 38,
81, 83, 118
attacks on mosques and
individuals 38, 120
attempt to dismantle racist
policies due to GWOT by
CAGE 170–1
citizenship withdrawal 151–2
conquest and colonization of
India 33, 47–8, 49, 161
counterterrorism policies
148–54, 164
critique of multiculturalism
118–19
cyber-attacks on Muslims
82–4, 120
end of rule in India 49–50
hostility towards immigrants
by main political parties
119–20
immigration of Muslims after
Second World War 33–4
increase in racist violence 36
Islam as second largest
religion in 32
London 7/7 bombings (2005)
37, 80–1, 118
London Bridge stabbings
(2019) 25
Muslim demographic
landscape 32, 34, 35, 38
Muslim histories and
relations 32–9, 59–60
and nationalism 110
and nationalist populism
117–20
Nationality and Borders Bill
151

PREVENT policy 2–4, 76,
120, 144, 148–54
"preventative" policing
152–3
and race/racial classification
17
reasons for Muslims' failure
to integrate 120
relations between Muslims
and the nation-state 32–9
relinquishing of Hong Kong
to China 133
representation of Muslims in
film and television 76–80,
104
representation of Muslims in
the media 75–84
representation of Muslims in
news media 80–2
resistance against anti-racist
activities and racialization
36–7, 170–1
and "Rushdie Affair" 37
success of Muslims in 38
Terrorism Acts (2000/2006)
152–3
terrorist attacks 37–8
Trojan Horse policy 120–2
use of GWOT to justify
increased surveillance/
discriminatory policies
against Muslims 60
see also Brexit
Britain First campaign 75–6
British Empire
colonization of India (1858)
33
decline of 34
expansion of 32
British National Party see BNP
Britishness 35, 82, 118, 119
"broken windows policing"
166–7
Brookings Institution 144

Browne, Simone
Dark Matters 20–1
Buffalo grocery store killings (2022) 166
Bush, President George W. 109–10, 137–8
meeting with Jiang Zemin 154
speech on War on Terror (2001) 111, 137
State of the Union Address (2002) 111–12
Bush, Laura 138
Byler, David
terror capitalism 159–60
In the Camps 157–8, 159

CAGE 152, 153, 170–1
Cameron, David 119
Campaign for Uyghurs 1, 174–5
capitalism
surveillance 159
terror 159–60
capitalist imperialism 11, 12
Center for Security Policy (US) 114, 115
Cháirez-Garza, Jesús F. et al 18
Channel 149, 150
Chelsea football team 31
China 12, 23, 54–9, 131–5, 176
anti-immigration sentiments 26, 91, 134
authoritative populism 109, 134
cadre program 86–7
counterterrorism policies 154–60, 165
Cultural Revolution 58
desire to build a New Silk Road 132
economic growth 133

ethnicity surveys 19
features of online right-wing populism 91
film production 85–7, 104
and Global War on Terror 154–60
and Hong Kong 133
Hui Muslims 92
language policies 135
Muslim histories and relations 54–9, 60
and nationalism 110, 133–5
and neo-orientalism 10, 12
news media 87–90
Patriotic Education Campaign 134
Regulation on De-Extremification Act (2017) 156–7
representation of Muslims in the media 63, 84–93
social media 84–5, 90–3, 134, 159
state censorship 84, 85, 93
and surveillance technologies 21
and Uyghur Muslims *see* Uyghur Muslims
China Daily 89
"China Dream" 134
Chinese Communist Party (CCP) 19, 57–8, 134
Chinese Exclusionary Act (1885) (US) 44
Choudhary, Vikas K. 52
Christianity
conflict with Islam 40–1, 46
citizenship 140
rules in India and exclusion of Muslims 27, 63, 130–1
withdrawal of 151–2
Citizenship Amendment Act (CAA) (India) (2015) 130–1, 172

Index

215

Civil Rights Act (1964) (US) 45
civilized/uncivilized dichotomy
137, 154, 168
"clash of civilizations" 9, 111,
137, 140
climate change 22
Clinton, Hilary 116
colonialism 2, 7, 12, 13, 18,
20, 23
settler *see* settler colonialism
Commonwealth Immigrants
Act (1962) (Britain) 35
communalism
in India 18, 19, 48–9, 51, 52,
53, 64
Conservative Party 34, 35,
119–20
Islamophobia in 38
Counter-Terrorism Committee
138–9
Countering Violent Extremism
see CVE
counterterrorism policies 29,
137–65, 167, 176
and Britain's PREVENT
policy 148–54, 164
China 154–60, 165
economic and capitalistic
motivations driving 156
and gender 165
global nature of 2, 4, 155
India 161–4, 165
institutionalization of 14–15
secrecy and non
accountability of 143, 166,
170
and surveillance *see*
surveillance
and UN Resolution 1373
138–9
United States 141–8, 153,
165
using new and emerging
technologies 139

COVID pandemic
news media frames of
Muslims during 81
role of Indian news media in
fueling anti-Muslim racism
during 97–9
cow slaughter (India) 52
cow vigilantes (India) 128–9
Crusades 32
cultural racism 12
Cultural Revolution 58
Curzon, Lord 48
Customs and Border Protection
(CBP) (US) 147
CVE (Countering Violent
Extremism) program
143–6, 169–70
United States 3, 4, 143–5
cyber-attacks
on Muslims in Britain 82–4,
120

Delhi riots 100, 172
Dhanak of Humanity 129
digital surveillance 159
Diouf, Sylviane 39, 40
Drabu, Onaiza 96
drugs
connection between War on
Terror and War on 146–7
Dyer, Brigadier 49–50

East India Company 32
Eastern Turkestan Islamic
Movement (ETIM) 155
Eastwood, Clint 69
Election Law (1953) (China)
19
Electronic Frontier Foundation
146–7
English Defence League (EDL)
30, 36, 82
ethnicity
surveys of in China 19

ethnonationalism 28–9, 80, 83, 107, 176
ethnonationalist populism 27, 67, 75–6, 107, 108, 109, 176
  in United States 91, 110, 115–16
European Union, creation of 108
Evolvi, Giulia 83
Executive Order 13769 (US) 46

Facebook 75, 100
  and anti-Muslim violence in India 100
facial recognition 21, 22, 139
Falah, Ghazi-Walid 73
Fanaa (film) 95
fanfang 54
Farah, Mo 38
Fazaga, Sheikh Yassir 143
FBI
  hyper-focus on terrorism 146
FBI v. Fazaga 143
Fear of Being Watched, The (film) 142
Federal Information Surveillance Act (FISA) 141
film 62, 104
  representation of Muslims in British 76–80, 104
  representation of Muslims in Indian 93–5
  representation of Muslims in United States 67, 68–71, 76, 104
  representation of Uyghur Muslims in Chinese 85–7, 104
First World War 49
flag flying, in United States 110–11
Fox News 74

fundamentalism
  linking Islam with 10, 37, 67
fusion centers 166–7, 169, 170

Gabriel, Brigitte 115
Gaffne, Frank 114–15
Gandhi, Indira 123, 128
Gandhi, Mahatma 50, 52
Garvey, Marcus 41
Geller, Pamela 75, 113
gender
  and counterterrorism policies 165
  and neo-orientalism 10–11
  and US media representations of Muslims 72–3
gendered racialization 4, 11, 12, 23–8, 114
  and GWOT 23–8, 66, 71, 78, 79, 173
  of Uyghur Muslims and nationalism 133–5
Gendron, Peyton S. 166, 167
genomics 12–13
George V, King 49
Germany 107–8
Gérôme, Jean-Léon
  Slave Market 107–8
Ghani, Nusrat 38
Gilroy, Paul 120
Global War on Terror *see* GWOT
globalization 108
Goderich, Miriam 115
Goebbels, Joseph 62
Golwalkar, M.S. 125
Good/Bad Muslim paradigm 70–1, 74, 120, 148
Great Replacement Theory 64
Grewal, Zareena
  Islam is a Foreign Country 8
Guangzhou (China) 54
Guantanamo Bay 170–1

Index

GWOT (Global War on Terror) 1, 2, 4, 22, 26, 59, 136, 137, 138, 164
  contextualizing 30–61
  and gendered racialization 23–8, 66, 71, 78, 79, 173
  and instigation of surveillance industry 139
  and media 63–6
  and orientalism/neo-orientalism 8–9, 10–11
  use of to justify oppression of Muslims 59, 60, 64, 65, 66, 93, 98, 107, 139

Hadiya case (2018) 130
Hassan, Mehdi 103
Heath, Edward 35
Henry Jackson Society 151
Henry VIII, King 32
hierarchies, racial 14
hijab 15, 73, 74, 84, 94, 142, 162
Hindi cinema
  representation of Muslims in 93, 94–5
Hindu Maratha Confederacy 48
Hindu right-wing movement 94
Hindus/Hinduism 18, 48, 123
  and partition of Bengal 48
  racialization of in United States 44
  relations and tensions with Muslims 48, 49, 51, 93, 94, 100
  and RSS 124–5
  and US Census 16
Hindutva ideology 53, 93, 94, 101–2, 123–5, 126–8
Hitler, Adolf 62
Hollywood 67
  diversity initiatives 104

representations of Muslims 63, 67, 68–70
Homeland (tv show) 70
Hong Kong 133
Huaisheng mosque (China) 54
Hui Muslims (in China) 92
Human Rights Watch 163
Huntington, Samuel 8–9
  "The Clash of Civilizations" 9, 111
Hussain, Nadiya 38
hyper-surveillance 141, 153, 158, 159, 165, 169, 176

Ibn Said, Omar 39
Immigration Act (1881) (US) 44
Immigration and Customs Enforcement (ICE) (US) 147
Immigration and Nationality Act (1965) (US) 44
Immigration and Naturalization Services (INS) (US) 147
immigration/immigration policies
  nationalism and rise in 108
  United States 44–6, 147–8
  see also anti-immigration sentiments
imperialism 13
  border 163
  capitalist 11, 12
India 2, 12, 23, 47–53, 122–31, 176
  Amritsar massacre (1919) 49–50
  "anti-nationals" 125
  assassination of Indira Gandhi (1984) 123
  banning of interfaith marriages 27, 129
  BJP's use of media to define male Muslim as threatening to women and the state 64

India (*cont.*)
  British conquest and colonization 33, 47–8, 49, 161
  and caste 122, 123
  Citizenship Amendment Act (CAA) 130–1, 172
  citizenship rules and exclusion of Muslims from 27, 63, 130–1
  and communalism 4, 18, 19, 48–9, 51, 52, 53, 64
  Constitution 51–2, 53
  counterterrorism policies 161–4, 165
  and Covid pandemic 97–9
  cow slaughter issue 52
  cow vigilantes 128–9
  cow-related hate crimes 101
  demand for independence and end of British rule in 49–51
  destruction of the Babri Masjid mosque and riots after (1992) 94, 126, 127
  economic growth 127–8
  Gujarat province riots and killing of Muslims (2002) 127
  Hadiya case (2018) 130
  Hindu-Muslim relations 48, 49, 52, 60
  and Hindutva 53, 93, 94, 101–2, 123–5, 126–8
  Jamia Millia Islamia protests 172
  and Lahore Resolution 50–1
  and Love Jihad 27, 64, 96, 129–30
  and Lucknow Pact (1916) 49
  and Mughal Empire 47, 48
  Muslim histories and relations 47–53, 60
  Muslims seen as threat to nation 124, 126–7, 131
  and nationalism 110, 122, 123
  and neo-orientalism 10, 12
  partition of (1947) 51, 127, 161
  partition of Bengal (1905) 33, 48–9
  political system 122, 123
  power and political domination of BJP 126
  Prevention of Terrorism Act (2002) 161–2
  and race/racial classification 18–19
  relations with Pakistan 163
  representation of Muslims in film 93–5
  representation of Muslims in the media 63, 93–102
  representation of Muslims in news media 96–9
  representation of Muslims in social media 99–102
  resistance to racialization 172–3
  and RSS 18, 124–5, 127
  secularism and religious minorities in the new domain of 51–3
  Shaheen Bagh protests 172–3
  surveillance of intimate relationships in 129
  terrorism laws 161
  tightening of border security and abuses committed on 162–4
  Unlawful Activities Prevention Act (UAPA) (India) 162
  use of GWOT to justify increased oppression of Muslims 60

Index

Indian Councils Act (1909) 49
Indian National Congress (INC) 49, 50, 51, 122
Indian People's Party *see* BJP
Instagram 75
Institute for Research and Education on Human Rights 113
Institute for Social Policy and Understanding (ISPU) report 45
insurgency/insurgents 24, 164
Iran 37
Iraq, invasion of 137
ISIS 97
Islam
  British/European representations of 37
  conflict with Christianity 40–1, 46
  linking of to fundamentalism 10, 37, 67
Islamic Revolution (1979) 45
Islamophobia 5–7, 102, 150
  and *Bodyguard* film 78
  in Conservative Party 38–9
  critiques of term 5–6
  online 83
  race/racism as central concept of 5
  social media 67, 75
  structural 139–40
  and whiteness 5–6
Israel 163

Jackson, Leonie
  The Monstrous and the Vulnerable 65
Jaffrelot, Christophe 124
Jamaat-e-Islami 98, 99
Jamia Millia Islamia protests 172
Japanese Americans
  internment of 63

Javid, Sajid 38
Jiang Zemin 154
Jihad Watch 75, 82
"jihadi brides" 65
Jinnah, Muhammad Ali 50
Jones, Sally 65
Jones, Stephen and Unsworth, Amy
  survey (2021) 39

Karmokar, Shyamol 164
Khan, Sadiq 38
Khan, Usman 25
Khomeini, Ayatollah 37
Kumar, Deepa 6, 11, 24
Kundnani, Aron 148
Kundnani, Aron and Hayes, Ben
  Countering Violent Extremism 2, 3
Kunlun Brothers (film) 85, 86–7
Kunming railway station stabbings (2014) (China) 88

Labour Party 119–20
Lahore Resolution 50–1
lascars 32
Latif v. Lynch 145
Latin American populations 60
Leidig, Eviane 101
Lewis, Bernard 8–9
Liverpool Football Club 30–1
London bombings (7/7) (2005) 37, 80–1, 118
London Bridge stabbings (2019) 25
Lopez, Ian Haney
  White By Law 16
Love Jihad 27, 64, 96, 129–30
Lucknow Pact (1916) 49
Luqiu, Luwei Rose 87–8

220 A Global Racial Enemy

Malmir, Bahareh 72
Malviya, Amit 99
Mamdani, M. 70
Mao Zedong 57
mass shootings 166
Massoumi, Narzanin et al 150
media 28, 62–105
  anti-Muslim portrayals and
    biased representations
    62–105
  and GWOT 63–6
  positive representations of
    Muslims 103–4
  representation of Muslim
    women 64–5
  representation of Muslims in
    British 75–84
  representation of Muslims in
    Chinese 63, 84–93
  representation of Muslims in
    Indian 63, 93–102
  representation of Muslims in
    United States 63, 66–75
  role in facilitating racism 63
  see also film; news media;
    social media; television
Mei Xinyu 90, 91
Mercurio, Jed 79
Migration Policy Institute 147
Miller, Todd
  Empire of Borders 163
Minto, Lord 49
Mischief Night (film) 77–8
Modi, Narendra 99, 123, 124,
  125, 127, 128, 173
Mohamed, Ahmed 23–4
Monteilh, Craig 142–3
Moorish Science Temple 41
mosques
  attacks on in Britain 38,
    120
  building of in United States
    and resistance to 113,
    117

destruction of Babri Masjid in
  India (1992) 94, 126, 127
receiving of CVE funding
  144
Mountbatten, Lord 51
Moussawi, Ghassan 11
Mughal Empire 47, 48
Muhammad, Elijah 41
multiculturalism 37
  criticism of in Britain
    118–19
Muslim Council of Britain 37
Muslim Justice League (MJL)
  169–70
Muslim League 50–1
Muslim women 26, 66
  and gendered racialization 4,
    11, 12, 23–8, 114
  representation of in British
    film and tv 77, 78–9
  representation of in the
    media 64–5
  representation of in US films
    70–1
  representation of in US news
    72–4
  and Shaheen Bagh protests in
    India 172–3
  wearing of hijabs seen as a
    threat at airports 15–16
Muslims
  seen as terrorists 10, 12, 15,
    22, 23–5, 26, 46, 78, 103,
    112, 140, 165, 176
  seen as a threat to national
    security and society 15, 20,
    22, 23, 26–7, 28, 31, 60,
    65, 72, 76, 107, 136, 140,
    142
Muzzafarnagar riots (2013)
  129

Naber, Nadine 13
Nahdi, Fuad 36

Index

Nation of Islam 41–2
National Front 36
National Health Service (NHS) 35
National Investigation Agency (NIA) (India) 162
National Security Entry-Exit Registration System (NSEERS) 141–2, 152
nationalism 23, 28–9, 61, 106–36, 136, 176
  Britain 110
  China 110, 133–5
  definition 107–10
  India 110, 122, 123
  and rise in immigration 108
  rise in 106–7
  role of anti-Muslim hostility in growth of 107
  United States 110
  and Uyghur Muslims 57, 131–2
Nazis 62
Nehru, Jawaharlal 50, 51, 52
neo-orientalism 10–11
Netherlands 140, 144
  Preventing Violent Extremism (PVE) program 3–4, 140, 144, 148
New York Times 72, 73, 115
news media 103
  representation of Muslims in British 80–2
  representation of Muslims in Chinese 87–90
  representation of Muslims in Indian 96–9
  representation of Muslims in United States 67, 71–4
Nigeria 6
9/11 9, 15, 21, 66, 80, 109, 136, 138, 141, 146
  increase in patriotism in US after 110–11

Nizamuddin Markaz (New Delhi) 98–9
Northern Ireland 117

Obama, Barack 112, 115, 143
  rumour of not being born in United States 115, 116, 117
Omar, Ilhan 74
Omi, Michael and Winant, Howard
  Racial Formation in the United States 13–14
One Voice One Step campaign (2018) 174
online anti-Muslim racism 82–4
  impact of Brexit on 83
  and offline anti-Muslim racism 83–4
  see also social media
Operation Flex 142–3, 146
orientalism 7–10, 11–12, 107
  neo- 10–11
O'Toole, Theresa 150
Ottoman Empire 32, 41, 43, 60

Pakistan 18, 144, 161, 163
  creation of (1947) 51
  and CVE 144
  relations with India 163
Pakistani Muslims
  discrimination against in British society 35
  representation of in British film 76–7, 78
Pakistanis
  racialization of in UK 2
Parivar, Sangh 127
PATRIOT Act (US) 21, 60, 141, 146–8, 153, 161
Pew Research Center 16
phenotype
  and racialization 12, 14
Plassey, Battle of (1757) 48

222 A Global Racial Enemy

police doorstepping 171
policing
    "broken window" 166–7
    "preventative" 152–3
Poole, Elizabeth 81, 82
Popular Front of India 162
populism 61, 106–36
    Britain and nationalist
      117–20
    China and authoritative 109,
      134
    definition 107–10
    ethnonationalist 27, 67,
      75–6, 107, 108, 109, 176
    and globalization 108
    right-wing 91, 106, 107,
      109, 114, 116, 136
    rise in and role of
      anti-Muslim hostility
      106–7
    United States 108–9
Powell, Enoch
    "Rivers of Blood" speech 35
PREVENT policy (Britain) 2–4,
    76, 120, 144, 148–54
Preventing Terrorist Extremism
    (PVE) 140
    in Netherlands 3–4, 140,
      144, 148
    see also PREVENT
Prevention of Terrorism Act
    (2002) (India) 161–2
Pugh, Martin 35
Puri, Jyoti 18–19, 109

Qing dynasty 55–6

Race Relations Act (1976) (UK)
    17
race theory 7, 13
race/racism
    biological 12–13
    as a central concept of
      Islamophobia 5

    and colonialism 20
    cultural 12
    as a cultural construct 168
    imperial 13
    scientific 13, 18
    seen as an illness 6
    21st century 20–3
    and white supremacy 20, 168
racial classification
    Britain 17
    India 18–19
    United States 16–17
racial profiling
    of Muslim plane passengers
      15–16, 142
racialization
    definition 13–15
    entailing of certain tropes
      about Muslims 4
    gendered *see* gendered
      racialization
    and hierarchies 14
    and orientalism/
      neo-orientalism 7–12
    and phenotype 12, 14
    shifting nature of 13
    and stereotypes 15
Rahman, Khalid 52
Rai, Amit 95
Ramy (film) 104
Rana, Junaid 13, 25
Rashtriya Swayamsevak Sangh
    see RSS
Ray, Adil 38
Reddit 75
Refugee Admissions Program
    (US) 46
resistance to racialization
    168–75
    Britain 36–7, 170–1
    India 172–3
    United States 169–70
Rigby, Lee, murder of (2013)
    37–8

Index

right-wing populism 91, 106, 107, 109, 114, 116, 136
Roberts, Sean 54–6, 57, 132, 157
Romney, Mitt 116
RSS (Rashtriya Swayamsevak Sangh) 18, 124–5, 127
Rushdie, Salman
The Satanic Verses 37

Sageman, Marc 145
Said, Edward 10, 11, 107, 167–8
"The Myth of the Clash of Civilizations" lecture 9
Orientalism 7–8, 9
Salah, Mohammed 30–1
Samaie, Mahmoud 72
Sanders, Bernie 109
Savarkar, V.D. 124–5
schooling, Muslim
portrayal of in the media 82
scientific racism 13, 18
Second World War 50
Selod, Saher 14
settler colonialism 7, 55, 60
and Uyghur Muslims 55, 58, 60, 131–3, 135
sexual orientation
and orientalism 11
Shah, Amit 100
Shaheen, Jack 63
Reel Bad Arabs 68
Shanghai Cooperation Organization (SCO) 155
Shanghai Five 155
"Shared Responsibility Committee" (US) 145
Sharma, Parth 98
Shawcross, William 151
Shebley, Eaman 15
Siddiqui, Kalim, *The Muslim Manifesto* 37
Sikander, Zainab 98

Sikhs/Sikhism 17, 43, 51, 118, 128
Singh, Jayant 128
slavery/slave trade 7, 39, 46, 59
United States 39–41, 42, 46
Snowden, Edward 141, 176
social media 28, 67
anti-Muslim content 75, 103
anti-Muslim hatred on US 75
anti-Muslim racism/hate crimes in Britain 82–4
impact of Brexit on online anti-Muslim racism 83
and Islamophobia 67, 75
portrayal of Uyghur Muslims in China 84–5, 90–3, 134, 159
representation of Muslims in Indian 99–102
South Asian Muslims 2, 5, 7
migration to the United States 42–7
Southern Poverty Law Center 113, 115
Soviet Union
and Uyghur Muslims 57
Spencer, Robert 75, 82
Squire, Megan 75
Stampnitzky, Lisa
Disciplining Terror 24
Stop Islamification of Europe 113
Stop Islamization of America (American Freedom Defense Institute) 75, 113
Stop Islamization of Nations 113
#STOPCVE campaign 169–70
structural Islamophobia 139–40
surveillance 20–2, 23, 139, 165, 167, 176
biometric 22, 152, 159–60

surveillance (*cont.*)
  of blackness in United States
    20–1
  and Britain's PREVENT
    policy 148–54
  and China 21
  and fusion centers 166–7,
    169, 170
  hyper- 141, 153, 158, 159,
    165, 169, 176
  instigation of by GWOT 139
  investment in new
    technologies 21
  and PATRIOT Act 141
  resistance against via Muslim
    Justice League (US) 169–70
  in United States 22, 141–3,
    144–6
  of Uyghur Muslims in China
    21, 25, 158–9
surveillance capitalism 159
surveillance industrial complex
    20–1, 25
Syrian refugee crisis 92
Syrians
  migration to United States
    43, 44

Taliban 11
Targeting Violence and
    Terrorism Prevention
    (TVTP) 145
Tattle Civic Technology 97
Tea Party movement 112–13,
    115, 117
Tea Party Patriots 113, 114
television 104
  representations of Muslims
    on US 67, 70
  representations of Muslims
    on British 76–80
Tell MAMA (Measuring
    Anti-Muslim Attacks) 82,
    83–4

Terman, Rochelle 73
terror capitalism 159–60
terror-industrial complex 25
terrorcraft 24–5
Terrorism Acts (Britain)
    (2000) 152, 153
    (2006) 152–3
terrorism/terrorists 24–5
  Muslims seen as 10, 12, 15,
    22, 23–5, 26, 46, 78, 103,
    112, 140, 165, 176
  see also GWOT
Theodoridis, Alexander 117
Thermo Fisher 161
Tiansham film studio (China) 85
Times, The 82
Tlaib, Rashida 74
Traitor (film) 70–1
Transportation and Security
    Administration (TSA) 15,
    142
Triple Talaq 96
Trojan Horse policy 120–2
Trump, Donald 45–6, 92, 106,
    145
  and birtherism 116
  questioning citizenship of
    Obama 116, 117
  and Twitter 99
Trump v. Hawaii 46
Turkistan Islamic Party (TIP)
    155
24 (tv series) 70
Twitter 75, 99

UK *see* Britain
UN (United Nations)
  attempts to combat terrorism
    139
  Security Council 167
  Security Council Resolution
    1373 138
United Kingdom Independence
    Party (UKIP) 118

Index

United States 22–3, 39–47
anti-immigration sentiments and policies 26, 42, 46, 111, 113, 115
anti-Muslim activism and movements in 112–17
anti-Muslim attitudes and policies 68, 72, 111–12
anti-sharia movement 114–15, 117
Bellingham riots (1907) 43
birther movement 115–17
border security 147–8, 163
Buffalo grocery store killings (2022) 166
Campaign for Uyghurs 174, 174–5
citizenship withdrawal 152
conflict between Islam and Christianity 40–1
connection between War on Drugs and War on Terror 146–7
Countering Violent Extremism (CVE) 3, 4, 143–5
counterterrorism policies 141–8, 153, 165
detentions and deportations of non-citizens 147–8
ethnonationalist populism in 91, 110, 115–16
FBI's Operation Flex 142–3, 146
fusion centers 166–7, 169, 170
global racialization of Muslims and rise of nationalism and populism 110–17
immigration policies 44–6, 147–8
increased militarization of the police 147
influence of Islam on African Americans 41–2
internment of Japanese Americans 63
invasion of Afghanistan 11, 72, 111, 137, 138, 147
migration of Muslims to and motives 23, 42–7
mosque building and resistance to 113, 117
Muslim histories and relations 39–47
Muslim Justice League (MJL) 169–70
National Security Entry-Exit Registration System (NSEERS) 141–2, 152
and nationalism 110
PATRIOT Act (2021) 21, 60, 141, 146–8, 153, 161
patriotism 110–11
populism in 108–9
portrayal of Muslims as cultural threat 27
racialization of Hinduism in 44
racism structured into society 45
reach and impact of the War on Terror in 146–8
relations between Muslims and the nation-state 39–47
representation of Muslims in films/Hollywood 67, 68–71, 76, 104
representation of Muslims in the media 63, 66–75
representation of Muslims in news media 67, 71–4
representation of Muslims on television 67, 70
resistance to racialization 169–70

226   A Global Racial Enemy

United States (*cont.*)
  "Shared Responsibility
    Committee" 145
  and slavery 39–41, 42, 46
  social media and anti-Muslim
    hatred 75
  storming of Capitol building
    by protesters (2021) 106
  surveillance 22, 141–3,
    144–6
  surveillance of blackness
    20–1
  Tea Party movement 112–13,
    115, 117
  use of GWOT to justify
    increased surveillance of
    Muslims 60
  view of race/racial
    classification 12, 16–17
  violence towards South
    Asians in 43–4
Unlawful Activities Prevention
  Act (UAPA) (India) 162
US Citizenship and
  Immigration Services
  (USCIS) agency 152
Uyghur Human Rights Project
  (UHRP) 175
Uyghur Muslims (in China) 11,
  23, 55, 55–9, 60, 131–5
  attempt to assimilate into Han
    culture by Qing dynasty 56
  atrocities faced by women in
    camps 158–9
  colonial relationships
    endured by 55
  crackdown on and atrocities
    against 25–6, 58, 64, 84,
    85, 174, 175
  de-extremification of 156–7
  desire for self-autonomy 132
  detention of and camps
    25–6, 27, 90, 93, 132,
    156–60

  establishment of the Second
    East Turkestan Republic
    (ETR) 57
  forced labor in camps
    and benefiting of by
    corporations 160, 175
  forced marriages of women
    to Han men 27, 65,
    134–5, 165
  forced sterilization of women
    27, 158, 175
  gendered racialization of and
    nationalism 133–5
  histories and relations with
    Chinese state 55–9, 131–2
  portrayal of on social media
    84–5, 90–3, 134, 159
  and "positive" propaganda
    89–90
  protests and grievances 156
  representation of in Chinese
    film 85–7, 104
  representation of in Chinese
    media 84–5
  representation of in Chinese
    news media 87–90
  resistance from women
    abroad 174–5
  rise in nationalism amongst
    57, 131–2
  seen as a terrorist threat 1–2,
    26, 58, 132, 154–5, 156,
    174
  seen as a threat to Chinese
    culture and society 135
  and settler colonialism 55,
    58, 60, 131–3, 135
  surveillance of 21, 25, 158–9
  and terror capitalism 159–60
  Xinjiang riots (2009) 87, 88

Vajpayee, Atal Bihari 125
Van Gogh, Theo, killing of 3
Velshi, Ali 103

Index

War Within, The (film) 70
Warsi, Baroness Sayeeda 38
Washington Post 73
Weibo 90, 92
Weiner, Melissa 14
Werbner, Pnina 37
Westminster Bridge attack (2017) 38
WhatsApp
  and facilitating of anti-Muslim violence in India 101
white savior trope 79
white supremacy 12, 20, 22–3, 41, 62, 64, 67, 75, 107, 168, 176
whiteness 16, 167, 167–8
  and Islamophobia 5–6
  as racial classification 16–17, 18
  and racialization of Muslims 167–8
  and US Census 16–17, 18
Williamson, Milly 81

Wings of Songs, The (film) 85–6
women, Muslim *see* Muslim women

Xi Jinping, President 25, 26, 134, 135, 155, 156
Xi Wuyi 90
Xinjiang riots (2009) 87, 88
Xinjiang Uyghur Autonomous Region (XUAR) 57

Yang, Fan 87–8
Yang Zengxin 57
Yasmin (film) 78
Ye, Meng 89
Yerushalmi, David 114
Ying Miao 92

Zajączkowska, Natalia 97
Zempi, Irene 84
Zhang, Chenchen 91
Ziawudun, Tursunay 158
Zuboff, Shoshana 159